The Natural History of

SQUIRRELS

The Natural History of

SQUIRRELS

JOHN GURNELL

Facts On File Publications
New York, New York ● Oxford, England

First published in the United States of America by
Facts On File, Inc., 460 Park Avenue South,
New York, New York 10016

Library of Congress Cataloging in Publication Data
Gurnell, J. (John)
  The natural history of squirrels.
  Bibliography: p.185.
  Includes index.
  1. Squirrels.   I. Title.
QL737.R68G87   1987   599.32'32   86–24096
ISBN 0–8160–1694–1

Printed in Great Britain
10 9 8 7 6 5 4 3 2 1

Contents

List of colour plates

List of figures

List of tables

Acknowledgements

Grateful acknowledgements to Ernest Neal for inviting me to write a book on squirrels, and to Mark Anderson, Don Broom, Paul Chanin, Gordon Corbet, Bruce Don, Angela Gurnell, Robert Kenward, Ian Keymer, Clare Ludolf, Frank Nowell, Ernest Neal, Harry Pepper and Richard Tinsley for commenting on various sections of the book in draft form.

I should also like to sincerely thank Bruce Don, Curt Halvorson, Jessica Holm, Robert Kenward, Clare Ludolf, Harry Pepper, the late Judy Rowe, Luc Wauters and many other friends, colleagues and students, too numerous to mention by name, for sharing with me their interest and enthusiasm for squirrels over the past many years.

Jo Little and Jean Warburton helped with the preparation of the text for which I am most grateful. My thanks to Michael Clark for his excellent illustrations and to the following for generously allowing me to use their photographs: Natural History Photographic Agency (Plate 19), Michael Clark (Plate 5), Peter Gasson (Plates 2, 13), Joseph G. Hall (Plate 1), L.P. Hansen (Plate 16), Jessica Holm, courtesy Nikon UK (Plate 4), Mike Jordan (Plates 10, 15), Robert Kenward (Plate 9), Stephen L. Lindsay (Plate 17) and D.A. Sutton (Plate 20). All uncited photographs are by the author.

The Mammal Society and Blackwell Scientific Publications kindly gave permission to reproduce Figures 6.4 and 7.5, and the Forestry Commission to use the data presented in Figure 8.5.

Finally, my warmest thanks to Angela and David for their encouragement, support and help throughout my many studies of squirrels and other animals.

Series editor's foreword

In recent years there has been a great upsurge of interest in wildlife and a deepening concern for nature conservation. For many there is a compelling urge to counterbalance some of the artificiality of present-day living with a more intimate involvement with the natural world. More people are coming to realise that we are all part of nature, not apart from it. There seems to be a greater desire to understand its complexities and appreciate its beauty.

This appreciation of wildlife and wild places has been greatly stimulated by the world-wide impact of natural-history television programmes. These have brought into our homes the sights and sounds both of our own countryside and of far-off places that arouse our interest and delight.

In parallel with this growth of interest there has been a great expansion of knowledge and, above all, understanding of the natural world—an understanding vital to any conservation measures that can be taken to safeguard it. More and more field workers have carried out painstaking studies of many species, analysing their intricate behaviour, relationships and the part they play in the general ecology of their habitats. To the time-honoured techniques of field observations and experimentation has been added the sophistication of radio-telemetry whereby individual animals can be followed, even in the dark and over long periods, and their activities recorded. Infra-red cameras and light-intensifying binoculars now add a new dimension to the study of nocturnal animals. Through such devices great advances have been made.

This series of volumes aims to bring this information together in an exciting and readable form so that all who are interested in wildlife may benefit from such a synthesis. Many of the titles in the series concern groups of related species such as otters, squirrels and rabbits so that readers from many parts of the world may learn about their own more familiar animals in a much wider context. Inevitably more emphasis will be given to particular species within a group as some have been more extensively studied than others. Authors too have their own special interests and experience and a text gains much in authority and vividness when there has been personal involvement.

Many natural history books have been published in recent years which have delighted the eye and fired the imagination. This is wholly good. But it is the intention of this series to take this a step further by exploring the subject in greater depth and by making available the results of recent research. In this way it is hoped to satisfy to some extent at least the curiosity and desire to know more which is such an encouraging characteristic of the keen naturalist of today.

Ernest Neal
Taunton

For Angela and David

1 Squirrels of the world

Squirrels are conspicuous and familiar animals. Apart from the polar regions, they are found throughout the world except in Madagascar, parts of North Africa, Australasia, and the southern parts of South America (Figure 1.1). In fact there are three types of squirrel which can broadly be described as flying or gliding, ground-dwelling and tree squirrels. I have included chipmunks, prairie dogs and marmots in the ground-dwelling group. Many countries contain examples of all three types but only the last, the tree squirrels, are found in the British Isles.

This book concerns tree squirrels; animals which many of us know from myths, legends, fairy stories, and children's stories such as Beatrix Potter's delightful *The Tale of Squirrel Nutkin*. Common names for squirrels vary from species to species and place to place; they include attractive names such as the chickaree, the fairydiddle and the tassel-eared squirrel. More

Figure 1.1 Zoogeographical regions and distribution of numbers of species of tree (T), flying (F), and ground-dwelling (G) squirrels (Family Sciuridae). (ig = grey squirrel introduced; ia = Mexican red-bellied squirrel introduced). Source: Corbet and Hill (1980)

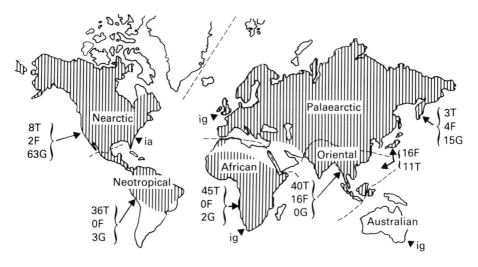

inauspicious is the name tree-rat which has been used to describe some species and rather spoils the image of these normally engaging creatures.

Throughout the book I concentrate on those species which live in North America, a continent often referred to as the Nearctic zoogeographical region, and Eurasia, which is often referred to as the Palaearctic region. These two are sometimes lumped together as the Holarctic region, and I shall use this word from time to time.

Holarctic tree squirrels live in cold-to-temperate, broadleaved and coniferous forests, and a great deal has been written about them in the last 50 years. This abundant literature results partly from the fact that tree squirrels have long been hunted for sport, fur and food throughout their range; today some species or subspecies in parts of their range are designated as pests while others are protected by law. In all there are ten species of Holarctic tree squirrel which belong to two genera, *Tamiasciurus* and *Sciurus* (Table 1.1).

In writing this book, I have used many sources of information and it has been impossible to cite every one. However, I have tried to include the most important or the most recent so that readers can follow up a particular topic if they so wish. My task has been made much easier by the many books which have been written about squirrels over the years, the most notable of which are Monica Shorten's *Squirrels* (1954), Dorcas MacClintock's *Squirrels of North America* (1970), Shirley E. Woods Jr *The Squirrels of Canada* (1981), and Keith Laidler's *Squirrels in Britain* (1980). I also enjoyed David E. Brown's *Arizona's Tree Squirrels* (1984). Lastly, the bibliographies in the articles by Flyger and Gates (1982a, 1982b) and the published symposium on the *Biology of Squirrels* (Gurnell, 1983) are rich sources of information.

This chapter and the next look at the world's squirrels in general, and the characteristics and habitats of tree squirrels in particular. These set the background for a detailed look at the behaviour and ecology of Holarctic tree squirrels in Chapters 3 to 8. The last chapter looks at the connections between squirrels and Man. Where possible, I not only describe the characteristics and behaviour of squirrels, but also try to give some explanation as to why they occur. There is much still to learn about squirrels and some of the ideas put forward will undoubtedly need revising in the future.

SQUIRRELS AND OTHER MAMMALS

Squirrels are rodents belonging to the order Rodentia of the class Mammalia. This order, containing about 1,650 species, is the largest group of living mammals, comprising some 40 per cent of all present-day mammal species. Much of the success of rodents can be attributed to their generalised body plan, grinding cheek teeth and very efficient gnawing front teeth. Indeed the very name rodent is derived from the Latin *rodere* which means 'to gnaw'. Rodents also breed fast and show an ability to adapt quickly to changing surroundings and to colonise new habitats. The first rodents may well have been forest living, squirrel-like animals; they appeared in the fossil record some 50 million years ago in North America and soon after that in Eurasia (Black, 1972). Since that time the rodents have spread widely. Now they are found in all continents and with a wide variety of life styles (Eisenberg, 1981).

Broadly speaking, there are three types of rodents which differ in the way their jaw muscles are attached to their cheek bones. Sometimes these groups are classified as suborders within the order Rodentia. They are: the mouse-like rodents or myomorphs with about 1,100 species, the porcupine-like rodents or hystricomorphs with 180 species and the squirrel-like rodents of sciuromorphs with 365 species in seven families. One of these families is the Sciuridae and it is here that we shall find the subject of this book, the tree squirrels, along with the flying and the ground-dwelling squirrels which we also look at.

TYPES OF SQUIRREL

All three types of squirrel probably evolved from a common ancestor which lived in North America sometime in the Eocene epoch, 54 to 37 million years ago (Black, 1972). The sequence of events since that time is complex and not fully understood. It is best known for the Nearctic region and, at least on the evidence from that continent, seems to be characterised by long periods of time with little evolutionary change interspersed with short bursts of time with more rapid change (Figure 1.2). Faunal exchanges have occurred between North America and Eurasia several times since the Oligocene which complicates evolutionary history. Squirrels also spread into Africa, possibly as early as the Miocene but certainly during the Pleistocene (Walker, 1983). These animals also moved into South America from North America after completion of the Panama land-bridge at the end of the Pliocene, three million years ago (Marshall *et al*, 1982). al, 1982).

Figure 1.2 Evolutionary history of Nearctic Sciuridae. Broken horizontal lines indicate presumed relationships without fossil evidence; asterisks indicate lines died out. Source: Hafner (1984)

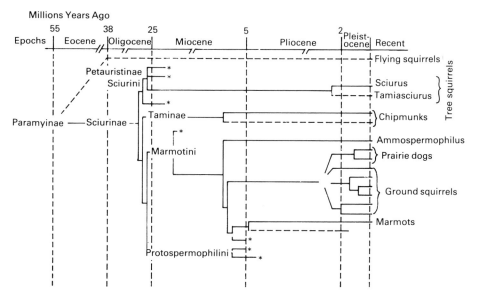

Table 1.1 Species of Holarctic tree squirrels

Species (Common name used in this book)	Other common names	Distribution	Habitat	Number of subspecies	Head and body length (mm)	Tail length (mm)
GENUS *TAMIASCIURUS*						
T. hudsonicus (Pine squirrel)	Red, Chickaree	Canada N.E. USA Rockies	Coniferous forests	25	270–385	92–158
T. douglasii (Douglas squirrel)	—	W. Canada W. USA	Coniferous forests	4	270–348	102–156
GENUS *SCIURUS*						
S. vulgaris (Red squirrel)	Common, Brown	Eurasia	Coniferous forests—also deciduous in W and S of range	40?	180–240	140–195

S. lis (Japanese squirrel)	—	Honshu, Shikoku and Kyushi, Japan	Coniferous and deciduous forests	1	180–240	140–195
S. anomalus (Persian squirrel)	—	Caucasus and Asia Minor. Lesbos in Greece	Coniferous and deciduous forests	1	180–240	140–195
S. carolinensis (Grey squirrel)	Eastern grey	E. USA Intr. England and S. Africa	Deciduous forests	5	383–525	150–243
S. griseus (Western grey squirrel)	—	W. USA	Oak/pine and redwood forests	3	510–570	265–290
S. niger (Fox squirrel)	—	E. USA	Savanna and open, deciduous forests	10	454–698	200–330
S. aberti (Abert squirrel)	Tassel-eared (subsp. Kaibab)	S. Central and N. America	Ponderosa pine montane forests	9	463–584	195–255
S. arizonensis (Arizona grey squirrel)	—	New Mexico and Arizona, USA	Montane forests	3	506–568	240–310

Flying squirrels, more appropriately described as gliding squirrels, are believed to be an early evolutionary offshoot of the main lineage (Figure 1.2). Today there are 36 species in Eurasia, North and Central America (e.g. Wells-Gosling, 1985). They are nocturnal, arboreal forest dwellers which eat fungi, flowers, fruits, seeds and insects. They have large flaps of skin between the fore and hind limbs which become taut when the limbs are spread out as they launch themselves to glide through the air. It may be that flying squirrels are nocturnal because their gliding habits would make them conspicuous and vulnerable to sharp-eyed, day-active birds of prey. Despite the similarities in their life style to that of the tree squirrels, the two groups are not now believed to be closely related (Hafner, 1984).

Tree and ground-dwelling squirrels seem to have diversified widely towards the end of the Oligocene (Figure 1.2; Hafner, 1984). From an arboreal or semi-arboreal forest-dweller feeding on nuts, seeds and berries evolved ground-dwelling squirrels, chipmunks and true tree squirrels. It is not clear why this radiation occurred but it may have been affected by climatic cooling which started in the Eocene and led to the southward shift of subarctic, temperate and tropical belts of vegetation (Chaney, 1947; Dorf, 1960). This would have led to the formation of patches of grass and scrub habitats suitable for ground-dwelling squirrels. Some exchange in ground-dwelling squirrels occurred between the Nearctic and the Palaearctic at this time (Black, 1972).

Chipmunks are ground or terrestrial animals but they may forage in trees; in this sense they can be considered to be intermediate between tree and other ground-dwelling squirrels. Chipmunks entered Asia from North America in the mid-Pliocene epoch and now there is one species in Eurasia and 20 in North America. They are mainly associated with grass and scrub-type habitats in forest clearings and along forest edges.

During the Miocene there was a rapid radiation of the other ground-dwelling squirrels in North America after the Rocky Mountains had become uplifted in the west (Figure 1.2). This major event created a rain-shadow in the interior which accelerated the drying and formation of grasslands. Another major radiation in ground squirrels occurred towards the end of the Pliocene epoch in North America as the mountain building in the west of the continent increased and habitats in the interior fragmented and diversified. A further migration of ground-dwelling squirrels (ground squirrels and marmots) from western North America into Eurasia occurred at about this time (Black, 1972). So today we find ground-dwelling squirrels, that is marmots, ground squirrels, and prairie dogs, throughout North and South America, Eurasia and also in Africa.

Ground-dwelling squirrels, in general, are fairly large, diurnal, vegetarians and many species live in exposed habitats such as grasslands, deserts and alpine meadows. During the last 30 years, these squirrels have become favourite research subjects for students of behaviour and ecology. As a group of species, they reveal interesting comparative relationships between their social organisation and the environment (see Murie and Michener, 1984). Unlike tree squirrels, most ground-dwelling species hibernate during unfavourable weather.

TREE SQUIRRELS—ORIGINS

The earliest records of tree squirrels are for a genus called *Protosciurus* from Oligocene fossil deposits in North America, and for 'Sciurus' dubius from slightly later in the same epoch in Europe. Both squirrels showed some similarities in generalised dental characters to present tree squirrels (Black, 1972). It appears on the available evidence, therefore, that tree squirrels first evolved in North America during the Oligocene epoch and soon after migrated westwards through Asia into Europe.

The place of origin of the modern genus Sciurus is not known but it has been found from the early Miocene in both North America and Europe. However, the history of Sciurus since that time is obscure (Black, 1972). Moore (1961) has suggested two or more invasions of the Palaearctic species Sciurus vulgaris into North America during the Pleistocene which subsequently diverged to produce at least some of the species now found on that continent. At one time Tamiasciurus and Sciurus were not believed to be closely related and this was based on differences in the characteristics of the baculum or penis bone (Pocock, 1923) and the skull (Moore, 1959). For example, Tamiasciurus only has a small or vestigeal baculum (Layne, 1954). However, new evidence from a variety of sources suggests that they are in fact closely related and so they are now grouped together within the same tribe (a taxonomic group which pools together closely related genera) called Sciurini (Table 1.1; Hight et al, 1974; Ellis and Maxson, 1980). Hafner (1984) has depicted that the two genera diverged towards the end of the Pliocene, some 3 million years ago.

It is worth just briefly mentioning that two other evolutionary lines of tree squirrels have been suggested, one giving rise to the South-east Asian squirrels and the Indian genus Funambulus, and the other to the giant squirrels of the genus Ratufa. A long time ago Ratufa was found in Central Europe but is now confined to India and the Oriental zoogeographical region (Hight et al, 1974). In addition, the tree squirrels from Central and South America could possibly have diverged from the Sciurus squirrels in North America as early as the middle Miocene period, long before the land connection between North and South America had formed (Ellis and Maxson, 1980).

HOLARCTIC TREE SQUIRRELS

There are two genera and ten species of squirrels living in cold and temperate forests in the northern hemisphere (Table 1.1). In North America I shall only consider those species which occur down to the Mexico border although I have not included Nayarit's squirrel (Sciurus nayaritensis) which, although mainly a squirrel of montane forests of the Sierra Madre in Mexico, does occur over the border a little way into New Mexico and Arizona (Figure 1.3). In fact Nayarit's squirrel is very similar to the fox squirrel, S. niger (E.R. Hall, 1981). Similarly, I do not consider other species of Central America, such as Allen's squirrel (S. alleni) and Peter's squirrel (S. oculatus) or the exotic Mexican red-bellied squirrel (S. aureogaster) which has been introduced into Florida (see Brown and McGuire, 1975).

There is a great deal of variation in the body weights of squirrels according to the time of the year and food availability. Table 1.1, therefore, shows a range of figures for the head and body, and tail measurements of the different species. The range is quite large for most species; this reflects their wide occurrence and regional variation in body size. In fact, most

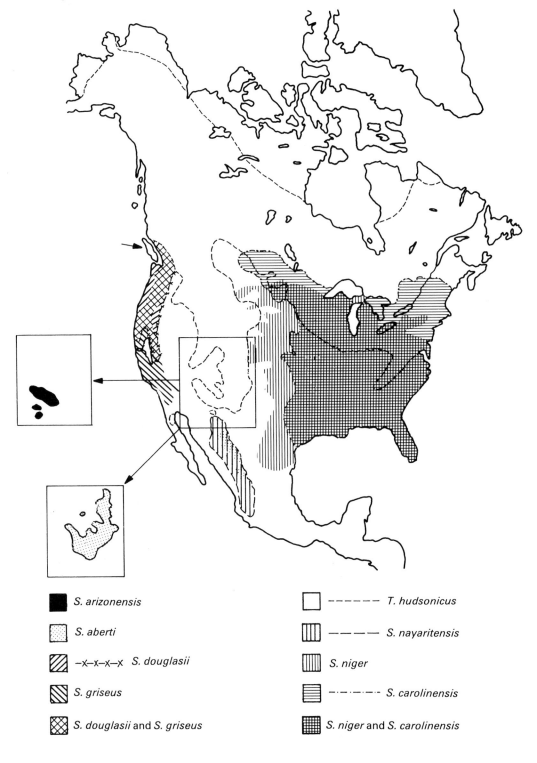

Figure 1.3 Distribution of Nearctic tree squirrels. Source: E.R. Hall (1981)

races or subspecies of squirrel (Table 1.1) have been separated on the basis of body size and coat colour. I shall examine some common features of these attributes among the squirrel species in the next chapter.

TREE SQUIRRELS OF THE NEARCTIC

There are seven native species of tree squirrel in North America which belong to the two genera, *Tamiasciurus* and *Sciurus*. Pine squirrels, *T. hudsonicus*, are often known as red squirrels but not so in this book in order to distinguish them from the Eurasian red squirrels. They are closely associated with cold, boreal and subalpine coniferous forests in Alaska and Canada, with extensions to their range stretching south in the Rocky Mountains to New Mexico and south in the Appalachians to South Carolina. Man has introduced the pine squirrel to many places including Newfoundland. Fishermen took several pairs of this species across the sea from Labrador to Hare Bay in 1963; the squirrels are now well established and spreading throughout the northern peninsula (Woods, 1981). Pine squirrels have dark reddish-brown backs with a white underside and a white eye ring. The separation of the dark back from the white underside is often marked by a dark line, especially during the summer. In the winter, pine squirrels sport small ear tufts, but they are not as splendid as the tufts on tassel-eared or red squirrels. Their tails, which have yellowish tips bordered with black, tend to be relatively smaller and flatter than squirrels of the *Sciurus* genus. Pine squirrels are known by a variety of other common names, many, such as barking squirrel, boomer and chatterbox, relating to their noisy habits which includes their scolding, territorial 'tchrrr' calls. Pine squirrels also go by the names chickaree, fairydiddle and *Adjidaumo*, a Red Indian name which means 'tail in the air' and which was used by Longfellow in his poem *Hiawatha* (MacClintock, 1970; Woods, 1981).

Not surprisingly, with such a large geographic range, many subspecies of pine squirrel have been described (Table 1.1). These tend to vary slightly in colour and body size. In general, they are the smallest of the Holarctic squirrels with body weights of between 200 and 250 g. Douglas squirrels, *T. douglasii*, are very similar to pine squirrels in appearance and habits and tend to be at the upper end of the pine squirrel's range in body size. They are found mainly in coniferous forests on the west coast of North America from southern British Columbia in Canada, through the Cascade Mountains in Washington and Oregon in the USA and down into the coastal forests and Sierra Nevada in California. The subspecies, *T.d. mearnsi* from the Sierra Laguna and Sierra San Pedro in Baja California has been raised to specific rank by Lindsay (1981). The upper surface of douglas squirrels has been described as dusky-olive to greyish-brown, the underside from yellowish-white to white suffused with orange. As in the pine squirrel, a dark lateral stripe separates the upper and lower coat colours. The tail has white tips bordered with black bands and the ears carry small tufts with longer brown hairs in winter.

In the Pacific Northwest (British Columbia, Washington and Oregon), the ranges of the pine and the douglas squirrel overlap slightly. From time to time hybrids between the two species based on, for example, coat colour, have been reported from these areas of overlap. However, a detailed analysis by Lindsay (1982) strongly suggests that no hybridisation has occurred and that the so-called hybrids can be ascribed to one or the other species. Therefore, the two species are reproductively isolated and the similarity in appearance between the two species in zones of overlap results from a convergence in adaptive features (e.g. coat colour) to those particular forest habitats.

The remaining five species of North American squirrel belong to the genus *Sciurus*. Two species, the fox squirrel (*S. niger*) and the Eastern grey squirrel (*S. carolinensis*) occur together over large areas of the eastern part of the USA. The range of the fox squirrel extends slightly farther west but not quite as far north as the grey squirrel which is found in parts of south-east Canada (Figure 1.3). The fox squirrel is the largest of the Holarctic tree squirrels and body weights may exceed 1,000 g. Various colour forms are found but the three commonest are: (1) grey with reddish colours on the limbs, a dark head and white on the nose and ears, (2) reddish black on the dorsal surface and reddish-yellow to light grey on the underside, with a mixed black and rufous tail and black soles to the feet, and (3) a black or melanistic form found especially in the southern parts of their range. Fox squirrels are found in a variety of habitats but they are mainly associated with open hardwood and mixed forests, often bordering on prairie and farmland, or in riverine and swamp forests and shelterbelts. Fox squirrels have been introduced into many locations in the western part of the USA (Flyger and Gates, 1982a).

In comparison with the fox squirrel, the grey squirrel is found in denser, more mature hardwood forests and as the relative proportion of forest to open land in an area increases, so the proportion of fox to grey squirrels declines. For example, where 10 per cent of the land is forested, fox and grey squirrels occur in equal abundance, when 70 per cent of the land is forested, the fox squirrel tends to be absent (Flyger and Gates, 1982a). Grey squirrels are moderately large with adult body weights between 500 and 600 g. As their name suggests, grey squirrels look grey in colour but on closer inspection they have a salt-and-pepper appearance. This is because the underfur is grey but the longer guard hairs have grey bases, and brown and black coloured shafts tipped with white. Very often the flanks, limbs and paws are reddish-brown and the ears are similarly light or reddish-brown. Usually, the underside of the body is white, but some varieties may be grey. Like fox squirrels, melanic greys are not uncommon but here black squirrels are mainly found in the north of their range. Both fox and grey squirrels are common in parks and gardens in urban areas throughout their range. Interestingly, in the mainly agricultural state of Illinois, grey squirrels will be found in some towns and fox squirrels in others, but why is not known.

Another similarity to fox squirrels is that grey squirrels have been introduced into various places in the Pacific states, but they have also been introduced further afield into parts of Canada, Britain, South Africa and Australia. Many of these overseas introductions occurred at the end of the nineteenth and the beginning of the twentieth centuries.

The grey squirrel in Australia was formerly found in garden suburbs in places like Melbourne, but they appear to have died out several years ago (Seebeck, 1984). The grey squirrel was first introduced into the South West Cape in South Africa by Cecil Rhodes in 1900, and it continues to flourish in the mild mediterranean climate of that region (Millar, 1980). The grey squirrel also thrives in Britain and has replaced the native red squirrel throughout much of England and Wales. We shall return to look at this more closely in Chapter 8.

The Western grey squirrel (*S. griseus*) is slightly larger than its counterpart from the eastern states of the USA. It has a blue-grey back sharply separated from its white underside. The tail is large and grey with dark bands and white edges. The eyes are ringed in white and one of its three subspecies has black hindfeet. It is mainly found in open, mixed, dry hardwood forests but also evergreen forests along the western coast of the USA from Washington and western Oregon in the north and along the coastal ranges and the Sierra Nevada in California into Baja California.

The Arizona grey squirrel (*S. arizonensis*) is in fact more closely related to the fox squirrel than to either the Eastern or the Western grey squirrel (Brown, 1984). Further, they are very similar to three other types of squirrel from north-central America which have been given specific rank in the past, the Apache squirrel (*S. apache*), the Chiricahua squirrel (*S. chiricahuae*), and the Nayarit squirrel (*S. nayaritensis*). E.R. Hall (1981) assigns the Apache squirrel and the Chiricahua squirrel as subspecies of the Nayarit squirrel. The upper parts of the Arizona grey are grizzled grey in colour with tinges of reddish-brown over the shoulders and back, and the underside is white. It has a noticeably large, very bushy tail with long fringes of white, a white eye ring and short round ears without tufts. They are found almost entirely in Arizona in dense riparian, mixed hardwood forests, particularly at elevations between 1,000 and 3,000 m. Consequently, they do not occur in higher evergreen forests or the more open woodlands of the flood-plain.

The last North American species to be mentioned, the abert or tassel-eared squirrel (*S. aberti*), is the most handsome of all squirrels. The name tassel-eared comes from their very long ear tufts which are especially noticeable in the winter. The tufts consist of black hairs which range in length from about 0.5 cm in July to 4 cm in February and then decrease to 2 cm in June (Nash and Seaman, 1977). They are large animals with adult weights of between 600 and 700 g. The tail, which is dark grey and fringed with white, is not particularly long but tends to be broad and bushy. The body comes in several colour phases the most common of which is a peppered charcoal grey back separated from the white underside by a black bar. In some regions there is a broad reddish-brown band down the back. A high incidence of a dark or melanic phase is found mainly in the northern part of their range in Colorado. Abert squirrels are confined to forests of ponderosa pine (*Pinus ponderosa*) which occur at elevations approximately between 1,800 and 3,000 m in parts of Wyoming, Colorado, New Mexico, Arizona, Utah and Mexico. The nine subspecies of abert squirrel tend to be rather isolated because of the discontinuous distribution of ponderosa pine. The best known subspecies is the beautifully coloured Kaibab squirrel from the Kaibab Plateau on the north rim of the Grand Canyon in Arizona. This squirrel sports a black belly with a whitish tail.

TREE SQUIRRELS OF THE PALAEARCTIC

The red squirrel (*S. vulgaris*), often called the common or brown squirrel, has perhaps the largest range of all squirrels and is found throughout the Palaearctic south to the Mediterranean, the Caucasus Mountains

Figure 1.4 Distribution of Palaearctic tree squirrels. Source: Corbet (1978)

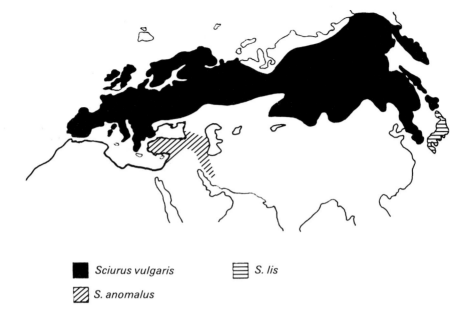

■ *Sciurus vulgaris*   ☰ *S. lis*

▨ *S. anomalus*

(between the Black Sea and the Caspian Sea), the southern Ural Mountains, the Altai mountains in central Mongolia, and north-east China (Figure 1.4). In the east it is found on Sakhalin Island off the coast of the USSR and the most northern of the Japanese Islands, Hokkaido. As in the case of the pine squirrel, it is not surprising that many subspecies have been suggested for the red squirrel, although the distribution of the species is for the most part continuous and the taxonomic status of all these subspecies is not clear (Corbet, 1978; Shorten, 1962). The dorsal colour varies between grey and brown, to bright red to black, whereas the underside is whitish. There are conspicuous ear tufts, and in some forms the colour of the ear tufts, tail and feet can be different to the rest of the animal. Reintroductions and transplantations of red squirrels between regions have often occurred in the past which makes it more difficult to identify particular colour varieties. This is so with the red squirrel which occurs in the British Isles. Formerly ubiquitous in the islands, its distribution has declined since the introduction of the grey squirrel, *S. carolinensis*, from eastern North America during the late nineteenth and early twentieth centuries (see Chapter 8). The red squirrel is now found mainly in Ireland, Scotland, Wales, northern England and one or two places in central and southern England. Its coat colour is very variable with some forms sporting whitish tails and ear-tufts in summer. It appears that population densities were very low at times during the seventeenth century in Ireland, the eighteenth century in England and the nineteenth century in Scotland (Chapter 8). As a result squirrels were imported from various places on the Continent and generally moved about the country. Lowe and Gardiner (1983) found no evidence that the present British squirrels are unique to Britain although it seems likely that at one time there was a distinct British race.

Lowe and Gardiner (1983) also comment on the other two species of Palaearctic tree squirrel, the Persian squirrel, (*S. anomalus*) and the Japanese squirrel (*S. lis*). Both species are similar in size to *S. vulgaris* but the pelage is distinctive and different from the many variants of red squirrel. The Japanese squirrel is found on the islands south of Hokkaido: Honshu, Shikoku and Kyushu (Figure 1.4); although very similar to the red squirrel, Lowe and Gardiner (1983) support Corbet (1978) in assigning it specific rank. It has an olive coloured, finely speckled dorsal pelage, a white ventrum, white tips to the hairs on the tail and ear tufts in winter. The status of the Persian squirrel, which is found on the Greek island of Lesbos, in the Caucasus Mountains and Anatolia, and south through the Zagros Mountains in Iran to the Persian Gulf (Figure 1.4), is less clear from Lowe and Gardiner's examination of skull shape. However, it appears distinctive. In comparison with the red and Japanese squirrels, it does not have conspicuous ear tufts or a second premolar in the upper tooth-row and it has a posterior pad on the sole of the hindfeet (Corbet, 1978). Its dorsal surface and the base of the tail is coarsely speckled and grey. Its flanks, shoulders, face and rest of the tail is brown, and its ventral surface is suffused with reddish brown (Gordon Corbet, pers. comm.). Very little is known about the ecology of this species.

TROPICAL TREE SQUIRRELS

Although this book is about Holarctic tree squirrels, it is worth noting that the greatest diversity of tree squirrels occurs in the tropics. Although tropical tree squirrels have by no means been as intensively studied as Holarctic tree squirrels, work carried out within the last 15 years in Africa and Malaysia has revealed some interesting variations in life style (e.g.

Table 1.2 Resource partitioning among eight species of African tree squirrel in the Gabon. All species are found in mature and secondary forest with dense shrub layers (from Emmons, 1980). The diet figures are the mean per cent dry mass per stomach. The long active period refers to squirrels being active all day, a short active periods refers to squirrels returning to the nest several hours before sunset

Species/vertical distribution	Body Weight (g)	Active Period	Diet (%)			
			Inverts	Fruit	Leaves	Bark
UPPER LAYERS						
Protoxerus strangeri	690	short	<1	85	9	
Heliosciurus rufobrachium	360	short	5	89	6	
Aethosciurus poensis	100	long	11	89		
Myosciurus pumilio	17	long?	37	33		30
INTERMEDIATE						
Funisciurus lemniscalatus	140	long	36	59	3	
F. isabella	110	long?	6	81	9	
FOREST FLOOR						
F. pyrrhopus	300	short	12	83		
Epixerus ebii	590	short	2	98		

Emmons, 1980). Whereas most northern forests contain just one or two species of tree squirrel, tropical forests contain up to eight or nine different types. The same general distinction between Holarctic and tropical habitats can be applied to flying squirrels and ground-dwelling squirrels. How can such a large number of similar species live within the same habitat? The answer is quite complex but essentially tropical forests are rich, varied habitats and each animal species has its own unique niche within these habitats. All tree squirrels are remarkably similar in appearance but tropical squirrels vary from the very small, pygmy and dwarf squirrels to the very large, giant squirrels, and, unlike Holarctic squirrels, confine their activities to distinct layers within the forest (Table 1.2). Some remain in the top canopy whereas others will live in the middle or lower layers and one or two even stay on the ground. They also tend to choose different foods. Only the large species are seed specialists, the others variously eat fruit, leaves, insects, bark and sap. It is also worth pointing out that they have to share the available resources with other arboreal animals, particularly primates. A result of this varied and complex community structure is that tropical tree squirrels tend to occur at low densities.

2 Characteristics, homes and haunts of squirrels

It is possible to describe the life style of a mammal from a simple examination of its teeth and feet; other clues come from body size, body posture, tail and skull characters.

HEADS, SKULLS, TEETH AND SENSES OF SQUIRRELS

Squirrels have powerful, upper and lower incisor teeth followed by a gap, called a diastema, where the canine teeth would normally be found in omnivorous animals such as primates, or carnivorous animals such as cats and dogs (Figure 2.1). The incisors are called evergrowing or open-rooted

Figure 2.1 Skull and teeth of a grey squirrel. Top: side view of skull and lower jaw; bottom: ventral view of skull

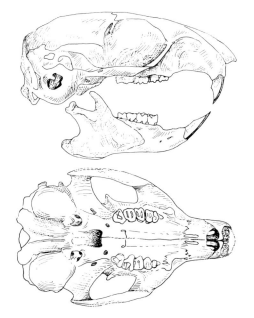

teeth because they keep growing throughout the life of the animal to compensate for the enormous amount of wear which they endure. They have chisel-shaped, self-sharpening cutting edges with hard enamel only on the front surfaces; the tips, therefore, have a typical bevelled appearance. If damaged so that the upper and lower incisors do not meet, then their growth is uncontrolled and bizarre forms may arise which eventually lead to the death of the animal. Behind the diastema come the cheek or grinding teeth which consist of premolars and molars. There are three molars in each jaw and one or two premolars. Some species, such as grey squirrels, have two upper premolars the first being small and close to the inner edge of the second premolar. Other species such as the fox squirrels do not have the first upper premolar. Therefore, the general dental formula of squirrels can be expressed as:

$$\frac{1.0.1\text{--}2.3}{1.0\ \ 1.\ \ 3} \times 2 = 20\text{--}22$$

The left-hand side of the expression refers to the number of the different types of teeth on the upper and lower jaws on one side of the skull (from left to right: incisors, canines, premolars, molars). In young squirrels the first premolars to develop are milk teeth and these are replaced by permanent teeth when they are between six and twelve months old. The cheek teeth have prominent enamel cusps which function as an aid in grinding up the food material (Figure 2.2). They wear away as the animals get older. Indices of tooth wear have been used to assess the age of animals (Chapter 7).

Figure 2.2 Cheek teeth of a fox squirrel. Top: oblique view of upper cheek teeth; bottom: oblique view of lower cheek teeth (posterior to right)

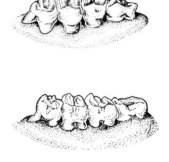

The jaws have two actions; in the first the lower jaw is pulled forward so that the upper and lower incisors meet for gnawing, and in the second the lower jaw is withdrawn slightly so that the cheek teeth can meet and grind up the food with a circular motion of the lower jaw. Different groups of muscles are responsible for these actions but particularly noticeable outwardly are the large masseter or cheek muscles (Figure 2.3). The skull is relatively high, short and broad, with a well-developed, slightly flattened zygoma or cheek bone and an incomplete post-orbital bar.

Squirrels have four sets of vibrissae on the head: above and below the eyes, on the underside of the head in front of the throat, and the large nose

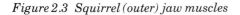

Figure 2.3 Squirrel (outer) jaw muscles

Temperalis

Masseter lateralis

Masseter superficialis

whiskers (Figure 2.4). Similar types of hair are found on the underside in the position of the mammae, at the base of the tail and around the feet (Laidler, 1980; Shorten, 1954). Vibrissae are tactile or touch receptors and provide the animal with information about its immediate surroundings. Squirrels have quite large eyes and good eyesight with a wide field of vision. They particularly have an ability to distinguish vertical objects which is essential in a tree-living animal. Squirrels are day-active and at one time were believed to have all-cone retinas. (Cones are light sensitive cells associated with colour vision and an accurate discrimination of detail; rods are cells sensitive to low light intensities.) Now it is known that the retina is a two-tiered structure with an inner tier (towards the centre of the eye) composed of rods and an outer tier of cones (Jacobs, 1981). Therefore, we can infer from this that squirrels are able to see in dim light. The present evidence suggests that in daylight squirrels have dichromatic colour vision (humans have trichromatic colour vision). Thus they are like humans with red-green colour blindness, that is they cannot discriminate

Figure 2.4 Squirrel head and manipulation of food with front feet

red from green but they can discriminate red or green from blue. The ears of squirrels are moderately large, and some species, such as abert or Tassel-eared squirrels and red squirrels, have prominent and attractive ear tufts. Little is known about the range of hearing in squirrels but they are certainly sensitive to the smallest noise or disturbance. Similarly, they have a well-developed sense of smell which they use in social communication (Chapter 5) and in detecting food buried under the ground. Interestingly, tree squirrels have relatively larger brains than ground-living squirrels but the reason for this difference is not clear (Meier, 1983).

FEET AND TAILS

Squirrels have long, strong hindlimbs and a hindfoot with five long digits, the fourth one being the longest (Figure 2.5). The forelimbs are smaller and the forefeet, and have four long digits and a very small thumb with a flattened nail which largely goes unnoticed. All the long digits bear tough, curved claws and greatly assist the animals in climbing. The ventral surfaces of the feet have prominent pads and may be slightly furred, especially in the winter. When walking or running the whole of the foot is placed on the ground; this is technically called a plantigrade stance. Squirrels are excellent climbers and can leap considerable distances using their powerful hindlimbs. When not on the move, squirrels usually squat on their hindlegs and are able to manipulate food or objects with their forefeet (Figures 2.4, 2.6). In their nests, squirrels curl up into a ball.

The tails of squirrels are probably their most distinguishing characteristic and the names of the two genera considered in this book reflect this. The generic name *Sciurus* is derived from the ancient Greek words *Skia*, meaning shadow, and *oura* meaning tail. Hence a squirrel is an animal which sits in the shadow of its tail. Similarly, the generic name *Tamiasciurus* has a prefix derived from the Greek word *Tamias* literally meaning an animal who caches food; again, as we shall see, this is a most appropriate description. Squirrel tails then are large and bushy and held over the back of a resting animal. The tail is stretched out behind during running and leaping. Tails are used for balance, but they have other functions as well. We shall see later in the book that the tail may be used in the regulation of body temperature or as a signalling device.

Figure 2.5 Squirrel feet. Left: front; right: back

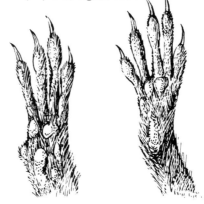

Figure 2.6 Squirrel skeleton and upright stance

THE MOULT AND COAT COLOUR

Like most mammals from northern latitudes, squirrels change their coat twice during the year, first in the spring and then in the autumn. All Holarctic squirrels seem to follow the same pattern of moulting. In red squirrels the spring moult occurs in April and May and lasts about six weeks. The moult occurs in a fixed sequence over the head and body. It begins on the nose and around the eyes, then spreads to the cheeks, forehead and base of the ears (Figure 2.7). The hands and feet may also moult at this time. The moult progresses to the shoulders, along the back, across the flanks to the underside. The tail and the tips of the ears moult only once a year. In the tail it starts at the base in June and continues towards the tip. This moult is prolonged and may not finish until September. The ear tufts, which are not found in all species, appear in September, grow until January and then slowly thin out so that by the summer most of the tuft has disappeared. The autumn moult starts in October and proceeds in the opposite direction to that of the spring moult.

19

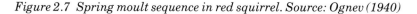

Figure 2.7 Spring moult sequence in red squirrel. Source: Ognev (1940)

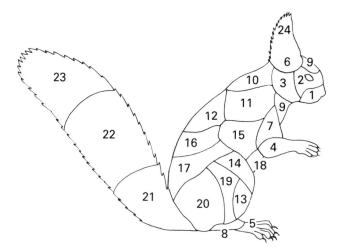

It starts at the base of the tail, spreads up the back over the flanks and forelimbs and lastly to the underside. Individuals in a population do not moult exactly at the same time or at the same rate; the timing partly depends on the physical condition of the animals. Adult males begin to moult first but the moult is more prolonged than in females. Young born in the spring moult out of their juvenile coat in June and July and then they moult again slightly later than adult males in the autumn. Adult females tend to moult after the spring-born young and the start of the autumn moult is deferred until after they have finished nursing summer-born young. Summer-born young moult in the autumn shortly after they have been weaned at about three months old. They do so quickly; they have little time left before the onset of winter (Ognev, 1940).

The appearance of a squirrel will depend upon the stage of the moult with the full winter coat tending to be more luxuriant and brighter in colour than the summer coat. Similarly, the tail is bushiest, the ears most furred and the ear-tufts, if present, most splendid in mid-winter. Furthermore, there is quite a variety of colour forms within and between species. These colour varieties can be considered to be adaptive in that they convey some protection to the animals from predators by matching their background. Thus, squirrels tend to match the tree bark of the dominant trees in their particular region. For example, Christopher C. Smith (1981) points out that grey fur of fox and grey squirrels matches the grey bark of beech trees and many species of maple and oak. Pine and red squirrels tend to have red or brown dorsal coats which match their habitats predominantly made up of pine, spruce, fir and cedar. Smith also proposed similar arguments for subspecific changes in colour form including the colour of the sides and the ventral fur. Pine squirrels which live in mixed deciduous and coniferous forests in the eastern USA (*T.h. loquax*), for example, have ashy-grey sides. Furthermore, many species of squirrel have pale undersides which tend to blend in with the sky or distant background when viewed from below.

Despite the above, coat colour may not simply be a form of crypsis.

All-white or albino squirrels turn up from time to time, but more interestingly a dark or melanic colour phase is found in many species. Melanistic fox squirrels, for example, frequently occur in southern parts of their range whereas black grey squirrels are abundant in the northern parts of theirs. Melanistic abert squirrels are found in northern Colorado and the strikingly attractive Kaibab squirrel has a dark body with a white tail. I have spent many an hour watching the very attractive melanic red squirrels in pine forests high in the Alps in Switzerland. In the particular small forest I visit, all the squirrels seem to be very dark or black, elsewhere on the Continent the proportion of black squirrels in a population varies. This has probably best been studied in Scandinavia.

Throughout Scandinavia, red squirrels exhibit three colour phases: a red phase, a melanic phase, and an intermediate or brown phase. The brown phase appears to be most common, followed by the red and then the black. The red phase, however, is much more common in Sweden than throughout most of Finland. Voipio (1970) suggests that the relative numbers of these phases vary throughout Fennoscandia but they are constant in particular regions according to climate and genetic back-ground. This is referred to as a balanced polymorphism. The melanic phase, for example, has longer underfur than the red phase and may have better insulating properties (Voipio and Hissa, 1970). Melanic abert squirrels also have longer guard hairs and underfur than grey morphs (Hancock and Nash, 1979) and there is evidence that melanic grey squirrels are better adapted to the cold than the normal, grey form (Chapter 4). The fact that melanic abert and melanic grey squirrels are both found to the north of their respective geographic ranges supports the idea that melanism is associated with thermoregulation. However, this may not be the whole story since melanic fox squirrels are found to the south of their range.

BODY SIZE

Body size is biologically very important. For example, small mammals are said to spend relatively (i.e. in relation to body mass) more energy on thermoregulation than large mammals. This is because rates of heating and cooling are influenced by the surface-to-volume ratio since a change in body temperature 'is proportional to the heat exchange with the environ-ment, which occurs through the surface, and is inversely related to heat storage, which in turn is a function of volume (mass)' (McNab, 1971). Therefore, in species which range over wide geographic areas we should expect individuals to increase in size as the climate becomes cooler, either at higher elevations or at higher latitudes. This is known as Bergmann's rule. Taking several species of *Sciurus* squirrel as a whole, body size (head and body length) does tend to increase with latitude (Figure 2.8), but the pattern is not particularly evident if trends in body size within species are examined. In addition, since the total amount of heat lost by a large mammal must be greater than that of a small one, the energetic explanation for Bergmann's rule may not be appropriate. Indeed, only about a third of all mammal species are larger at northern latitudes, and pine squirrels are the smallest tree squirrel in North America and yet live in the coldest, most northerly climates. It has been suggested that the size of seed foods and the presence of competing species affects body size trends

Figure 2.8 Relationship between length of head and body of North American squirrels and latitude. Source: Heaney (1984)

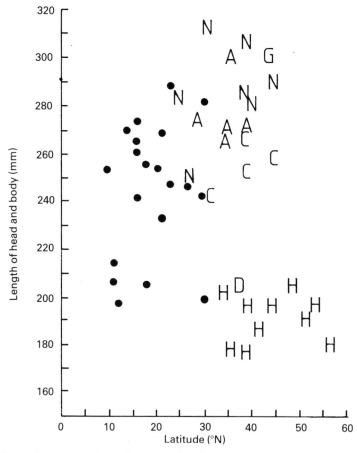

A = *Sciurus aberti* C = *S. carolinensis* G = *S. griseus* N = *S. niger*
D = *Tamiasciurus douglasii* H = *T. hudsonicus* ● = Central and South American squirrels

in North American tree squirrels but more detailed analyses are required to test these hypotheses (Heaney, 1984; McNab, 1971). It is also possible that lightness of foot and an ability to forage well out on thin branches could influence the body size of, for example, pine, red and douglas squirrels which predominantly live in coniferous habitats.

SQUIRREL HABITATS

Natural communities of plants and animals which are adapted to a particular range of environmental factors, such as temperature and rainfall, are called biomes (Figure 2.9). Squirrels are forest animals, and forest biomes are widespread throughout much of the Holarctic region (Figure 2.10). Historically, modern forests can be traced back to the end of the Palaeozoic Era, more than 225 million years ago. Thereafter conifers diversified greatly and became abundant; deciduous trees similar to those found today did not appear until the end of the Cretaceous Period, some 65

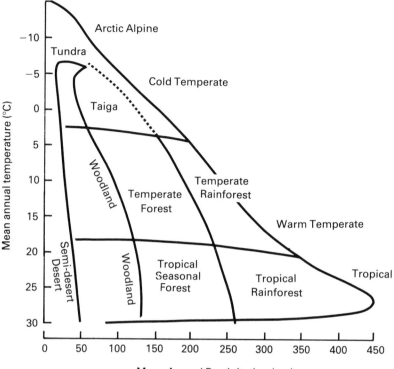

Figure 2.9 Classification of major terrestrial biomes with respect to mean annual precipitation and mean annual temperature. Source: Whittaker (1975)

million years ago. In Chapter 1 tree squirrels were traced back to warm Eocene times when, in England for example, tropical trees were found as far north as London. Thereafter there was a widespread cooling of the climate and the temperate forests came to dominate most of the Northern Hemisphere during the Miocene (Dorf, 1960; Spurr and Barnes, 1973). The climate continued to cool, albeit interspersed with warm periods, until the Pleistocene when there were several major periods of dramatic climatic change called the Ice Ages.

The alternating warm and cold periods of the Ice Ages resulted in respective northerly and southerly migrations of tree species. It can reasonably be assumed that squirrels and other forest animals moved with the forests. The last Ice age, called the Wisconsin in North America, the Weichsel in north-west Europe and the Devensian in Britain, lasted between about 70,000 and 12,000 years ago. At the greatest extent of the Wisconsin ice sheet, spruce and pine trees grew as far south as Georgia in North America (Cox and Moore, 1985).

After the last Ice Age, there was a general warming of the climate which reached its maximum between 7,000 and 5,000 years ago. Tundra and open spruce and pine forest parkland were the first vegetation types to inhabit open country. As the climate continued to warm, boreal spruce and pine forest became established, to be replaced by temperate, deciduous forests. Many land bridges, which allowed the free movement of plant and animal species between land masses, such as those between Britain and

Figure 2.10 Distribution of major terrestrial biomes of the Nearctic and Palaearctic regions. Source: Cox and Moore (1985)

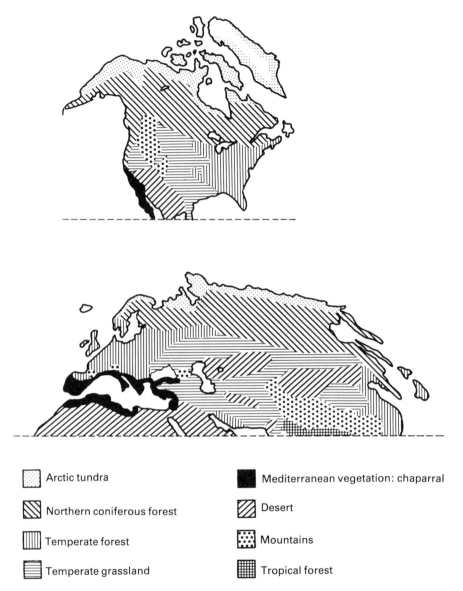

▥ Arctic tundra		■ Mediterranean vegetation: chaparral	
◩ Northern coniferous forest		▨ Desert	
▥ Temperate forest		▥ Mountains	
▤ Temperate grassland		▦ Tropical forest	

Europe, and between Siberia and Alaska, were broken during this time as the ice sheets melted and sea levels began to rise.

Today, temperate and boreal floras in North America and Eurasia are still remarkably similar in structure and plant genera. However, at mid-latitudes the western European forest flora is much poorer in species than those in eastern North America. This is significant for tree squirrels in relation to tree seed variety and availability. One theory why this should be is that the northwards return of some plant species during the Pleistocene was impeded by east-west mountain ranges and by the

Mediterranean in Europe. This was not the case in North America because the mountain ranges run closer to north–south leaving corridors in between. The result is that the European flora became relatively impoverished during the Pleistocene. Over the last 5,000 years the climate in the Northern Hemisphere has generally been slightly cooler and more humid.

Today northern coniferous forests extend in a belt right across North America and Eurasia but they are also found at lower latitudes on high mountain ranges such as the Rockies and the Alps. Northern forests are characterised by long, cold winters and the dominant trees are needle-leafed conifers such as spruces, firs and pines which are able to resist drought and to photosynthesise at any time of the year. Typically, in North America and Eurasia large tracts of coniferous or boreal forest (sometimes called taiga) consist of just one or two tree species. The cones and buds of these trees, along with fungi, form the bulk of the food for pine, red and other coniferous forest squirrels. The deciduous larch, and broad-leafed birch trees are also found in coniferous forests, especially in the most northerly, open forests, and poplars and aspen (often as secondary forest) may be associated with conifers in some regions. Understorey, shrub and field plants are infrequently found in mature, northern coniferous forests, except in damp places. Therefore, berries and other potential squirrel foods from these types of plant are not abundant.

In North America, two regional types of coniferous forest association are worth mentioning, the Pacific coastal forest of the north-west and the so-called 'lakes-forests' around the Great Lakes in the east. The Pacific coast forest has a high rainfall and moderate climate and is the densest coniferous forest in the world. It also contains the largest tree species such as the coastal redwood (*Sequoia sempervirens*), and douglas fir (*Pseudotsuga taxifolia*). The lakes-forests have moderate rainfall and wide extremes of temperature. It is a very mixed forest consisting of associations of white pine (*Pinus strobus*), red pine (*P. resinosa*), hemlock (*Tsuga canadensis*) and various broad-leafed tree species. *Tamiasciurus* squirrels are found in both types of forest.

Pine trees are worth a mention in their own right and are particularly important for tree squirrels in certain areas. They are the most widespread group of trees in the world consisting of more than 100 species, and they are found from cold, boreal regions through to the equator. They inhabit coarse, dry soils such as sands, gravels and glacial till and they are often found in areas subject to frequent burning (e.g. the closed cone pines—see Chapter 3) or in areas subject to wide temperature variations (Spurr and Barnes, 1973). We have already noted that the abert squirrel is found only in dry ponderosa pine forests on mountains in the mid-southwest of North America, and several species of pine including white pine, Scots pine (*P. sylvestris*) and cedar pine (*P. sibirica*), often in mixtures with spruce or other conifer trees, provide optimum habitats for squirrels in boreal forests.

The natural climax forest in much of Europe and eastern North America consists of a mix of broad-leafed, deciduous trees such as oak, beech and maple, variously in association with other hardwoods such as limes, elms, ashes, walnuts and chestnuts. These provide a variety of seed foods, many of a large size, for squirrels such as the fox and grey squirrels in North America. As pointed out above, the mixed hardwood forests in eastern

North America consist of as many as twelve or more tree species, whereas those in Europe may consist of as little as two or three species. Therefore, red squirrels in European hardwood forests lack the variety and stability of tree seed supplies that their counterparts have in North America (Chapter 3). In addition, an understorey of trees such as hazel are often present in mixed deciduous forests, and where the canopy is open a rich shrub and field layers develop. These supply a variety of additional foods for squirrels. A further feature is that the climate in these deciduous forests is considerably wetter and milder than in the northern coniferous forests, although the winters can still be very cold.

As elsewhere in the world, many of the northern forests either have been eliminated (particularly temperate deciduous forests) or greatly affected by human activity. This, to a small extent, has restricted the range of some squirrels but none, other than one or two subspecies, are particularly in danger of dying out. Finally, it should not be forgotten that, even though squirrels require large, mature trees in order to survive, they are, like other rodents, adaptable animals and can be very successful in man-made landscapes such as farmland, parks, gardens and urban areas.

SQUIRREL NESTS

There are four types of nests used by squirrels: winter dreys, summer dreys, dens and holes in the ground. Dreys are conspicuous twig and leaf nests built in trees, the winter forms being by far the most elaborate. They are compact, nearly circular structures (Figure 2.11), mostly between 25 and 45 cm in diameter, although they may be as large as 100 cm depending upon the individual and the species. The entrance to the drey (sometimes two entrances) is not usually noticeable as the nest material tends to move back and obscure it as the squirrel moves in and out. They are waterproof and made of an outer coarse layer of interwoven twigs, which the squirrels usually remove from the tree in which the drey is built (often with leaves still attached). There is a softer inner lining consisting of moss, bark, leaves, fur, feathers, lichens and similar material (Tittensor, 1975; Laidler, 1980) and dreys which are used by females to rear young tend to be very well-padded. In one part of the forest in which I study grey squirrels in southern England, the squirrels have learnt to strip the soft, spongy bark from a small group of exotic, giant redwood trees (*Wellingtonia* sp.) during the winter to line their winter breeding dreys. A squirrel takes from one to several days to construct a drey, and they will maintain it and add to it as and when required. Summer dreys are much simpler affairs and may be no more than twig and leaf, saucer-shaped platforms on exposed branches on which the squirrels rest during hot weather (Shorten, 1951). Dreys made in deciduous woods are more visible than those built in coniferous woods, especially during the winter when the leaves on the trees have disappeared. Often they may be seen as rough balls of dead leaves; this is in contrast to coniferous dreys which clearly show the neat, outer layers of twigs. Disused winter dreys may persist in the trees for several months until they eventually get blown apart. Summer dreys usually fall apart fairly quickly after the squirrels abandon them.

Winter dreys have to withstand high winds and inclement weather, and be as secure as they can be against predators (e.g. Shorten, 1951; Brown and Twigg, 1965; Sanderson *et al*, 1976; Rothwell, 1979; Vahle and Patton,

Figure 2.11 Drey with squirrel

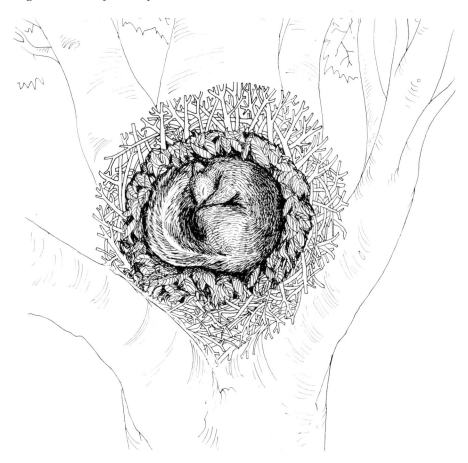

1983). Therefore, dreys will not be built close to the ground or near the tops of the trees unless well protected. Brown and Twigg (1965) found that grey squirrels in England tended to build dreys halfway up the trees. In general, it seems that dreys are seldom built lower down than 3 m, and usually up to a height of 8 m to 10 m or more, depending on the height of the tree (e.g. Tittensor, 1970; Rothwell, 1979; Vahle and Patton, 1983). Many dreys will be situated in the fork of a large branch close to the main trunk, but by no means all. Tree selection is also important, and most dreys will not be found in isolated trees. Surrounding trees offer protection from the weather, escape routes from predators and a nearby source of food (Rothwell, 1979; Vahle and Patton, 1983; Brown, 1984).

Squirrels which live in coniferous forests have less choice about which species of tree to build their dreys in than squirrels living in mixed deciduous wood, and usually they will be found in the dominant species such as pines or spruces. Squirrels living in deciduous woods exhibit preferences depending upon the tree species available. Shorten (1951), for example, found that grey squirrels in England preferred to build their dreys in oak trees, then blackthorn and maple, while Brown and Twigg (1965) found that sweet chestnut, beech and lime were also quite popular.

Sanderson *et al* (1976) found that grey squirrels built 54 per cent of all dreys in oak trees, and that hickories, yellow-poplar and maples were also preferred in West Virginia. Oak trees were also preferred by Arizona grey squirrels (Brown, 1984), but they in fact build dreys in a large number of other species including sycamores, walnuts, alders, and maples. Pine squirrels in coniferous forests in North America tend to build their dreys near their large winter stores of conifer cones called middens, and this would minimise the distance they have to go to and from the middens during the cold winters (e.g. Rothwell, 1979; Vahle and Patton, 1983; Gurnell, 1984). It is possible that there is an association between good food supplies or food stores and drey sites in other species. Dreys are considered again in Chapter 7 where I explore the possibilities of using drey counts to estimate habitat use.

Tree dens are another major type of nest used by tree squirrels. These are holes or cavities in the main trunks of trees which have been left by branches falling away or they have been made by birds such as woodpeckers. Dens may be either nest dens and are lined with nesting material, or they may simply be escape dens. Some dens may be found in dead trees but most occur in live trees, and in a variety of species in mixed deciduous woodland (Sanderson *et al*, 1976). Clearly, large, mature trees are needed to contain cavities of sufficient size to be of use to squirrels. For example, grey squirrels in West Virginia preferred trees of >40 cm diameter at breast height for nest dens (Sanderson *et al*, 1976). Interestingly, and in contrast to the red squirrel, Persian squirrels appear to mostly use tree dens.

The last type of squirrel nest is built in a hole in the ground. This may seem curious for arboreal species, but pine squirrels in cold coniferous forests in North America have often been known to nest underground. I found pine squirrels in the subalpine forests of the Rocky Mountains living in rock holes, burrows in the ground and burrows within their middens (Gurnell, 1984). This makes sense, however, when one considers the advantages of the insulation afforded below the ground in harsh climates, and if your food is on the doorstep, then it is even better. Interestingly, red squirrels in similar environments in the Old World still seem to use tree nests, and this is probably related to the fact that they forage mainly in the canopy of the trees for seeds throughout the winter. It is rare for other species to nest in the ground but occasionally there are reports of squirrels doing so. Recently, for example, during some very cold weather in February in southern England, a rabbit worker using a ferret flushed out a grey squirrel with a litter of suckling young from a hole in an embankment on the edge of a beech wood (Harry Pepper, pers. comm.). It is interesting to consider whether the rather sudden very cold spell drove the female underground to give birth to her litter.

3 Food and feeding

Squirrels are granivore-herbivores and a comprehensive list of all the food items eaten by a particular species can be long and impressive (e.g. C.C. Smith, 1968; Moller, 1983; Brown, 1984). However, this in itself only tells us that squirrels can be opportunists and generalists and turn to a wide variety of food items if necessary and when they are available. More characteristically, squirrels rely on only a few important types of food which, with the exception of fungi, are closely related to the products of the trees in the habitats in which they live.

METHODS OF STUDYING DIET

The diet of wild squirrels has been studied in three ways: direct observation in the wild, stomach and gut content analysis, and captive feeding experiments. There are problems with all three methods of quantifying all the items of food which an individual eats, and out of the 154 papers cited in Henrik Moller's (1983) excellent review of the diet of red and grey squirrels, only 17 provided quantitative information. The reasons for this are fairly clear. For example, different types of food have different rates of digestion, and so the estimation of volume or bulk of different food items in the gut, rather than simply their occurrence, is a problem. In the case of direct observation, squirrels sometimes can be quite easy to observe from a distance, but they frequently remain high up in the leafy canopy, and getting close enough to monitor accurately what they are eating without disturbing them is very difficult. In fact, you often hear squirrels feeding before you see them. The noisiest squirrels I have heard were fox squirrels eating walnuts in a forest in Illinois; I could hear them from quite a long way off, but it took me a considerable time to locate them, where they were perched on top of branches in the tree canopy. I have also found it easier to observe feeding in some squirrels species than others; North American pine squirrels in the subalpine forests of the Rocky Mountains were easier to observe than red squirrels in the subalpine forests in Switzerland, and I never got good sightings of Western grey squirrels feeding in California. It is difficult, therefore, to identify the types of food in the diet of squirrels from direct observation and, in most instances, there is no way of knowing the quantity of the food being eaten.

Some idea of the number of tree seeds eaten by squirrels can be obtained by counting shells or the seeds removed from conifer cones. In fact squirrels leave many characteristic signs of their feeding on the ground. These include gnawed bark, the terminal twigs of trees from which buds have been removed (particularly conifers such as spruce, fir and larch but also some deciduous trees such as beech), and the remains of feeding on fungi as well as seeds. Seeds eaten by squirrels can be distinguished from those remains left by mice, voles and birds and there are good field guides (e.g. Bang and Dahlstrom, 1974) which show how this can be done (Figure 3.1). Squirrels feeding on seeds high in the trees let the shells, scales and cone-cores fall to the ground; these remains may be clumped under a favourite feeding perch, or scattered under the trees. Squirrels feeding on the ground often carry their food to a feeding perch such as a tree stump, log or mound where the remains will accumulate. Feeding remains can tell us which particular trees are exploited for their seed or buds, and when (Brown, 1982; Moller, 1983).

Squirrel feeding has also been studied in captivity and here the approach is to feed the animals different combinations of food types to see which they prefer and how the food affects their body weight and condition. Studies of this nature must be interpreted with caution as it is known that the feeding behaviour of squirrels may be severely affected by confinement

Figure 3.1 Squirrel feeding remains of spruce cone (a), pine cone (b) and hazel nut (c). In the middle of (a) is a spruce seed with wing; only the seed contents are eaten, the wing and the seed coat being discarded

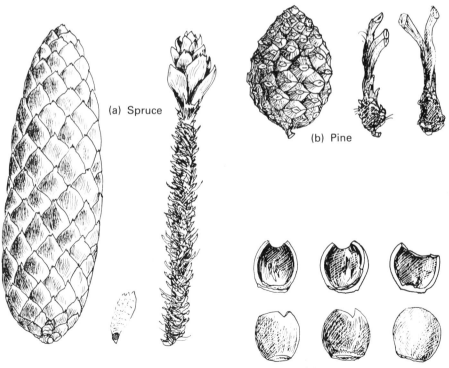

(a) Spruce

(b) Pine

(c) Hazel nut

(Knee, 1983) and also the squirrels are being forced to make unnatural choices.

A combination of these methods appears to offer the best way of studying the composition of the diet of squirrels, and perhaps more rewarding work on captive squirrels could be carried out in large, semi-natural, field enclosures.

COMPOSITION OF DIET

Despite the problems associated with the methods of study, it is known that the main or primary foods of squirrels are tree seeds and fruits (Figures 3.2, 3.3; Moller, 1983). The availability of tree seeds is of such pervasive importance to the behaviour and population dynamics of squirrels that I shall return to it several times throughout this book. Secondary foods, include berries, epigeal (appearing above-ground) fungal fruiting bodies, and hypogeal (remaining underground) mycorrhizal fungi. Many species of fungi are eaten by squirrels and it could be argued that they are a primary rather than a secondary food, although often they appear in the diet in inverse proportions to the amount of seed and fruit. Christopher C. Smith (1968) lists 45 species of fungi eaten by pine squirrels in the Cascade Mountains, British Columbia, including truffles and false truffles. At certain times of the year, fungi can make up the bulk of the diet. Jessica Holm has observed that red squirrels on the Isle of Wight spent 90 per cent of their active time during the month of December feeding on the mycelium of *Vuilleminia* under the bark of dead or dying branches in the canopy of oak trees. This behaviour has also been reported from Finland (Pulliainen and Salonen, 1966). Grönwall and Pehrson (1984) report that 46 g (wet weight) of fungi were found in one red squirrel shot in March in Sweden, and they estimate that it is possible for red squirrels to satisfy at least half their daily energy requirements by consuming fungi. They are also a valuable source of nitrogen; I shall return to this aspect later. In their turn, squirrels are important agents of spore dispersal (Kotter and Farentinos, 1984).

Lastly, there is a mixture of other types of food, which include buds, growing shoots and other green plant material, flowers, bark and lichens, which are rarely selected in large quantities. They are generally of low energy content per unit weight, and if they are eaten in bulk they may be difficult to digest quickly enough to satisfy the individual's energy requirements; this is sometimes called a digestive bottleneck. Nevertheless, these foods can be important; for example, tree buds are relied on as a source of food during the spring when seeds become scarce (Grönwall, 1982), or even during autumn and winter if the seed crop fails (Pulliainen and Salonen, 1965; M.C. Smith, 1968). Occasionally, animal food, such as invertebrates, birds' eggs and young, and even dead squirrels, will be eaten, especially in the summer. Occasionally more exotic foods such as roots, bulbs and soil (possibly as a source of roughage) contribute to the squirrel's diet.

FOOD QUANTITY

Naturally, the squirrels' diet depends upon what is available and this varies according to the habitat and the time of the year (Figure 3.4).

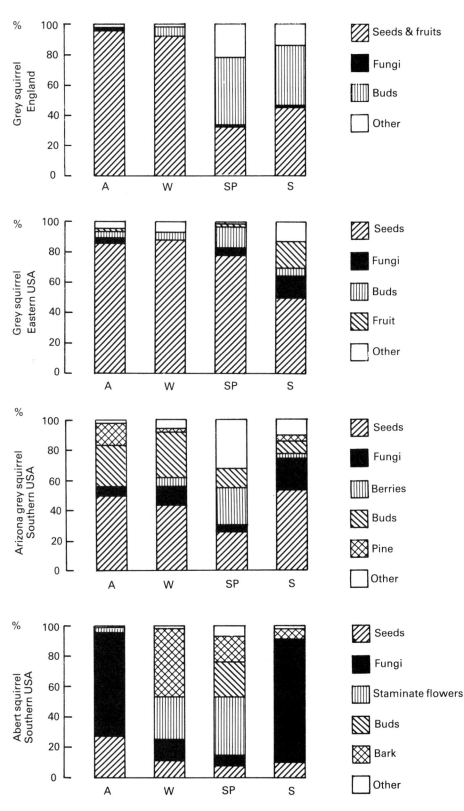

Figure 3.2 Diet of grey, Arizona grey and abert squirrels (grey squirrel data from England expressed as per cent importance others as per cent stomach volume). Sources: Mackinnon (1976) in Moller (1983), Nixon (1968), Brown (1984), Stevenson (1975) in Brown (1984)

Figure 3.3 Diet, as proportion of stomach volume, of red squirrels from the combined regions of Skane, Södermanland and Varmland in Sweden in years of different cone production. Source: Grönwall (1982)

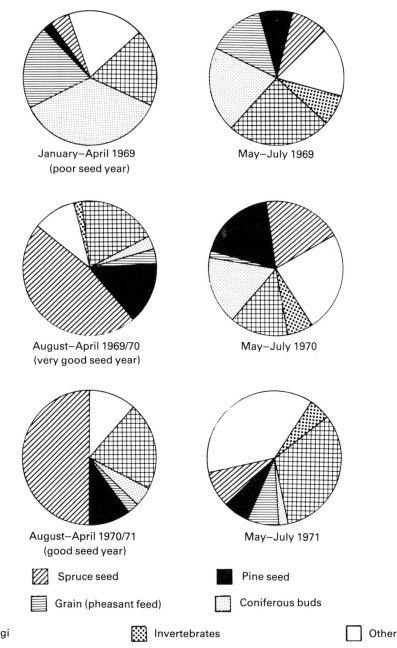

January–April 1969 (poor seed year)	May–July 1969
August–April 1969/70 (very good seed year)	May–July 1970
August–April 1970/71 (good seed year)	May–July 1971

Spruce seed   Pine seed

Grain (pheasant feed)   Coniferous buds

Fungi   Invertebrates   Other

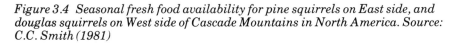

Figure 3.4 Seasonal fresh food availability for pine squirrels on East side, and douglas squirrels on West side of Cascade Mountains in North America. Source: C.C. Smith (1981)

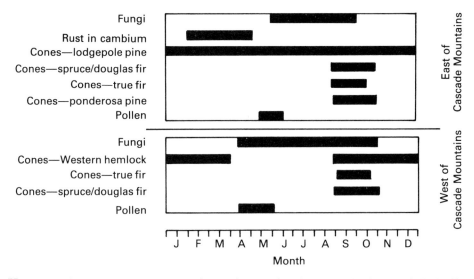

However, it is not quite as simple as this and to be straightforward, I shall consider below mainly the primary squirrel food, tree seeds.

Seed availability not only varies between seasons of the year but also between years. Most temperate and boreal tree species produce seed crops which vary in abundance from one year to the next. Sometimes the crops are large, sometimes they are non-existent, whilst in other years they may be of intermediate size (e.g. Figure 3.5; C.C. Smith, 1970; Gurnell, 1981). The phenomenon of very large crops, called mast crops, is well known, not only in temperate deciduous trees but also in conifers. Various environmental factors are known to influence seed crop abundance. Weather, especially, temperature and rainfall, can affect all stages of the tree reproductive cycle and even the weather in previous years can be important (Harper, 1977). One familiar example of the effects of weather is that of late air frosts during the spring which damage flowers and result in a reduction in fruit or seed yields (e.g. Goodrum *et al*, 1971). Another factor is how long it takes a tree to build up energy and nutrient reserves since its last large seed crop. This often takes one year but may take considerably longer and can be affected, for example, by the depredations of leaf-defoliating caterpillars which remove leaves during the spring and summer. One of my oak wood study areas in southern England is particularly affected by green tortrix moths (*Tortrix viridana*) and winter moths (*Operophtera brumata*) so that by early summer in some years the trees are devoid of all leaves. Lastly, disease or parasites can affect the yield of healthy seeds. One particular example is that of the acorn gall-forming cynipid wasp (*Andricus quercus-calicis*), which has been spreading throughout southern England in the last ten years. This wasp is responsible for the large acorn knopper galls found on the ground during the autumn. There is no field evidence that galls are taken by seed-eaters, although squirrels eat them in captivity. Losses of healthy acorns can on occasions be high which will reduce acorn availability to squirrels and

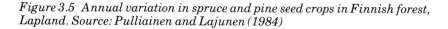

Figure 3.5 Annual variation in spruce and pine seed crops in Finnish forest, Lapland. Source: Pulliainen and Lajunen (1984)

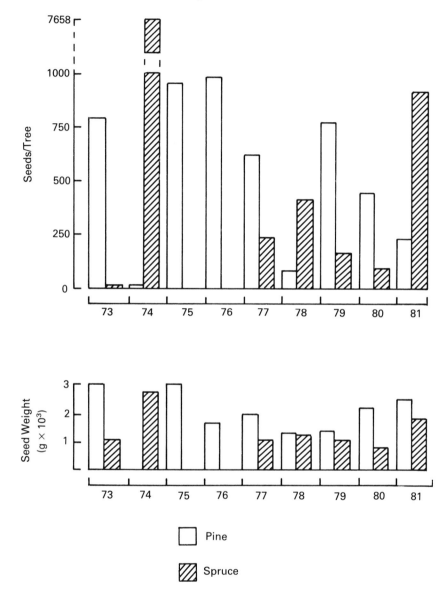

other animals (Crawley, 1983). Trees appear to benefit from producing seed crops of variable size from one year to the next. Woodland rodents, for example, respond to good autumn seed supplies by increasing in numbers, but this does not occur sufficiently fast for the animals to eat all the crop. This is especially so if a stand of trees produces a poor crop one year followed by a good crop the next. This will result in small populations of seed-eaters in response to the poor seed year feeding on the large crop the following year. Consequently, many seeds will escape being eaten which will improve the chances of some seeds successfully germinating.

Most coniferous and deciduous trees produce mature seed within a year from the setting of the seeds. However, some pine trees, such as Scots pine, are an exception and in this species the cycle is two years; flowering and pollination occur in the spring of one year, but fertilisation and cone and seed development do not occur until the summer of the second year. In the first year the pollinated female flowers, called conelets, remain small and compact and are not eaten by squirrels. Therefore, a good spring for setting seed in a forest mixture of spruce and pine trees may produce, all other things being favourable, a good spruce seed crop the same year and a good pine seed crop the following year. Weather may influence the size of the seed crop of several tree species occurring together over large areas. However, seed crop size is also known to vary spatially within the same species and across small geographic areas. For example, I have found quite different yields of acorns from different oak woods within a few miles of each other in southern England. In addition, there can be quite a wide variation in seed yields between different trees, and, equally important, between different species within a wood. The number of species of tree within a forest can, therefore, be important to squirrels. British deciduous forests naturally contain few tree species but deciduous forests of the eastern USA contain twelve or more species of tree (Chapter 2). It can be seen that fluctuations in seed supplies between years, and hence fluctuations in squirrel numbers, will be much greater in British than American deciduous forests. Similarly, there will be differences in the stability of squirrel numbers between managed forest plantations which are usually monocultures, and naturally occurring, mixed forests.

As we can see, trying to work out in advance what seed will be available to squirrels in any one year is a very complex problem, and, if biologists have great difficulty in predicting the size of a crop, then squirrels and other seed-eaters probably do too. Nevertheless, squirrels, like other animals, are sensitive to indicators concerning quantitative aspects of their environment and I shall discuss ideas relating to this later.

As well as the number of seeds available, there are other factors which influence the squirrel–seed relationship. Many of these relate to food quality and will be examined below, but first the pattern of seed maturation and dispersal which different tree species adopt will be considered. Squirrels will remain foraging and feeding in trees while seeds, flowers and buds are present. The proportion of the year that squirrels can do this depends largely on how long the mature seeds remain on the trees (Edlin, 1968). This can be illustrated by comparing Scots pine forests in cold latitudes with oak forests in temperate latitudes. Squirrels start to feed on new pine cones when they are green and not fully ripe and this occurs in June and July (Grönwall, 1982; Moller, 1983). They may then continue to feed on the cones in the canopy until the following spring when the cones start to open and disperse their seed. At this time squirrels will be seen on the ground feeding on windblown or buried seed, but it is also at this time that feeding on tree buds and flowers reaches a peak. Squirrels in oak woods start to feed on green, maturing acorns in the trees towards the end of the summer in August. This continues until seed fall, which occurs over a period of just three or four weeks in October and November (Gurnell, 1981); thereafter and throughout the winter squirrels forage on the ground for acorns and other foods. It is perhaps worth mentioning that there are differences in the amount of ground or tree foraging between squirrels in similar habitats, and this is discussed in Chapter 4.

One benefit of remaining in the trees to feed is that squirrels are probably less vulnerable to predators than on the ground. Feeding in trees enhances predator-detection, ease of escape and the use of refuges such as tree dens.

FOOD QUALITY

Although everyone has an intuitive idea as to what is meant by food quality, defining it is extremely difficult. Indirectly, it is possible to infer the quality of the food by considering the performance of the animals feeding on it. In other words, whether the animals grow normally, are healthy and survive to reproduce successfully.

Alternatively, the food squirrels eat can be examined to establish certain properties, such as nutrient and energy contents, which are believed to be indicators of food quality. Such information, however, takes on a greater significance if these properties of different foods are considered in relation to the foods that the squirrel chooses to eat. For example, a food which contains a high concentration of energy but is difficult to procure or energetically expensive for the squirrel to process, may not be preferred. Henrik Moller (1983, 1986) has considered in some detail the selection by squirrels between food types and selection within and between food species. Here I shall mention only some of the important factors affecting food preference and it is a good idea to bear in mind that food selection in animals which eat many types of food (that is, polyphagous animals) depends upon the availability of potential food items. If all food items are equally available then squirrels can afford to select food which will maximise their nutrient and energy intake. When food availability declines then the food choice options open to squirrels will decline and eventually, at times of food shortage, squirrels will have to eat any foods they can get. Primary, secondary and tertiary foods of squirrels have already been mentioned in relation to their importance in the diet. Nutrient content, digestibility, seed packaging and foraging behaviour can now be more closely examined.

Nutrient Content

Nutrient content of seeds and other food items (Table 3.1) varies between times of the year, and within and between species and geographic areas. Generally, nitrogen has the highest concentration in seed foods followed by potassium and phosphorus, whilst sodium has the lowest. Havera and Smith (1979) found from feeding studies on captive, female fox squirrels that sodium and calcium were deficient for all the foods which they tested, whereas potassium, magnesium, phosphorus and nitrogen were generally in excess. Their work suggests that seeds satisfy the nutrient requirements of squirrels with the exception of sodium and calcium; other studies suggest that nitrogen and phosphorus may also be in short supply in certain seeds or habitats (Short, 1976). Deficient nutrients would need supplementation from other sources, especially in the case of females during pregnancy and lactation when nutrients are very important. Havera and Smith (1979) note several reports of salt-seeking behaviour by squirrels such as gnawing bones and licking salt off roads; this is discussed

Table 3.1 (a) Nutrient contents of selected squirrel foods. Mean per cent dry weight ($\times 10^3$) of sodium (Na), potassium (K), calcium (Ca), magnesium (Mg), phosphorus (P) and nitrogen (N); (b) Energy content (KJ.g. dry weight) of selected squirrel foods. Original articles should be referred to for sample size and standard error of means

(a) Food	Na	K	Ca	Mg	P	N	Notes
SEEDS							
White oak[1]	3	918	38	70	99	1120	Tannin content = 5.6%
Black oak[1]	5	950	99	82	114	1290	
Red oak[1]	3	923	62	62	87	1000	
Shagbark hickory[1]	4	558	99	152	361	2530	Tannin content = 0.5%
Black walnut[1]	5	670	62	230	631	5330	
Scots pine[2]	35	680	107	400	700	4420	Crude fat = 20.5%, crude fibre = 28.2%
Scots pine[6]	17	630	39	300	750	3500	
Norway spruce[2]	61	620	100	250	440	2750	Crude fat = 24.3%, crude fibre = 29.3%
Norway spruce[6]	8	790	20	310	660	2200	
BUDS/FLOWERS							
Scots pine buds[2]	36	790	500	200	410	2750	
Norway spruce buds[2]	72	930	670	210	780	4740	
FUNGI							
Av.14 species[5]	30	3740	90	92	520	3440	

(b)

Food	Energy content	Food	Energy content
SEEDS/FRUITS			
White oak[1]	18.8	Western hemlock[4]	28.5
Black oak[1]	22.6	Douglas fir[4]	29.7
Red oak[1]	20.5	Subalpine fir[4]	29.7
Pedunculate oak[7]	18.6	European larch[7]	27.1
Sessile oak[7]	18.3	Blueberries[4]	22.2
Hazel[7]	32.9		
Beech[7]	29.1	**BUDS/FLOWERS**	
Elm[7]	23.2	White oak buds[3]	19.3
Lime	25.2	Hickory buds[3]	20.1
Shagbark hickory[1]	31.8	Elm buds[3]	18.8
Black walnut	29.3	White oak staminate flowers[3]	19.3
Scots pine[7]	27.0	Hickory flowers[3]	18.4
Norway spruce[7]	25.1	Elm flowers[3]	18.0
Ponderosa pine[7]	31.8		
Lodgepole pine[4]	28.5	**FUNGI**	
Swiss stone pine[7]	32.3	Av.4 species[3]	17.6
Englemann spruce[4]	28.5	Av.8 species[4]	20.5

1. Havera and Smith, 1979. 2. Grönwall, 1982. 3. Montgomery et al, 1975. 4. C.C. Smith, 1968. 5. Grönwall and Pehrson, 1984. 6. Pulliainen and Lajunen, 1984 (testa and endosperm). 7. Grodzinski and Sawicka-Kapusta, 1970

in more detail by Weeks and Kirkpatrick (1978). Further, the ingestion of animal food, fungi, buds and soil may be important for making up the requirements of these nutrients.

Given a choice, squirrels would be expected to prefer seeds or buds with a high nutrient content. In some respects, red squirrels in Scandinavia appear to follow this rule since they forage on spruce buds in trees which have higher average nitrogen values than occur in non-foraged trees (Grönwall, 1982). However, although Scots pine seed contain larger amounts of nitrogen and phosphorus than spruce seed, squirrels show a preference for spruce seed. Other factors such as size, shape and hardness of cone, and resin content are probably more important than nutrient content in this case.

The nutrient content of fungi is high, as shown in Table 3.1, and overall is similar to that of primary foods. This reinforces the idea that fungi are very important foods for squirrels, especially in cold coniferous forests when cone crops fail and there are few other foods available.

Digestibility

Plants (or parts of plants) have evolved several types of defensive mechanism against herbivores. These include chemical deterrents, such as toxins and substances which decrease digestibility, and physical deterrents such as hard outer layers, hairs and spines. Plant material which a particular herbivore finds hard to digest will be less favoured than a plant material which is easy to digest. Plants have cellulose cell walls which are difficult to break down and herbivorous vertebrates require microorganisms to accomplish this since they do not naturally have the necessary digestive enzymes. They also need modification to the gut such as fermentation chambers or long intestines to allow a greater retention time for digestion to occur. Seed endosperm (i.e. the nutritive tissue which nourishes the plant embryo inside the seed) is much more digestible than green plant material and squirrels, which are seed specialists, tend to have quite short intestines. Red squirrels which have to feed on quite large quantities of green plant food have been reported to have longer intestines than those which do not (Karpukhin, 1979). This suggests there can be changes in gut morphology in response to changes in diet as has been found in song birds such as starlings (Sibly, 1981).

Not much is known about the chemical defences of foods where squirrels are concerned. The digestibility of seeds is high (88 to 96 per cent) compared with leaves and stems (60 to 70 per cent). However, digestibility varies between seeds from different tree species and some of this variation has been attributed to tannin content. Tannin is a chemical found in many plant tissues which forms complexes with proteins giving them an unpleasant taste and making them indigestible (Short and Epps, 1976; Moller, 1983). Hence, some workers (e.g. Ofcarcik et al, 1973; Short and Epps, 1976), but not all (C.C. Smith, 1968; C.C. Smith and Follmer, 1972), suggest that this is why fox and grey squirrels take white acorns in preference to red and black oak acorns. Recent laboratory studies with pine squirrels (Mould, 1983) show that squirrels select food with low tannin content and that this preference may be influenced by taste.

Fat content also affects the digestibility of seeds and this may be why hickory nuts (29 per cent fat) are preferred to black and white acorns (5 and 10 per cent fat respectively) (C.C. Smith and Follmer, 1972), despite the fact that squirrels take longer to extract hickory seed, and receive a lower rate of energy intake, than from acorns (Lewis, 1982).

FORAGING AND FEEDING—OPTIMAL PATTERNS OF BEHAVIOUR

Individual trees and their supplies of seed can be thought of as patches of food and, when observing foraging squirrels, we might ask why a particular squirrel is feeding in a particular tree and what determines when it should give-up feeding in that tree. Similar questions can be asked about squirrels feeding under trees on the ground.

These sorts of questions on the, so-called, 'decision rules' made by animals when faced with choices, are studied by behavioural ecologists. Another interesting question is, 'do squirrels exhibit optimal foraging behaviour?'; that is do they forage and feed in the most economical way possible in specific circumstances (e.g. Krebs and McCleery, 1984)? To try and answer this it is necessary to assess the costs of the particular foraging and feeding strategy of an animal in relation to the benefits gained. The energy and nutrient intake are obvious gains, whilst costs refer to the energy and time taken to find certain foods and to eat them, including the costs involved with handling the food before it is eaten. It may be said that evolution has shaped the behaviour of an animal so that it maximises the result of the benefit minus cost equation. However, it should be remembered that the behaviour of an animal at any time results from a compromise between different motivations, such as looking out for predators and feeding. Also, as a mere observer, the behavioural ecologist may not be able to work out all the costs and benefits of any particular behaviour. Finally, individual variation in behaviour, one of the ingredients for the natural selection of individual traits, generally complicates matters.

In the case of squirrels, I shall consider two types of behaviour in terms of their costs and benefits. The first concerns foraging and feeding behaviour; the second, food hoarding.

FORAGING AND FEEDING BEHAVIOUR

It has been shown above that the quantity and quality of seeds and buds varies within and between tree species and I have suggested that this affects food preference. The most detailed studies on squirrel feeding behaviour have been carried out on animals feeding on cones in coniferous trees, and I shall concentrate on two aspects of the behaviour of squirrels in these habitats, namely which patch of food a squirrel chooses to feed in, and which food items within the patch the squirrel selects to eat.

Generally, it is well known that feeding squirrels frequent and return to certain trees more often than others. Henrik Moller (1983, 1986), in his studies of red squirrels in a Scots pine forest in Scotland called these favoured (F) trees and he was able to carry out some elegant work on the cone crops and the behaviour of squirrels in F trees compared with those in randomly selected (R) trees. F trees had up to twice as many cones as R trees during the summer and although there was a gradual depletion of cones in F trees, the average density of cones at the end of the following March was still greater in F trees than R trees. In a few instances, cone density in an F tree did fall below the average for R trees but squirrels would still feed in the F trees suggesting that there were other reasons why it was still more profitable to do so.

Moller found that, although the external dimensions of cones between F and R trees did not differ significantly, the weight of viable seeds within similar sized cones was up to 50 per cent higher in F trees. Therefore, seed size (or total seed weight within a cone) appeared to be an important determinant of which patches of food a squirrel selected for feeding. Overall, adults took less time to eat cones of a given length in F trees than R trees. Eating time is analagous to handling time because it refers to the cost from the time the squirrel sits on its feeding perch with a cone until the time when seed extraction is complete and the cone core is dispensed with. The time a squirrel took in eating a cone was lowest in June when the cones were young and green, but this increased quickly until August when eating time stabilised until the following year. The average time a squirrel took to locate, pick and carry a cone to a feeding perch (i.e. the search time) was lowest in June, increased in July and then declined slightly and levelled off until it increased during the following spring and summer (probably because more cones had partially or completely split to shed seed by this time and thus intact cones were more difficult to find). In the spring, in fact, squirrels tended to favour trees with lower than average proportions of split cones, which lowered their search times within these trees.

Moller used this information to calculate the dry weight of seed swallowed per unit time spent finding, picking, carrying and eating cones. This ingestion rate can be used as a measure of relative benefit from feeding on certain cones. Overall, ingestion rate was higher in F trees than R trees. In June, squirrels picked much larger than average cones to eat, suggesting that they were maximising their ingestion rates. This trend continued until August when squirrels selected more middle-sized cones (35 to 44 mm) to eat than small (<35 mm) or large (>45 mm) ones. As the number of middle-sized cones declined squirrels turned more and more to small cones rather than large ones. This does not agree with the idea that squirrels should maximise their rate of ingestion. Moller was unable to find a convincing reason to explain why large cones were the last to be used. Perhaps the large cones became too tough or heavy to handle efficiently or perhaps in other ways they were of a lower quality.

Differences between Squirrels in Feeding Behaviour

Interestingly, squirrels, like humans, are either right-handed or left-handed and when handling cones grip them between their forepaws with the blunt end or base uppermost and angled either to the right or the left. The squirrel removes a scale with its teeth, and then the underlying seed, possibly by flicking it up into its mouth with one of its fingers (Reynolds, 1981). It then rotates the cone with its forepaws to the next scale. Eventually the squirrel works its way to the top of the cone leaving the characteristic cone-core. Extracting seeds from cones can be a laborious and energetically costly process and different species of cone vary widely in this respect (C.C. Smith, 1968).

Moller (1983) divided his red squirrels into two sorts, those squirrels which neatly clipped the scales off of the cones, the so-called 'clippers', and those which tore off the scales, the so-called 'tearers'. Clippers took 32 per cent longer than tearers to eat the middle-sized cones but there was no difference in the size of cones selected. It does not appear, therefore, to be advantageous to be a 'tidy-eater' if you are a squirrel! Further, it took young squirrels longer to search for cones than adults, partly because they approached and rejected more cones than adults, and partly because they appeared to move more slowly and be less sure-footed. Young squirrels also picked smaller cones to eat than adults. This is compatible with the hypothesis that squirrels try to maximise ingestion rate since young squirrels are less efficient than adults at handling cones, particularly large ones. Young squirrels appear to learn to handle cones and seeds efficiently by trial and error. Weigl and Hanson (1980), however, have shown that this process can be improved if they are able to observe experienced squirrels handling food.

Moller's study shows how squirrels may be observed with respect to contemporary ideas on foraging and feeding behaviour. The results from several other studies are consistent with the notion that squirrels tend to maximise their rate of ingestion. For example, red squirrels prefer large hazel nuts to small ones, hazel nuts to spruce or pine cones and spruce cones to the much tougher pine cones (Grönwall, 1982; Moller, 1983). Red squirrels also prefer beech nuts to spruce seeds (Zwahlen, 1975). Lewis (1982) was able to rank the preference of grey squirrels for three species of acorn according to their rate of energy intake. As pointed out above, however, the preference for the hard-shelled hickory nut could not be predicted on this basis. Pine and douglas squirrels from western North America take cones of different species in the order of the food energy contained in each cone, namely Pacific silver fir first, followed by douglas fir, then engelmann spruce and lastly Western hemlock. Pine squirrels also prefer douglas fir cones to the hard, serotinous lodgepole pine cones (see below; C.C. Smith, 1968, 1970), and among lodgepole pine cones they select ones which contain the largest number of seeds (C.C. Smith, 1968; Elliott, 1974).

Some questions about red squirrels' foraging behaviour have not yet been answered such as when should a squirrel leave one tree or patch of food and move on to another. In relation to stands of trees, the trees on the edge of a stand are likely to carry higher seed supplies than centrally located trees; thus squirrels may selectively forage at the edges of stands (Larsson and Schubert, 1970). In addition, Lewis (1980) found that grey squirrels tended to selectively forage on the ground in high density patches of lower energy, less preferred tree seeds rather than low density patches of high energy seeds. In this case it was the net energy intake from the food patch which was maximised.

It must also be added that some trees may be favoured for other reasons than to maximise ingestion rates. Grönwall (1982) has shown that peripherally located spruce trees within a stand have higher nitrogen, magnesium, sodium and calcium content than centrally located trees and thus may be favoured. Fox squirrels appear to find acorns of the white acorn oak group more palatable than the acorns of the black acorn oak group (Short, 1976). Tassel-eared squirrels feed extensively on the inner bark of ponderosa pine twigs during winter and spring and feeding trees are thought to be selected on the basis of their higher protein and lower monoterpene (a toxin) content (Capretta and Farentinos, 1979; Capretta et al, 1980). Damaged, diseased or parasitised buds or seeds are sometimes less preferred to healthy buds and seed (Lloyd, 1968; Grönwall, 1982) although not in all cases, and parasitic larvae may be valuable sources of protein (Korschgen, 1981; Grönwall, 1982).

FOOD HOARDING

Many types of animal hoard or cache food, ranging from insects to birds and mammals (Smith and Reichman, 1984). The process of storing food obviously varies between species but generally it can be expensive to do so in terms of time, energy and the risk of predation. Clearly, an individual which indulges in this costly business of caching food should gain some benefit from doing so. Food is cached at times when it is abundant; that is, there is surplus food to the animal's immediate requirements. The caching habit is often seen in captive animals which, although they do not need to do so, will frequently take food into their nests or hide it away in other places within their cages. In the wild, if the surplus food is not cached then the chances are that it will disappear before the animal can make use of it. Therefore, an animal which caches food should extend the period of availability of that food to itself as it can retrieve the cached food when other foods are in short supply. Competition for cached food can be strong, both from an animal's neighbours within the same population (intraspecific competition) and from animals of different species within the same habitat (interspecific competition). This means that it must be profitable for an animal to cache food despite the risks involved from other animals finding that food and eating it. The animal can minimise these risks by either defending the caches or by caching the food in such a way as to minimise the amount taken by other animals. Squirrels store two types of food, fungal fruiting bodies and tree seeds.

Fungi

Fungi are particularly stored by pine and red squirrels in coniferous forests. Many types of fungi are taken, notably in the autumn (C.C. Smith, 1968; Grönwall 1982); they are gnawed off near the base of the stem and either cached in a scrape or pit in the ground or carried up trees where they are wedged in the branches to dry. Drying fungi preserves them so that they will be a valuable source of food for some time into the future. Squirrels may exert a considerable amount of effort to store fungi. I saw a pine squirrel in a lodgepole pine forest in the Rockies cut a fruiting body of the fungus *Cortinarius* sp. quite as large as itself. Then, with apparent difficulty, it dragged the fungus to the base of a tree some 10 m away where it cut it up into sizable chunks. These it carried one by one up into the tree to cache.

Scatterhoarding Seed

There are similarities in the way pine and red squirrels cache fungi; however, there are major differences in the way they cache seeds. In fact, there appears to be a consistent difference here between the squirrels in the *Tamiasciurus* genus, and the squirrels in the *Sciurus* genus. Let us first consider the *Sciurus* squirrels. These exhibit a seed caching strategy generally called scatterhoarding. This involves redistributing individual seeds (or cones) taken from the canopy or from the ground, in small groups of ones and twos in shallow, covered scrapes or pits; these caches are widely scattered over the ground. Squirrels are unable to defend caches stored in this way and *Sciurus* squirrels are not territorial. Also, it is unlikely that the positions of the separate caches are remembered by the squirrels but it is possible that the general area of caching is remembered. There has been a suggestion, made particularly with reference to fox squirrels, that scatterhoarded areas around favoured feeding trees or nest sites are defended (Nixon *et al*, 1984), and, in situations where this occurs, it will affect the relative costs and benefits of hoarding discussed below. Individual caches appear to be located by smell from short distances (see Gurnell, 1983; C.C. Smith and Reichman, 1984).

Scatterhoarding food reduces competition from visual, diurnal seed-predators such as jays and woodpeckers. However, many seed-eaters locate their food by smell including rodents other than squirrels. Therefore, it has been suggested that squirrels must distribute their caches in such a way that they recover more of them than other seed-eaters (Stapanian and C.C. Smith, 1978). How this is done is not known for sure, but it is possibly connected with whether a naive seed-eater (that is a squirrel or other animal which did not store the food) on finding one cache will successfully find the next cache, and so on. If the competitor is successful and finds several buried caches fairly quickly then it will stay within the patch of cached food and undoubtedly find more caches to the cost of the squirrel which buried them. If the competitor is not successful within a certain time then it is likely to forage elsewhere. The success of the competitor will decline in proportion to decreasing cache density. Therefore, it would seem that the squirrel will have to cache seed in a way which will deter a continuous search by a naive seed-eater within that area, taking into account the distance the squirrel will have to carry the seeds from where it finds them to where it caches them. There should be, therefore, an optimum density of caches for scatterhoarding food.

Stapanian and C.C. Smith (1978) tested whether fox squirrels cached walnuts in a manner predicted by a model based on the above ideas. In general, they found that fox squirrels scatterhoarded walnuts such that the average cache density gave low rates of loss to naive seed-eaters; thus this supported the basic assumptions underlying the model. However, there was not total agreement, for example, the observed cache density (0.03 walnuts/sq m) was greater than the predicted cache density (0.008 walnuts/sq m). Also Stapanian and C.C. Smith's model was based on a central source of walnuts and they predicted that to minimise the total distance travelled to cache the walnuts the squirrels should use the full 360° arc around the source. The fox squirrels never used the entire 360°. This was further tested by Kraus (1983), this time using grey squirrels and walnuts. He found that the squirrels only used a small proportion of the full 360° arc. Thus the model does not completely predict caching behaviour and there are undoubtedly differences in the 'rules' employed by different squirrels species to cache different seeds in different habitats. Further, in most forests there will not be a single point source of seeds (e.g. one tree); and so, many seeds will be widely dispersed.

Scatterhoarding seed is common in deciduous woodland where the seeds, such as acorns, walnuts, beech mast, hazel and hickory nuts, are fairly small and compact. Cones, however, are also stored just under the surface of the ground in coniferous woods. Abert squirrels in ponderosa pine forests have been known to bury cones singly in shallow scrapes but generally they do not seem to cache many cones (Brown, 1984). Luc Walters (pers. comm.) has seen red squirrels cut Scots pine cones from the tops of trees in Belgium in September and October, and carry them down to the ground where they are buried in ones or twos (deciduous seed is also carried down to the ground by squirrels to cache). Since the pine cones stay on the trees over winter before shedding their seed in spring, it can be suggested that the advantage of burying the cones is to prevent bird seed-eaters from exploiting the seed. Even so, it would seem easier for the squirrels to drop the cones and let them fall to the ground rather than carry them down the trees. Pine squirrels, which do not scatterhoard food, usually drop cones in North American coniferous and deciduous forests (Layne, 1954; Gurnell, 1984). It is not clear whether red squirrels in cold boreal forests store many cones. Olavi Grönwall (pers. comm.) has only seen red squirrels storing single items in Sweden. The squirrels pick up cones from the ground, move them one or two metres and hide them in mosses close to tree roots, under stones or in dry grass in open areas. I noticed that pine squirrels in Colorado stopped caching cones shortly after snow settles permanently on the forest floor (Gurnell, 1984), and it would be energetically expensive to scatterhoard and retrieve cones through snow. However, red squirrels will dig through snow to obtain food if necessary and it is possible that cones buried in the autumn would be a useful source of food after the snows melt in spring or early summer; whether squirrels 'plan' for this is not known.

Squirrels and White Oaks

An interesting adaptive behavioural trait has been observed in North American grey squirrels feeding on acorns (Fox, 1982). Oaks (genus *Quercus*) can be divided into two groups: the white oaks (e.g. *Q. alba*, *Q. macrocarpa*) and the red oaks (e.g. *Q. rubra*, *Q. vetulina*). After dispersal, acorns of the red oak group remain dormant on the ground until the following spring when they germinate. Acorns of the white oak group, on the other hand, germinate soon after they fall in the autumn and they produce a large taproot (the radicle of the seed) which stores much (about 50 per cent) of the winter food reserves. The presumptive leaves and stem grow little until the following spring. I have found between 25 and 50 per cent of the acorns of *Q. robur* germinating soon after they fall in forests in southern England (Gurnell, 1981), although they do not seem to produce such large taproots as the white oaks in North America. The acorns work their way down into the surface of the soil under the litter and largely go unnoticed to the casual observer; this helps seeds 'escape' from predators. Squirrels do not seem to like to eat taproots or seedlings; they cut off the taproots before eating the rest of the acorn. Therefore, the early germination of white oak acorns means a loss of potential food to the squirrels. White oak acorns are cached by squirrels (although red oaks are more favoured for caching), but before they are cached the squirrels skilfully cut out the seed embryos, thereby effectively killing them and preventing germination. Squirrels do not kill the acorns of the red oak group. These observations show that killing white oak autumn-germinating acorns is an adaptation by squirrels which prevents future food loss. Adults seem to do this more often than juveniles, indicating that they learn how to do it. Seen from the tree's point of view, it is possible that white oak acorns germinate early as a tactic to minimise losses to squirrels (Barnett, 1977).

Larderhoarding

The caching strategy adopted by pine squirrels, and their cousins the douglas squirrels, in North American coniferous forest is very different than that which has been described for *Sciurus* squirrel species. During late summer and autumn, and up until the time that snow has permanently settled, the squirrels cut closed cones from the trees and let them fall to the ground. I have seen squirrels cut many cones from one tree before moving on to the next one.

The cones may be left for a few hours or longer before the squirrel carries them back to one, or occasionally more than one, large central store of cones. These cone stores are called middens (not to be confused with collections of droppings or food remains of carnivores) and are well-established sites going back over many years. The squirrels feed on the stored cones over winter and large amounts of cone scales and cores accumulate to build up the characteristic piles of debris. New cones are stored in pits within the cone debris; 20 or more cones may be buried in each pit. The middens provide a cold, moist environment for the cones which therefore remain closed almost indefinitely. Birds certainly cannot use this food and other rodent seed-eaters, such as deermice (*Peromyscus* spp.), do not seem to be able to cope with the tough cones when they are buried in this way (C.C. Smith, 1981). Furthermore, large central caches of food can be defended and indeed pine and douglas squirrels are territorial in coniferous forests. The squirrels are solitary; one squirrel, whether male or female, will defend an area of forest centred on the midden(s) against all other squirrels throughout the year. Therefore, by adopting this central or larderhoarding caching strategy, the squirrels reserve a supply of food entirely for themselves, and with the added benefit that they do not have to forage for food through the cold, harsh winters. In a sense, then, territories and their middens are economically defendable; this is to say that the benefits gained from defending an area of forest and harvesting cones from within that area and caching them in one central location outweigh the costs involved in caching the food and defending the territory. Caches can be very large and contain enough food for one or two winters (e.g. M.C. Smith, 1968). However, in poor seed years, when there are few cones to store, the territorial system may break down as squirrels leave their territories, often in large numbers, and move off in search of food (M.C. Smith, 1968). Mortalities in such circumstances are very high. A squirrel which has large supplies of stored food from previous years will be immune to such a disaster.

Hélène Lair found in Canada that territorial defence varied with diet in pine squirrels in a mixed deciduous and coniferous forest in southern Quebec (Lair, 1984). Within a large deciduous habitat, mainly composed of sugar maple (*Acer saccharum*), yellow birch (*Betula alleghaniensis*) and American beech (*Fagus grandifolia*), were two small, mixed conifer stands of balsam fir (*Abies balsamea*) and red spruce (*Picea rubens*), 6.6 ha and 2.1 ha in size. The squirrels concentrated their activities in the conifer stands and only used the deciduous habitat intermittently. Although most squirrels defended territories in coniferous habitats, some (about a quarter of the animals studied) defended territories in the deciduous habitat at least some of the time during the 3-year study. The latter occurred only when cacheable foods (seed cones, birch catkins and beech seed) were widely available. This was reflected by territories being defended only when the squirrels were able to spend more than 40 per cent of their time feeding on cached food. Hélène Lair observed that the same individuals stopped and later resumed territorial defence according to cacheable food availability, and defended territories in both coniferous and deciduous habitats. The flexibility in social organisation of pine squirrels revealed in this study can also be related to the economic defendability of food as well as the availability of cacheable food. It can be suggested that there was little competition from other seed-eaters in the deciduous habitats when food supplies were good. Also, the squirrels were able to defend territories when they did not have to spend long periods foraging for food. I know of no examples of douglas or pine squirrels maintaining permanent territories over long periods of time in deciduous habitats; further discussion on this can be found in Chapter 6.

There is quite a lot of variation between individuals in the intensity of caching behaviour and how they go about it. I have seen some squirrels cache many cones quickly and they appear to be very efficient cone harvesters. Others leave cones scattered about for a long time before gathering them up. Some build compact discrete middens, others diffuse middens over a larger area. Hélène Lair found that pine squirrels in her study described above defended several small-to-medium sized larderhoards rather than one large midden. In addition, as well as not being as adept at eating cones as adults (see above), young squirrels appear to be inefficient harvesters and cachers of cones.

Squirrels and Lodgepole Pine

Squirrels which are efficient harvesters probably cache as many cones as they have time for during the shortening autumn days. Feeding, territorial defence, building dreys and general maintenance behaviour will take up much of a pine squirrel's time (see Chapter 4). This is to say they do not stop caching when they have stored enough food for the coming winter, and it has been suggested that to have enough food to last two winters may be very profitable for the squirrels if the next seed crop fails. I came to this conclusion after carrying out some fascinating studies on pine squirrel territoriality and caching behaviour in a lodgepole pine (*Pinus contorta*) forest on the east slope of the Front Range of the Rocky Mountains in Colorado. These lodgepole pine forests, at an elevation of nearly 3,000 m, were most interesting because a substantial proportion (70 per cent) of the trees carried a form of the tough, small cone which remained closed on the trees for many years. These cones are described as being serotinous and this is an adaptation by the trees to living in the very dry, rainshadow area to the east of the Rockies. Here the forests in the past have been frequently devastated by fire. During such a fire the resin seal of the lodgepole pine cones on the trees is broken by the intense heat and this releases the seeds for recolonising the area after the fire has passed on. Other species of tree, for example pitch pine, (*P. rigida*) and jack pine (*P. banksiana*), also shed seed irregularly. On the other hand, lodgepole pine forests away from the danger of fire to the west of the Cascade and Rocky Mountains in North America do not exhibit serotiny.

Lodgepole pine cones only contain 20 to 30 very tiny seeds, are extremely tough and take a long time to handle and eat (C.C. Smith, 1968, 1981). For this reason, lodgepole pine cones are the least preferred of other cone species which occur in subarctic or subalpine coniferous forests.

However, in pure stands of lodgepole pine there is not much other food available. Christopher C. Smith demonstrated that pine squirrels which feed a great deal on lodgepole pine cones have a heavier and stronger jaw musculature than those which do not. There is one major advantage, however, to the squirrels living in fire subclimax lodgepole pine forests with their poor quality cones. Because the cones remain on the trees for many years, there is a fairly constant and predictable supply of food available and potential competitors such as birds are unable to cope with the tough cones. Poor seed years are not so important. Here there is a situation, therefore, where it would seem unnecessary for squirrels to harvest and cache cones. Rather like red squirrels in taiga forests, the squirrels can feed off of the cones in the trees. However, I found that squirrels did store lodgepole pine cones, although not in vast numbers. Because the energy content in each cone was small, supplies of cached cones would only last for two to four weeks. If the squirrels had stored the larger, more energetically rewarding engelmann spruce or subalpine fir cones (trees found in the neighbouring forests at slightly higher elevations), then the stores would probably have lasted 3 to 5 and 15 to 25 times as long, respectively. In fact it appears they cached as many cones as they could, since it may take squirrels 6 to 9 hours a day just feeding on lodgepole pine cones to get enough energy to sustain themselves. Therefore, it is likely that there was insufficient time to cache more (C.C. Smith, 1968, 1981; Gurnell, 1984; see Chapter 4).

A major benefit of having a large store of food near home is that it circumvents the problem of foraging for food, in the trees or under the snow, in the very hostile winter weather which occurs in cold coniferous forests. Pine squirrels may even build nests within their middens. However, squirrels living in serotinous lodgepole pine forests may have to expend a greater amount of time defending their supplies of food on the trees against intruders throughout the winter. In other types of coniferous forests, the cache and its immediate area would be all that the squirrel would have to defend during the winter months. Therefore, it seems that there is no breakdown of the normal territorial, larderhoarding behavioural strategies in serotinous lodgepole pine forests. However, at the edges of their geographical range where pine or douglas squirrels move into deciduous woodland, and overlap their range with other tree squirrel species, then there is no larderhoarding and no territoriality. Here the squirrels behave like *Sciurus* squirrels (e.g. Deutch, 1978) and this seems to be related to the fact that caches of deciduous tree seeds are not in the long term economically defensible.

4 Activity and energetics

Tree squirrels are active during the day; that is, they are diurnal animals and, contrary to popular belief, they do not hibernate. Such a belief probably stems from the fact that squirrels may stay within their nests for one or several days during very cold weather giving the impression that they pass the long winter months in a deep 'sleep'. True hibernators, such as dormice or ground-dwelling squirrels hibernate with greatly reduced metabolic rates and usually low body temperatures. Later it will be shown that the body temperatures of tree squirrels may vary slightly but within fairly narrow limits and certainly they do not enter the physiological state of true hibernation. In fact squirrels can be out and about during very cold weather and indeed the patterns of activity of squirrels at different times of the year result mainly from a balancing act between, on the one hand, staying in the nest and conserving energy and, on the other hand, foraging and feeding to obtain more energy. Hence activity and energetics are intimately tied together.

GENERAL PATTERNS OF ACTIVITY

Studying the activity of animals in cages or enclosures is straightforward but can give a false impression of the activity of free-living animals. As an example, Clarkson and Ferguson (1972) found that diurnal running-wheel activity in pine squirrels was greater in the winter than the summer which is contrary to our knowledge about relative amounts of activity during summer and winter in free-living squirrels.

Direct observation is an obvious way of studying free-living squirrels, but it suffers from the same drawbacks encountered earlier in relation to trying to quantify what animals eat by direct observation (e.g. Benson, 1980). Here the technique of radiotelemetry can greatly further our knowledge. This involves fitting a small radiotransmitter to an animal, usually by means of a collar, and either regularly pinpointing the position of a squirrel thus mapping where it goes, or locating and closely following the animal during the course of its normal activities using a hand-held radioreceiver (Kenward, 1982). Where clear sightings are obtained it is possible to record what the animal is doing, for example, feeding, grooming, dozing and so on. Even when direct sightings cannot be obtained it is still feasible to infer something about what the animal is doing by changes in the signals from specially designed radiotransmitters. These can pass on information about surface body temperature, the orientation of the body of the animal and whether the animal is moving about or curled up in a nest. In certain types of study, the activity and position of squirrels can be recorded automatically (e.g. Connolley, 1979). One of the main drawbacks of radiotracking squirrels is that it is labour intensive and not many animals can be followed at the same time.

Mel Tonkin has carried out some interesting studies radiotracking red squirrels in northern England and she provides us with very detailed information as to when squirrels are active and what they are doing (Tonkin, 1983). This information can be applied to other species of northern tree squirrel since they all exhibit similar gross daily activity patterns which vary according to the season of the year (e.g. Bland, 1977; Deutch, 1978; Thompson, 1977; Tamura and Miyashita, 1984). Since squirrels are diurnal it is not surprising that the length of the day governs the time of onset and cessation of activity (Bahnak and Kramm, 1977). This probably interacts with an internal rhythm of activity but not a great deal is known about this in the case of squirrels (see Kramm, 1975). Squirrels are early risers and more often than not become active at first light. Exceptions to this can occur. For example, some squirrels may delay the start of their activities for an hour or two. Such delays have been recorded at all times of the year but the reasons why they occur may be many and varied. Occasionally delays may occur because young or subordinate animals are avoiding adults or dominant squirrels (Tonkin, 1983). Also factors such as food availability or air temperature may affect

Figure 4.1 Red squirrel seasonal activity patterns. Arrows denote times of first and last light. Source: Tonkin (1983)

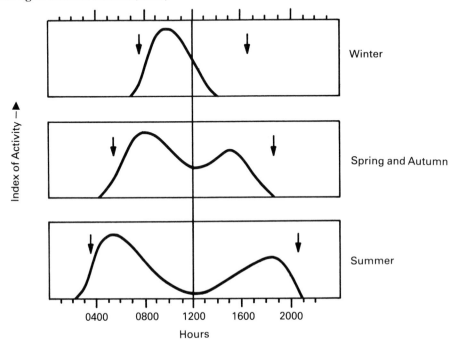

the timing of the onset of activity after sunrise, and the luxury of a 'lie-in' may be related to energy conservation (e.g. Deutch, 1978).

During the short winter day all squirrels have one main active period, with activity finishing sometime between midday and the end of the afternoon (Figure 4.1). During the long summer days there are two phases of activity interrupted by a rest period. The morning phase peaks 2 to 3 hours after sunrise, and the afternoon phase 2 to 3 hours before sunset with the animals retiring well before dark. The morning peak in winter may shift towards midday in cold, northerly climates (e.g. Pauls, 1978 on pine squirrels). Lemnell (1970) found that a male red squirrel in Sweden reduced its active period to 1 to 2 hours in the middle of the day in severe winter weather and Russell Hampshire found that grey squirrels kept in enclosures in England reduced their daily activity to 3 hours in December with a peak towards the afternoon. In general, the cessation of activity is less influenced by the onset of nightfall than the onset of activity is influenced by daybreak. In the autumn and spring the general patterns of

Table 4.1 Mean values for the activity of squirrels from two studies carried out in mixed deciduous woodland using radiotracking and direct observation methods: (a) red squirrels from northern England, 55°N (Tonkin, 1983); (b) grey squirrels from Maryland, USA 38°N (Hougert and Flyger, 1981). No figures are available for travel, resting/dozing, maintenance or interaction times from the grey squirrel study. Foraging times include feeding and caching

Behaviour	Time of the year							
	Dec–Feb		Mar–May		Jun–Aug		Sept–Nov	
	(a)	(b)	(a)	(b)	(a)	(b)	(a)	(b)
Total Hours Active	4.8		8.2		11.2		8.7	
Total Active Period (Hours)		5.6		10.6		14.0		11.2
% daylength active	51	31	52	65	63	74	71	53
% time foraging in trees	27	7	49	29	74	36	69*	25
% time foraging on ground	57	73	36	51	9	31	16	34
% time travelling	6		7		8		7	
% time resting/dozing	<1		5		7		5	
% time maintenance (grooming etc.)	1		1		1		1	
% time direct interaction	4		1		<1		<1	

*About 50 per cent of the time in October was spent caching seed from the canopy of trees

activity are intermediate between those of the winter and summer. Mel Tonkin found that the winter activity phase was half as long as the summer phase (Table 4.1; also see Hougart and Flyger, 1981; Knee, 1983).

It is important to remember that the timing of activity varies greatly between individuals and that the above gross activity patterns are composite pictures based on many individuals. Counts of numbers of squirrels seen at certain locations and at certain times are not, therefore, very informative unless individuals are recognised. A failure to follow specific individuals and differences in how activity is measured are the main reason why conflicting accounts occur as to the importance of the influence of environmental factors on activity. For example, Lampio (1967) believed that temperature alone did not influence daily activity in Finnish red squirrels whereas Naumov (1930, in Ognev 1940) in northern Siberia did. Another example is that Dice (1921) reported that he seldom saw pine squirrels in interior Alaska when air temperatures dropped to −32°C, but Murie (1927) reported them to be active all the year. When temperatures drop extremely low it is now believed that pine squirrels confine their activity to nests and burrows under the snow such as in middens or under the ground; that is to say they become subterranean and subnivean animals (Hatt, 1929; Pruitt and Lucier, 1958; M.C. Smith, 1968; Zirul and Fuller, 1970). Interestingly, red squirrels are reported to be entirely supranivean during the winter even in very cold climates (Pulliainen, 1982). Therefore, it should not surprise us that particular populations or individuals do not conform to the general pattern of activity but it is interesting to find out why a particular individual is active when it is. This will depend on factors such as whether the individual is an adult or juvenile, breeding or non-breeding, and also upon environmental factors such as weather and food supply. The influence of these environmental factors will now be considered.

Effects of Weather on Activity

Despite some early uncertainties concerning the role of temperature in influencing activity (e.g. Lampio, 1967), it now seems clear that in certain situations temperature is of overriding importance. This has been shown by a variety of techniques from studies of squirrel tracks in snow (Pulliainen, 1973 on red squirrels), to studies of captive animals in outside pens (Bahnak and Kramm, 1977 and Pauls, 1978 on pine squirrels; Hampshire, 1985 on grey squirrels) and laboratory cages (Bahnak and Kramm, 1979 on pine squirrels). Throughout much of their geographical range red and pine squirrels live in very severe climates and so the influences of temperature may be more readily observed in these animals. Mel Tonkin (1983) found that air temperature did not influence the time spent out of the nest or the amount of activity in red squirrels in the cool-temperate climate of northern England, but (as seen above) the effects of very low temperatures on activity by pine and red squirrels in cold boreal climates may be considerable. This is further substantiated by Pauls (1978) in Canada, who found that the time spent out of the nest and the amount of daily activity of pine squirrels in Winnipeg (which has a continental climate) were highly associated with mean daily air temperature. Therefore, at low temperatures squirrels will spend longer in the nest and will be less active outside the nest. In fact in severe weather conditions, squirrels may 'hole-up' in their nests for one to several days (e.g. Sharp, 1959; Hougart and Flyger, 1981). Squirrels may also become inactive out of the nest at high temperatures thus contributing to the lull in activity usually seen during the middle of the day in the summer.

Rainfall, unless heavy (Bland, 1977; Layne, 1954), does not greatly affect activity (Tonkin, 1983). Similarly, only heavy snowstorms are believed to affect activity but I noticed that pine squirrels in subalpine forests in Colorado distinctly avoided being active when the first snows of the year were falling in November, even though the snow falls were not particularly severe.

There are many reports that squirrels avoid being active in high winds, especially in the canopy of trees (Ingles, 1947; Layne, 1954; Pack et al, 1967; Pauls, 1978; also see Tonkin, 1983). There is no doubt that this is partly related to the difficulties of moving about in trees in high winds but, and especially during the winter, it must also be related to the excessive cooling effect of the wind on the body, the so-called chill factor (see below).

Effects of Food Availability on Activity

During active periods squirrels spend a greater portion of their time foraging for food, feeding and caching during the autumn (Table 4.1). Foraging and feeding is affected by the distribution, abundance and quality of food (see Chapter 3). On average, 60 to 90 per cent of a squirrels' time spent out of the nest is engaged in foraging, feeding, or caching food; Mel Tonkin's work on red squirrels gives a yearly average of 80 per cent. However, there are variations beween months and between years according to food availability. From the discussion in Chapter 3 it is easy to understand that there will be an increase in foraging activity when food is of low energy content, requires long search times to find it, or long handling times to process it. Feeding and foraging time will be lowest during the autumn and winter when seed is present, although there will often be an autumn peak in activity in relation to food caching. On the other hand, foraging and feeding activity are often high during the spring when squirrels turn to tree buds as a major source of food. Differences in the amount of time foraging in the canopy and on the ground are evident according to the time of the year and can be related to where the food is to be found. Squirrels spend least time foraging in the trees in late winter and most time in summer (Table 4.1). However, an interesting observation is that grey squirrels consistently spend relatively more time on the ground than red squirrels in similar types of woodland (Table 4.1). For example, grey squirrels in deciduous woodland in England spent 14 per cent of their active time throughout the year in the canopy of the trees compared with 67 per cent for red squirrels in similar habitat (Kenward and Tonkin, 1986). This shows that there are differences between the two species in relation to habitat and food utilisation and this has implications with respect to interaction between red and grey squirrels in Britain which is discussed in Chapter 8. Deutch (1978) found that wild squirrels provided with extra winter food spent less time out of the nest, less time foraging, and finished their daily activity earlier than squirrels without the extra food. Artificial sources of food which occur in parks and gardens also influence the normal activity periods of squirrels living in these habitats (Tamura and Miyashita, 1984).

Other Behaviours in the Activity Budget

Apart from foraging, feeding and caching food, most of the rest of the time that squirrels are out of the nest is spent up in the canopy on maintenance behaviour such as grooming, dozing or resting, or simply in moving through the trees (Table 4.1; Figure 4.2). Of course, occasionally squirrels must descend to the ground to cross from one tree to another if the trees are too far apart for the squirrels to jump between them. Squirrels doze or rest outside the nest for 20 to 30 per cent or longer of their time spent out of the nest in summer months (Hampshire, 1985; Hougart and Flyger, 1981; C.C. Smith, 1968). Sometimes squirrels will rest under cover such as in tree holes, but more often they will 'lie-up' in exposed locations (C.C. Smith, 1968). In these situations squirrels either may be taking advantage of solar radiation and sunbathing, or, in hot weather, they may be resting in such a way as to try and keep cool. They do this by lying spreadeagled on a branch with their tails hanging down (these ideas will be further discussed later); it should be noted that body posture is important to the heat economics of these animals. For example, squirrels resting in cold weather will adopt a nearly spherical posture with their tails folded over their backs; this is to conserve body heat (Ingles, 1947; Pauls, 1978; Muchlinski and Shump, 1979).

Few studies have described differences in activity between adults and juveniles, and breeding and non-breeding animals. Christopher C. Smith (1968) presents detailed activity budgets for three pine squirrels during the summer (Figure 4.2). He found two important differences in activity between a lactating female and an adult male. Firstly, the female did not spend any time caching seed while she was suckling her young and this is shown by the low 'food gathering' category in Figure 4.2; the male on the other hand stored pine cones and fungi at this time. Secondly, the female returned to the nest up to an hour later than the male at dusk. She therefore spent as much time as possible feeding during daylight hours to provide for her offspring. After the young were weaned the activity of the female became similar to that of the male. This may not be the case in other squirrel species such as grey squirrels. If the food supply is good, then the lactating female may in fact reduce its out of the nest activity and its range of movement. Thus she will spend as much time as possible with or near her young to look after them.

Christopher C. Smith found that juveniles just out of the nest (at about 50 days of age) but not weaned, and up until about two weeks after weaning (about 75 to 80 days of age) spent time exploring around the nest, gradually moving further afield, and learning about food and objects in a trial and error manner. They also indulged in play such as sexual play with their siblings or their mother (about 3.5 per cent of their time) and, in this territorial species, territorial behaviour (about 1.7 per cent of their time). About 5 to 8 per cent of the time of all animals was spent in predator-defence activities which included freezing, that is becoming motionless and observing the area of a disturbance (frequently the observer), alarm calling and rushing to a protected area or nest site.

The behaviour of squirrels will be returned to in Chapter 5 but it is worth mentioning that squirrels spend very little time on direct behavioural interactions with other squirrels; the intensity of this activity will vary according to the time of the breeding season and, for example, the time of

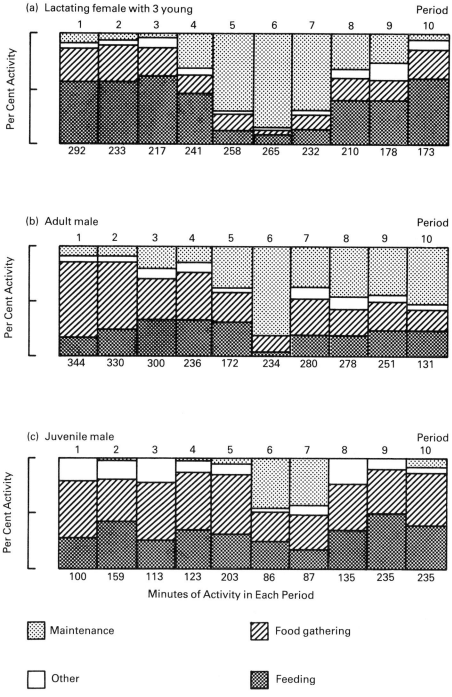

Figure 4.2 *Activity budget of pine squirrels. Day divided into ten periods with variable number of minutes in each period. Food gathering includes picking and carrying food which was either eaten or cached, and general movement through the forest. Maintenance activity includes dozing, resting and grooming. Source: C.C. Smith (1968)*

the establishment of territories in pine squirrels. Territories in pine and douglas squirrels, for example, are established or reaffirmed in the autumn as juveniles vie for 'places' in the habitat and caching the winter's food supply takes place. At this time territorial activity may be high for short periods. However, once established, territorial activity may not occupy much of the day's activity (e.g. <1 per cent of the time, C.C. Smith, 1968). The same relative amount of time in adult interaction probably occurs in all species. Nevertheless, despite this small amount of time spent in direct interaction, squirrels are undoubtedly always aware of the presence of their neighbours and communicate with them from a distance using visual signals, vocalisations and scent marking.

THE ENERGY BUDGET

It has been established that squirrels spend a great deal of their active day foraging and feeding. Food is the source of energy for the squirrel, and before discussing the interrelationship between energy conservation and activity, I shall, consider what happens to the food, and particularly the energy in the food, after it has been eaten by a squirrel.

Digested Energy

In all animals a proportion of the energy ingested is not absorbed or assimilated from the gut into the body, but is lost in the faeces (Figure 4.3). This has been discussed in Chapter 3; the proportion not assimilated depends on the type of food the squirrel has been eating, being 10 to 20 per cent for seeds and of the order of 20 to 40 per cent for plant food (measured mainly in other rodent species, e.g. Grodzinski, 1985). A consequence of this is that more food with low digestibility has to be passed through the gut for the same amount of energy uptake compared with food with high digestibility. Furthermore, green plant food with a low digestibility usually takes longer to process in the gut than, say, seeds and this will further lower the rate of energy uptake. In extreme circumstances an animal feeding for long periods on food of a low digestibility will still not obtain enough energy for its normal daily requirements and the animal will lose weight: this is sometimes called a digestive bottleneck and may occur in squirrels when they have to eat foods of a low quality (see Chapter 3). There is no direct evidence for digestive bottlenecks in squirrels but some indirect evidence comes from studies carried out in Alaska. M.C. Smith (1968) found that pine squirrels on average lost 24 per cent of their initial body weight over a 6-day period when fed on a mixed diet of a laboratory rodent food and buds of the white spruce; progressively smaller amounts of rodent food were presented until none were given on day 6. Thereafter the squirrels survived on a pure diet of buds for seven days but lost further weight. One squirrel died on day 6 and another on day 8 during the experiment. The squirrels recovered their lost weight within four days of returning to a 100 per cent rodent food diet.

Energy Lost in Waste Products

Some energy passes out in the waste products of metabolic activity, that is in the urine (termed U; Figure 4.3), and although few studies have measured U directly, it is believed to be between 1 and 5 per cent of that consumed (Knee, 1983).

Figure 4.3 Idealised squirrel energy budget

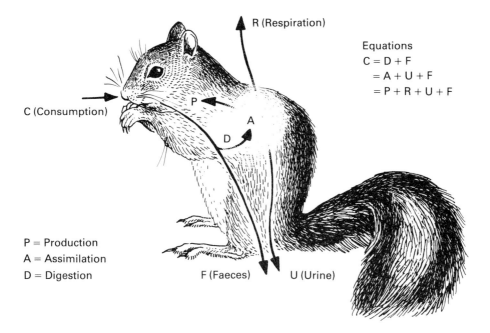

Equations
C = D + F
= A + U + F
= P + R + U + F

C (Consumption)

R (Respiration)

P = Production
A = Assimilation
D = Digestion

F (Faeces)   U (Urine)

Energy and Production

Looking at Figure 4.3, it can be seen that some of the assimilated energy goes into the production of new tissues (termed P). This formation of new tissues is usually referred to as an increase in biomass and can either be associated with the growth of the body (Pg) or it can be associated with reproduction, that is the production of offspring (Pr). Technically, when squirrels lose weight there is a loss of tissue but work can be done and heat is produced in the process.

Young squirrels will obviously divert energy into growth. Shorten's (1951) data on the growth of hand-reared grey squirrels suggests that, on average, an animal which is between 10 weeks old (that is when it is just weaned, which occurs at about 200 to 220 g in weight) and 20 weeks old will put on 3.14 g in weight a day. Studies on fox and grey squirrels in North America show that the average energy equivalent of squirrel body tissue is 8.1 KJ/g wet weight (Ludwick *et al*, 1969; Husband, 1976). Thus about 25 KJ of energy were put into growth by Monica Shorten's young squirrels each day. In addition, it is believed that young squirrels have higher metabolic rates than adults (see below) and thus the relative amount of energy required each day by a 250 to 300 g squirrel (i.e. in KJ/g/day) will be greater than that required by an adult. Clare Ludolf (pers. comm.) has found that the consumption rate of young grey squirrels in the laboratory can be represented by the equation: $y = 16.9 + 1.08x$, where y is consumption in KJ/animal/day and x is body weight in grams.

Adult squirrels also undergo changes in body weight often on a seasonal basis. This varies between species, food conditions and whether weight change is measured in captive animals or field animals (Knee, 1983). However, in general, body weight can increase by 10 to 15 per cent in the autumn in some of the smaller species (e.g. red) or up to 25 per cent in some of the larger species (e.g. grey). This is a period when fat is laid down in the body, mainly in the abdominal cavity (e.g. Short and Duke, 1971). The timing of weight loss is not so predictable. Obviously, if food is in short supply then body reserves will be used at that time. If not, then weight loss may not occur until the following spring or summer.

There have been few comprehensive studies on the additional energy required each day by squirrels during lactation. Havera (1979a) found that the total energy required by female fox squirrels over the 10 weeks of lactation was 1.75 times that of non-lactating squirrels (Figure 4.4). C.C. Smith (1968) found that lactating pine squirrels, on a daily basis, consumed 1.76 times as much as adult males. No figures are available for the increased amounts of energy required by a female during pregnancy, but Havera (1979a) presents figures from five other studies on rodents which show that on average this is of the order of 0.23 of that used in lactation. Thus the energetic costs to the female of raising a litter is considerable. For a period of about 45 days during pregnancy, and then for another 75 days during lactation, there is an increasing energy demand (Figure 4.4). This will depend upon litter size, and it is pertinent that, although squirrels are capable of having between five and eight offspring, the number of young weaned is nearer two or three (Chapter 7; Gurnell, 1981). Havera (1977) analysed the body composition of lactating and non-lactating squirrels and found that the total carcass fat was lower in squirrels which had finished lactating possibly because of the high energy demands of lactation. Further, he suggested that squirrels may require some minimum level of condition before entering oestrus. Thus the nutritional status of the female at the time of the mating season may determine whether she conceives or not.

Figure 4.4 Daily ingested energy of lactating fox squirrels as a percentage of that ingested by non-lactating squirrels. Average for two females, one with litter of 3 young and one with litter of 4 young. Source: Havera (1979a)

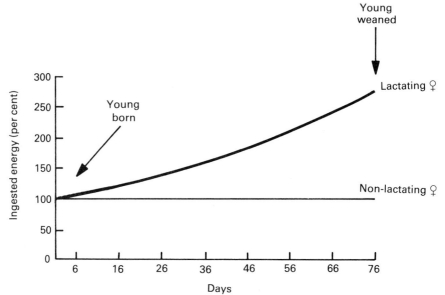

Energy and Metabolism

Most of the assimilated energy is used in work carried out during metabolism in the body. Metabolism refers to chemical processes involved with: (a) the breaking down of organic compounds with the liberation of energy which can be used by the squirrel during its various activities; and (b) the building up of simple compounds into complex compounds consuming energy. The use of energy in these life processes is called respiration (not to be confused with breathing) and is given the symbol R.

All the elements of the energy balance equation are referred to a time base and, as will be seen below, the rate of respiration or metabolism must be sufficient to maintain the body temperature of the squirrel and for muscular and other activities. For example, the harder that muscles have to work the more energy is used up and the greater the amount of heat produced. The metabolic rate in running squirrels, for example, is 1.4 to 2.8 times that of resting squirrels (Wunder and Morrison, 1974). In fact, different measures of metabolic rate are recognised: Basal Metabolic Rate (BMR) refers to the minimum expenditure of energy which occurs when the squirrel is at rest, without food in the gut (the postabsorptive state), and within its 'thermoneutral zone'. The thermoneutral zone is the range of environmental temperatures where metabolism is at a minimum, bounded each side by a rising metabolic rate (Mount, 1979). The basal rate of metabolism is sufficient to provide enough heat to maintain the body temperature of the squirrel above a certain level, called the lower critical temperature (Tlc). At temperatures lower than Tlc, energy has to be provided for maintaining body temperature; the Resting Metabolic Rate (RMR) takes this into account and is the BMR plus the energy used in thermoregulation, and plus the specific dynamic effect or action (SDA) of food in the gut. The term SDA needs further explanation. Shortly after feeding, the metabolic rate of an animal rises; this is partly due to the manipulation of the food in the gut and the process of digestion itself. It is this heat of food metabolism which is referred to as SDA and it varies according to a number of factors including type of food and meal size (see Brafield and Llewellyn, 1982, for a more thorough discussion). There are three other measures of metabolic rate and energy utilisation which should be mentioned. Active Metabolic Rate (AMR) refers to RMR plus the energy used when the squirrel is active; Average Daily Metabolic Rate (ADMR) is the average metabolic rate over a 24 hour period which includes periods of rest and periods of activity; and the Daily or Yearly Energy Budget (DEB or YEB) which is the total amount of energy used by an animal in a day or a year, respectively, including energy used for growth and reproduction. Metabolic rates will be discussed further below.

Each of these terms in the energy budget equation represent complex energy transformations and require special methods for their estimation. Metabolic rate may either be measured directly as the amount of heat liberated from a unit area of the body surface of the squirrel per hour (direct calorimetry; Innes and Lavigne, 1979) or indirectly from the amount of oxygen consumed or carbon dioxide liberated per unit body weight of the squirrel per hour (indirect calorimetry; Bolls and Perfect, 1972). Further, the amount of energy digested can be found from the difference between the amount of energy ingested and that lost in the faeces (gravimetric method). The details of these methods need not concern

Table 4.2 Energy requirements from selected studies of fox and grey squirrels (from Knee, 1983)

Method	Species	Mean body weight (g)	Energy required KJ/g/hr	Authority
Direct calorimetry RMR	Grey	570	0.013	Innes, 1978
Indirect calorimetry RMR	Grey	440	0.017	Bolls and Perfect, 1972
Indirect calorimetry ADMR	Grey	630	0.015	D. Wood in Knee, 1983
Gravimetric Daily Assimilation	Grey	610	0.024	Merson et al, 1978
Gravimetric Daily Assimilation	Grey	590	0.035	Knee, 1983
Gravimetric Daily Assimilation	Grey	530	0.056	Ludwick et al, 1969
Gravimetric Daily Assimilation	Fox	880	0.026	Havera, 1979
Gravimetric Daily Assimilation	Fox	740	0.032	Husband, 1976

us here although the different methods of estimating the energy requirements of squirrels do not produce concordant results (Knee, 1983). The
techniques used at present, therefore, need further evaluation. What
should be remembered is that the energy budget should balance in the long
run, and so, in a healthy adult with a constant body temperature and
constant body weight, the energy taken into the body should be balanced
by energy lost from the body.

The figures in Table 4.2 give some typical values for the rate of energy
required by fox and grey squirrels derived from several different methods
of study, and Table 4.3 gives examples of DEBs for three different squirrel
species.

Stress and Metabolic Rate

Several factors affect the energy budget, including stress, body size, and
the squirrel's thermal environment. The last two items will be explored
more thoroughly below but the effects of stress are not as well known and
evidence of stress in squirrels comes mainly from trapping or laboratory
studies. Heart rate responses to fear in fox and grey squirrels have been
studied using transmitters implanted into the abdomen of the animals

Table 4.3 Energy budgets of squirrels

Species/subject(s)	(Mean) weight (g)	KJ/animal/day				Comments	Authority
		Consumpt. C	Resp. R	Prod. P	Faeces + Urine FU		
Pine/adult male	243	523	376		147	Feeding observed in wild	C. C. Smith, 1968
Pine/subadult	134	348	251		97	Feeding observed in wild	C.C. Smith, 1968
Grey/3 adults	(527)	1006	514	201	291	Laboratory commercial rodent food	Ludwick *et al*, 1969
Fox/3 adults	(744)	727	507	80	140	Laboratory commercial rodent food	Husband, 1976

Note: in the grey squirrel study the captive animals ate 20 per cent more energy than required

(E.N. Smith and Johnson, 1984). In the field it was shown that fear resulted in a drop in heart rate if cover was available to the squirrels. If there was no cover available then the animals fled exhibiting an increased heart rate. An extreme form of stress has been seen in trapped squirrels (Guthrie *et al*, 1967) where very occasionally a trapped animal may appear to be uncoordinated in its actions and even have convulsions, become unconscious and die.

Physiologically, this sort of shock is associated with a reduction in body temperature (rectal temperatures fall to 27°C), a reduction in adrenal glucocorticoids, hypoglycaemia and an elevated packed cell volume. Specific studies indicate that these characteristics of stressed squirrels are not associated with lack of food or cold (Merson *et al*, 1978). Pack *et al*, (1967) suggested that shock mortality in live traps was greater among low ranking individuals but there was no real evidence to support this. However, Havera (1977) found that fox squirrels which died in live traps in his study were in poor condition with significantly lower average fat levels compared with controls. A good live trapping technique should aim at minimising stress in the captured animals and there are two important ways of achieving this. First, the traps should be visited two or three times during the day and especially at dusk so that animals are never left in traps for long, and especially overnight. Second, the traps should either incorporate a wooden nest box or be covered completely so that the inside of the trap is reasonably dark and protected from the weather; squirrels tend to sit quietly in nest boxes or well-covered traps (Chapter 7). Following these procedures I have been fortunate and not had any squirrels die in traps despite many years of trapping in all sorts of weather.

Some wild squirrels do not survive the trauma of being captured and placed in captivity and this is probably related to stress as described above. Clare Knee (1983) also believes that stress in squirrels resulting from confinement affects the study of their behaviour and energy requirements. This may be influenced by cage size, handling and food type, and frequently recently-caged wild squirrels will not feed properly and lose weight. This may also occur after cage cleaning, feeding, weighing or other disturbances. A result of animals being in stress is that they have higher metabolic rates (up to 16 per cent) than expected. After confinement or other disturbances this elevated metabolic rate in conjunction with a disrupted food intake, results in weight loss.

It is worth pointing out that juvenile and subadult squirrels do not appear to become as stressed as adults following capture or confinement. Where possible, therefore, squirrels required for behaviour or energetics studies in captivity should be taken from the wild as young animals. Also, following on from Clare Knee's work, observation cages or enclosures should be as large as possible.

BODY TEMPERATURE

Squirrels, like other mammals, are homoiothermic. That is they maintain a fairly stable deep body temperature, whether active or not and irrespective of the temperature of their surroundings (i.e. environmental or ambient temperature). However, body temperature is not absolutely constant. Tree squirrels normally have a body temperature which in fact varies between about 37°C to 40°C (Bolls and Perfect, 1972; Golightly and Ohmart, 1978; Reynolds, 1985a). Slight differences have been found between species, location, and the method of measurement (e.g. skin or rectal temperature; see Innes and Lavigne, 1979), but also, and most interestingly, it has been shown that body temperature varies within an individual according to whether the squirrel is active or not. The body temperature of a squirrel drops when it is at rest, especially during the night in the nest.

This phenomenon is sometimes called heterothermy and is illustrated by work carried out by Golightly and Ohmart (1978) on abert squirrels in Arizona and by Pauls (1979) on pine squirrels in Manitoba. The general picture to emerge is the same from both studies. For example, during the night the body temperature of abert squirrels dropped to an average value of about 38°C. Shortly before leaving the nest at daybreak the body temperature increased slightly, and when they were out of the nest and generally active the temperature reached about 40°C (also see Figure 4.5 for an example on pine squirrels).

The metabolic rate of squirrels follows this daily cycle of body temperature and activity (Grodzinski, 1971; Golightly and Ohmart, 1978).

Figure 4.5 Body temperature of pine squirrels in relation to air temperature: (a) outside nest during the day and (b) inside nest during night, and in relation to before and after animal leaves the nest, (c) for 4 exits with air temperatures of 4.6°C to 14.8°C and (d) for 11 exits with air temperatures of −17°C to −31°C. Means with 95 per cent confidence intervals. Source: Pauls (1979)

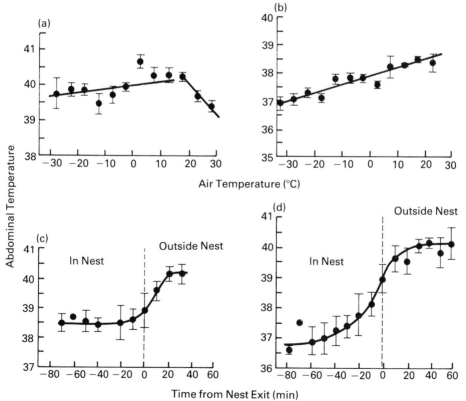

For example, the metabolic rate of squirrels is known to increase as they 'warm up' before they leave the nest. Golightly and Ohmart found that if the squirrels were very active, such as when they were running, then the body temperature of the squirrels would increase even more to about 41°C. After such bouts of intense activity, the squirrels would rest in a tree in the shade and often their faces would be moist with saliva to facilitate evaporative cooling (see below). Squirrels may also lose moisture, and hence heat, from sweat glands on the soles of the feet. In cool but sunny weather, abert squirrels made use of solar radiation and spent a good deal of their time sunbathing (about 40 per cent of their time in winter); in this way they intercepted about 18 KJ of energy per hour. Sunbathing is common in all tree squirrel species and the effect is enhanced by the low reflectance properties of the squirrel pelage.

Sunning abert squirrels with their tails up and pressed onto their backs had higher body temperatures than those with their tail down, and therefore it can be seen that the tail can have a dual purpose; it can either act to intercept solar radiation or to shade the body in very hot weather. In the latter instance the tail would be held above the back of the animal rather like a sunshade (see Viljoen, 1985). Fanning the tail over the back may aid cooling. The lowest body temperature recorded in an abert squirrel was 35.2°C in a rain-exposed individual; here the wet fur reduced insulation and increased heat loss from the body surface.

The body temperature of squirrels then varies over a range of 3 to 4°C. Why should this be? A high body temperature in active animals is necessary for efficient foraging, alertness, and quick reactions, coordination and movement which may be required when the animal has to escape from a predator. This is probably why squirrels pause to 'warm up' before leaving the nest. A further increase in body temperature with intense activity is understandable; this occurs in all animals. Finally, the lowering of body temperature during prolonged periods of rest is probably an adaptation to conserve energy and may be critical at certain times of the year. During the cooler night it will take less energy to maintain the lower body temperature. The evidence from the study on abert squirrels in fact suggests seasonal acclimatisation as well as diurnal cycles in body temperature. Body temperatures in summer and autumn were significantly higher than those in winter and spring.

The lower lethal temperature in abert squirrels appears to be about −20°C (Golightly and Ohmart, 1978); this means that if squirrels have to endure such temperatures for some time without nest insulation, they are unable to maintain their deep body temperature and so die. This emphasises the importance to squirrels in the wild using nests so that they can survive cold weather for several days, even with a reduced food intake.

I have left to last one more possible variation in body temperature which has potential adaptive significance. The problem here is that more studies are required to understand how common or extreme this form of body temperature variation is. There is some evidence from studies on red and grey squirrels that the body temperature can drop well below the normal range of heterothermy (Innes and Lavigne, 1979; Jessica Holm, pers. comm.) For example, a rectal temperature of 27.2°C was observed in a winter grey squirrel in the laboratory which had been deprived of food for 48 hours and exposed to −20°C for 3 hours (Innes and Lavigne, 1979). The squirrel recovered from this condition in about 10 minutes at 20°C without any apparent ill-effects. This suggests that squirrels are able to undergo a form of adaptive hypothermia or torpor which undoubtedly would be an important form of energy conservation. This could occur when squirrels 'hole-up' in their nests during periods of intense cold.

THE THERMAL ENVIRONMENT

When we consider that northern tree squirrels often live in cold climates (Chapter 1), that they are homoiotherms, and that they have to spend a considerable amount of time out of the nest foraging and feeding each day, then it is easy to see why environmental or ambient temperature has an important influence on the activity and behaviour of the animals. The thermal environment of squirrels is outlined in Figure 4.6.

In brief, heat is gained from resting metabolic activity, radiation, shivering and other muscular activities, conduction from the surface of the ground or objects, and non-shivering thermogenesis. Non-shivering thermogenesis refers to the metabolism of brown fat which has a high thermogenic capacity; adult pine squirrels are known to have brown fat in the thoracic and cervical region of their bodies which increases in quantity during the autumn (Aleksuik, 1971).

Heat loss from an animal occurs by convection, radiation, evaporation and conduction. Conduction is probably not very important in Holarctic tree squirrels. Squirrels will take measures to minimise heat loss (heat conservation) by reducing blood flow to the peripheral parts of the body, such as to the tail by raising the fur and trapping a layer of insulating air, by using a compact body posture, by using a nest (drey, den or burrow) which increases insulation, by huddling with other squirrels, and by varying activity according to weather conditions. Heat loss can be increased by an extended posture, and conduction loss may occur in very hot weather (Bakken, 1959), by increasing blood flow to the peripheral tissues, and by evaporative cooling. Evaporative cooling is known to occur in tree squirrels which have an elavated body temperature following high activity, especially when the ambient temperature is high (see above and Viljoen, 1985, concerning African tree squirrels). Sandra Viljoen also noted that conduction loss may occur in very hot weather in African tree squirrels.

Metabolic Rate and Body Size

Under stable conditions, the rate of heat loss from the surface of a squirrel should be balanced by the rate of heat produced through metabolism. The rate of heat loss depends upon the surface area of the animal, and hence larger squirrels (species or individuals) should lose heat more quickly than smaller individuals. Therefore the metabolic rate of larger animals will be higher when measured in terms of KJ of energy used per hour per animal. However, the surface area of larger animals is *smaller* in relation to body mass or volume compared with smaller animals, and therefore the metabolic rate in terms of KJ of energy per hour per gram body weight will be smaller. Using simple mathematical equations it is possible to calculate a predicted metabolic rate for an animal of given body size. It is then interesting to compare the predicted metabolic rates with those measured in living animals and see whether any differences can be related to aspects of their biology.

Figure 4.6 Thermal relationships between squirrels and their surroundings. Ta = ambient temperature which varies according to squirrel location; Tb = body temperature; B = body and tail posture; CV = heat convection (affected by air movements); RO = thermal radiation from objects; RA = thermal radiation from air; CD = heat conduction (affected by contact area); E = evaporative cooling (affected by humidity and air currents); dreys, dens, burrows and ground nests provide insulation. (The same relationships hold for the squirrel in the tree and that on the ground)

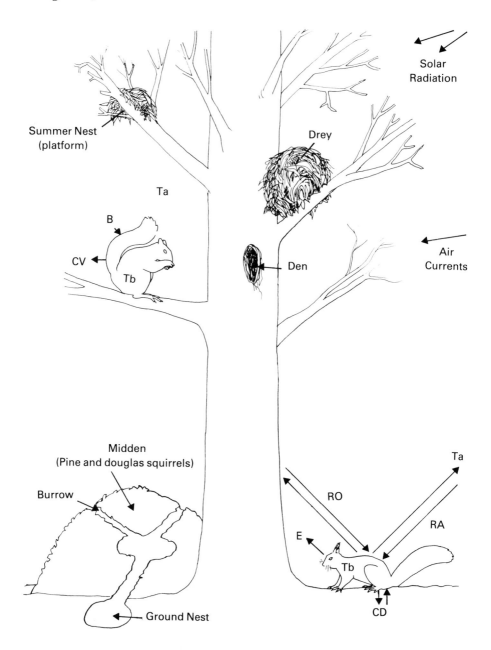

Figure 4.7 Relationship between basal metabolic rate (BMR) in KJ/g/day and body weight (g). Source: Reynolds (1986)

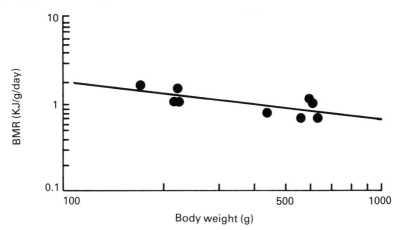

In Figure 4.7 the relationship is shown between BMR and body weight from 9 squirrel studies, 4 on grey, 4 on pine and one on abert, based on the analysis by Reynolds (1985b). Some of the variation in this relationship undoubtedly stems from different methods used by the different experimenters. Viljoen (1985) found that African tree squirrels adapted to warm, dry climates had metabolic rates 13 to 34 per cent lower than expected whereas Reynolds (1985c) found that Holarctic tree squirrels, the ones which particularly concern us here, had metabolic rates 3 to 80 per cent higher than expected. Despite some possible inaccuracies in the size of these figures, the overall conclusion is that the higher than expected metabolic rate in Holarctic tree squirrels is an adaptation to the cool/cold climate in which they live.

There are few data on the energy requirements of young, growing squirrels but in general it appears that metabolic rates (KJ/g/day) are higher in juveniles than adults (Grodzinski, 1971; Knee, 1983) as expected from the discussion above. Knee (1983) quotes Wood who found that the metabolic rate of juvenile grey squirrels was 1.8 times that of adults in laboratory respirometry studies.

Metabolic Rate and Ambient Temperature

As ambient temperature falls, the gradient between the internal and external body temperature increases and, proportionately, the rate of heat loss from the body increases (Figure 4.8). Consequently, the squirrel has to increase its metabolic rate to replace the heat loss and maintain its body temperature. For example, the abert squirrel, which has a body temperature of about 40°C, has to triple its metabolic rate when the ambient temperature drops from 20°C to −20°C. The slope of each line in Figure 4.8 is a constant for a particular species (or individual) and is sometimes referred to as the thermal conductance of an animal. As can be seen, this value will vary between species and individuals and whether, for example, the animal is winter or summer acclimatised (Reynolds, 1985a).

Body Insulation and Use of Nest

Squirrels do not appear to lay down large amounts of subcutaneous fat for extra insulation, although they may increase body fat reserves elsewhere within the body during the autumn ready for the winter. However, squirrels undergo a spring moult and an autumn moult (Chapter 2), and pelage characteristics will aid heat conservation during the winter and heat dissipation during the summer. For example, guard hairs of grey squirrels can be 3 cm longer in their winter coat. There is evidence that winter acclimatised animals have lower rates of heat loss compared with summer acclimatised animals and this, in part at least, must be due to changes in coat insulation (Figure 4.8; see Reynolds, 1985a).

There are many variations in the colour of the fur of squirrels and in many cases these can be explained as cryptic coloration (Chapter 2). However, in several species such as grey, abert, red and fox squirrels, there are two distinct forms; a normal one and a dark or melanistic one. As described in Chapter 2, the dark forms appear to occur more frequently in the northern parts of the ranges of grey, abert and red squirrels, but not fox squirrels. A black coat aids the uptake of radiant heat by sunbathing animals but it is believed that the reasons may be more complex than this. Melanic red squirrels have been shown to have slightly longer hairs at a higher density than the normal form which will increase insulation and

Figure 4.8 Relationship between metabolic rate (cc $O_2/g/hr$) and ambient temperature. Horizontal lines indicate position of lower critical temperatures. 1. Ngoye red squirrel from Africa (Viljoen, 1985); 2. pine squirrel—summer (Pauls, 1981); 3. grey squirrel (black and grey forms)—summer (Innis and Lavigne, 1979); 4. pine squirrel winter (Pauls, 1981); 5. abert squirrel (Golightly and Ohmart, 1978); 6. grey squirrel (black and grey forms)—winter (Innis and Lavigne, 1979); 7. grey squirrel (grey form)—winter (Innis and Lavigne, 1979); 8. grey squirrel (black form)—winter (Innis and Lavigne, 1979)

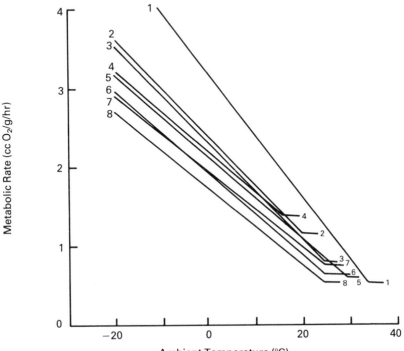

lower heat loss (Voipio and Hissa, 1970). However, a study conducted in Canada, directly aimed at looking at this problem in melanistic and normal grey squirrels in Ontario, found no differences between the thermal conductance of these two forms (Figure 4.8; Innes and Lavigne, 1979). On the other hand, melanic grey squirrels in the winter (but not the summer) were found to be better adapted to the cold; they had lower costs of thermoregulation and lower BMRs which may have been associated with lower body temperatures. This does not seem to clarify the situation very much since no link has been established between a lower body temperature and melanism. In addition, C.C. Smith (1981) makes the observation that few melanistic individuals have been found in pine squirrels despite the fact that they live in very cold climates. He puts this down to the fact that melanism would be counter-productive in winter conditions since the animals would stand out against the white, snow background and be at a greater risk of predation. (White coats too would make a squirrel obvious against the dark bark of trees, and indeed squirrels do not have white winter coats like blue hares or weasels.) It seems that further comparative studies on the adaptive significance of melanism are necessary.

Another way a squirrel increases its body insulation and reduces heat loss is to use a nest, whether it be a drey, a den or a burrow. In a way we can consider that the nest is rather like a thick overcoat and when in the nest the squirrel can greatly reduce its metabolic costs of thermoregulation. In a study using nest boxes, Havera (1979b) found that significant increases in metabolic rate for heat production in a fox squirrel were not necessary until the ambient temperature fell below $-8°C$. This points to a remarkable saving in energy consumption, and this was also found by Pauls (1981) in laboratory studies where pine squirrels which had nest boxes in winter had an average thermal conductance which was 60 per cent less than squirrels without a nest box (see Figure 4.9).

Studies of squirrels in natural nests have not provided such detailed information. However, Pulliainen (1973) found that red squirrels in Finland could maintain nest temperatures some 20-30°C above ambient temperatures of $-5°C$, following an initial warming up period after entering the nest, and Rasporov and Isakov (1935, in Havera, 1979b) found that the average nest temperatures of red squirrels in Russia during January, February and March was 18.5°C. I have not received any reports that red squirrels, like pine squirrels, go underground during the cold, harsh winters in the northern parts of their range. That they are able to stay above ground is a tribute to the remarkable insulation of their dreys. Pine squirrels have dreys, but as we have seen they use burrows in their middens or under the ground during very cold weather. I have also observed pine squirrels in the Rocky Mountains using rock holes as the weather deteriorated at the onset of winter.

Because they are solitary animals, there is another piece of adaptive behaviour which pine and douglas squirrels do not use but which other squirrels do. This is to huddle together in small groups within their nests. There have been no studies on the benefits of huddling in squirrels but considerable energy savings have been found in small rodents (Grodzinski, 1985).

In connection with nests, we have mainly looked at winter living quarters. During the summer, winter nests may become too hot for the

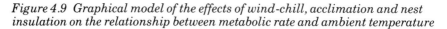

Figure 4.9 Graphical model of the effects of wind-chill, acclimation and nest insulation on the relationship between metabolic rate and ambient temperature

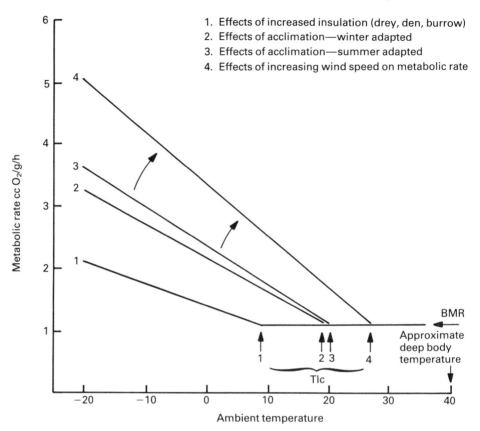

squirrels and so they build special summer nests. These are often no more than leafy platforms and allow the animals to keep cool (Chapter 2).

Metabolic Rate and the Effects of the Wind

It has been established that squirrels do not like being out and about in high winds, and this is particularly so when ambient temperatures are low. The reasons for this are twofold: (1) the difficulty in moving through trees when their branches are being whipped around by the wind, and (2) the cooling or wind-chill effect of the wind. Wind ruffles the fur and disturbs the insulating layer of air contained therein, and transfers heat away from the squirrel by the movement of the air; this is convected heat loss. The amount of heat lost depends upon wind speed and the difference between the surface temperature of the squirrel and ambient temperature. Figure 4.9 indicates how wind will greatly increase the metabolic cost of thermoregulation.

COMMENTARY

There are many things in this brief review of activity and energetics which I have only touched upon, but it should be clear that the behavioural tactics that a squirrel employs each day of its life take into consideration a complex of influencing factors. These include intrinsic factors which affect energy requirements such as age, sex, state of breeding, body condition, thermoregulation, foraging, and predator avoidance. These in turn interact with external factors such as ambient temperature, wind speed, relative humidity, and food supply. A higher than predicted metabolic rate on the basis of body size seems to be an adaptation to the all the year round activity of these animals in their cool, northern climates. Seasonal acclimatisation, heterothermy, and perhaps voluntary hypothermia, are further physiological adaptations.

At certain times during the day an individual will have to 'decide' whether it should continue to rest and conserve energy or whether it should become active, and use energy to seek food or indulge in other activities. The behaviour of squirrels then, is geared to the need to conserve heat at low ambient temperatures and the need to dissipate heat at high temperatures. Hence in very cold weather when the ground is frozen and food hard to obtain, it may profit the squirrel to remain in its highly insulated nest. On the other hand, during the summer, squirrels abandon their winter quarters and take to light, leafy summer nests. Other specific behaviours that have been mentioned include sunbathing, adjusting body posture, huddling and altering the length of time that the animal stays out of the nest. The total active period during the winter, for example, is much less than during the summer. This works all right when autumn seed supplies are good. These energy rich foods mean that sufficient energy during the coldest part of the year can be obtained during the short active days, aided by caches set up in the previous autumn. When food supplies are good, then squirrels will start breeding in mid-winter. It is when seed supplies are poor that the squirrels are in difficulty. Alternative foods may be of lower quality and take longer to obtain. This puts pressure on the length of the active day and squirrels may find that they have an energy deficit. It is easy to see how an animal may lose weight and condition and even die when food supplies are poor and weather conditions bad. Squirrels do not come into breeding condition during the winter when food supplies are poor (Gurnell, 1983).

Thus, we have seen the complexity of the decisions which a squirrel has to continually make every day of its life. Squirrels must feed for most of the time they are active. Also at certain times in the life history of an animal, it will have to 'decide' unconsciously whether it should divert energy into growth or reproduction. These ideas are related to the principle of the allocation of energy (Wunder, 1978; see Figure 4.3). In simple terms this works as follows: the squirrel will have to allocate its energy income (from feeding or the breakdown of reserves) according to certain priorities. Thus, energy must first be used in thermoregulation and general maintenance activities. Additional energy to this must then be diverted into foraging and feeding. It is only when these requirements are satisfied that 'surplus' energy can be diverted to growth, usually in young animals, or reproduction in mature animals. These ideas underlie many aspects of ecological and behavioural energetics.

Lastly, as if all this was not enough for a squirrel to take into consideration, there is the behaviour of the other members of the population which may make things much more difficult. I shall turn to behaviour in the next chapter.

5 Behaviour

My first encounter with a pine squirrel was in the subalpine forests of the Rocky Mountains in Colorado. Within five minutes of my first walk in the forests, I was taken completely by surprise by a loud 'tchrring' noise; I had not seen the perpetrator who had disrupted the quiet of the forest. It was a pine squirrel, no more than 3 m away, who was scolding me for entering its territory. This territorial call along with other aspects of the behavioural ecology of these fascinating animals were soon to become very familiar. Pine squirrels, and their close relatives the douglas squirrels are territorial and solitary animals in prime coniferous forest in North America. Some aspects of this behaviour have been discussed in relation to food caching in Chapter 3. On the other hand, squirrels which belong to the genus *Sciurus* have a different social and spatial organisation and, in some ways, these two groups will have to be considered separately. Nevertheless, there are many similarities between the behaviour of territorial and non-territorial squirrels, particularly in connection with how they exchange information with each other, how they mate and how they rear their young. These will be considered here. In the next chapter, the use of space, dispersal and social organisation will follow from these discussions.

COMMUNICATION

All squirrels are active during the day, spending their time moving through a complex, three-dimensional habitat and, in the main, leading a fairly solitary existence. Nevertheless, they are well aware of the presence of their neighbours and when necessary can communicate with them in a variety of ways using all the main senses: sight, sound, smell and touch. The main elements of communication have been summarised within these categories in Tables 5.1 and 5.2.

It is difficult to synthesise such a diverse array of ethological data from a variety of different studies in this way. For example, techniques of study, observer objectivity, interpretation and analysis differ markedly. It would take too long to present comprehensive behaviour descriptions here or, for example, sonograms of all the vocalisations from all species. Instead I have tried to explain the adaptive significance of some of the important patterns of behaviour.

Table 5.1 Visual, olfactory, tactile and vocal signals of squirrels

VISUAL
Piloerection	e.g. aggressive postures
Tail fluffing	e.g. disturbance
Tail waving	e.g. social interaction; male approach female at time of mating
Tail shivering	e.g. hesitant approach by male when near to female at time of mating
Tail flicking/flagging	e.g. investigation; alarm
Body postures	e.g. aggressive, submissive, defensive
Foot stamping	e.g. alarm, agonistic encounters (also sound)

OLFACTORY
Individual body odour	e.g. individual recognition
Sweat from foot pads	e.g. marking home range?
Urine	e.g. marking home range? breeding condition
Anal-dragging	e.g. home range marking in grey squirrels?
Cheek-rubbing	e.g. home range marking in pine squirrels— non-territorial
Face-wiping	e.g. expression of dominance in fox squirrels
Vaginal secretions	e.g. stage of oestrus in females

TACTILE
Mother–infant comfort reactions
Social groom	e.g. between siblings
Aggressive groom	e.g. dominant—subordinate interactions

VOCALISATIONS
(reference letters refer to function of calls described in Table 5.2)

Young	
Isolation/contact seeking	A
Disturbance	B
Distress	C
Mating—during mating chase	
male follow female	D
male approach female	E
male in response to other females	F
female approached by male	G
female during chase	H
Agonistic	
Aggressive or defensive threat	I
Subordinates when chased	J
Alarm	
Mild disturbance	K
Disturbance threatening stimuli	L
Distress/fright	M

Tree squirrels are exclusively diurnal animals and they make use of visual signals to communicate with other members of the population. Not surprisingly, the large fluffy tail is frequently used and can be effective

Table 5.2 Characteristic calls of grey (Lishak, 1982a, 1982b, 1984) and pine (C.C. Smith, 1978) squirrels. Additional information on grey squirrels can be found in Horwich (1972) and Bakken (1959). All calls are 0.01 to 0.6 sec. duration. Calls of abert squirrels are described by Farentinos (1974), fox squirrels by Zelley (1971) and douglas squirrels by C.C. Smith (1978).

Species	Call name	Dom. freq. (KHz)	Freq. range (KHz)	Repeat interval(s)	Function (see Table 5.1)
Grey	Buzz	3—6	0.3—12	0.03	L,M
	Kuk	2—5	0.5—16	0.31	K, L; F (Horwich)
	Quaa	2—5	0.5—16	0.63	L, M; (extended Kuks)
	Moan	1.2—2	1.2—6	Variable	K, L
	Squeak	5.8—9.6		0.2—0.3	B, C; 4—38 days of age
	Growl	0.45	0.45—12	0.06—0.63	B, C?; 23/30—98 days of age
	Scream	1.9—6—1.7 (3 portions to note)	1—9—16	Single or sequence of 2/3	C, M; From 28 days of age
	Tooth Chatter	1—4	0.05—14	0.07	L, J; From 54 days of age
	Lip-smacking	(With muk-muks)		Variable	Onset of nursing, feeding
	Muk-muk (young)	0.05—14	0.05—34	0.01	A; solicitory from 36 days of age
	Mating	0.26—14	0.26—34	0.33	D, F
Pine	Squeak	1—2	0—8		A
	Chirp	0.5—2	0.5—8	Variable	L
	Rattle			0.03—0.07	I; territorial call
	Screech			Variable	I; intruder seen
	Growl	0.5—2	0.5—5	c. 0.05	I, H, L
	Buzz	5—6.5	0.8	<0.01	E, A; intruder—appeasement

77

from quite some distance, although this is limited by the density of vegetation which will vary from forest to forest. Other visual signals include body postures which are used in close encounters between members of the same species. Tactile communication may also occur during close contact, but is particularly important between a mother and her young in the nest.

Olfactory communication is used more than many people realise, and, for example, squirrels leave scent marks throughout the home range for other squirrels to find. Marking with urine is common, and specific marking points have been recognised (e.g. Taylor, 1968, 1977). In grey squirrels these are often found in the crook of the underside of large branches (which will protect them from the rain), and they may be associated with scratches on the bark or bark removal. Such marking may also occur along exposed roots or along branches. Regularly used marking points become darkly stained by urine and perhaps other secretions.

Although it has not been fully investigated, it seems that grey squirrels may also mark their home range by anal-dragging. In this case secretions from anal glands, and perhaps faecal material, would act as the signals. I

Figure 5.1 Face-wiping marking behaviour in fox squirrels. Source: Benson (1980)

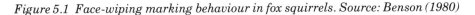

have noticed that branches placed in cages with captive animals develop long dark marks on them. Sandra Viljoen (1983) has observed anal-dragging in species of *Paraxerus* (African tree squirrels). She also describes another form of marking in these animals, called mouth-wiping, which involves wiping the lower and upper lips, including their inner surfaces, and cheeks against branches. This occurs during self-grooming but was also observed to occur at habitual marking points. Similar types of behaviour have been seen in fox and pine squirrels. In fox squirrels it has been called face-wiping (Figure 5.1), and in pine squirrels, cheek-rubbing (Ferron, 1983). It seems that saliva, and secretions from sebaceous glands on the inside of the lips (fox squirrel) and the corners of the mouth (pine squirrel) are deposited by these actions. The function of this type of marking seems to differ between fox and pine squirrels. Older fox squirrels face-wiped more than young animals, and dominant animals more than subordinates. This association with age and social position suggests that scent marking by face-wiping is an expression of dominance (Benson, 1980). In the territorial pine squirrel, on the other hand, it seems that cheek-rubbing occurs at feeding, grooming and resting sites, and Ferron (1983) suggests it is a type of scent marking which is, 'self-oriented to maintain the animal's familiarity with its home range'. It is worthy of note that Taylor (1977) suggests that grey squirrels may also face-wipe at marking points, and Jessica Holm has seen face-wiping in red squirrels on the Isle of Wight (Holm, 1985). These observations suggest that this form of marking is quite common.

It would appear that olfactory communication can function by signalling an individual's occupation of a home range, but it also may indicate some attribute of the individual such as its social position or its breeding condition. Squirrels moving throughout the forest will come across these odours deposited by others and will respond accordingly. This is well illustrated by female squirrels as they approach oestrus. Urine and vaginal secretions advertise to the male members of the population that the female will be ready to mate within a few days or hours. This occurs indirectly, from scent left within the female's home range, and directly, when males approach and sniff the ano-genital region of the female during the mating chase.

Vocal communication between squirrels is perhaps most obvious to us, as observers. Calls have a variety of functions and some of them are listed in Table 5.1 with some specific examples in Table 5.2. Analysing squirrel calls from the literature is particularly difficult. Calls are often a graded continuum of sounds with one type of call blending into another. Similarly, field workers usually describe calls in onomatopoeic terms. This is an obvious and useful thing to do and maintains continuity within a study, but it then becomes difficult to compare the calls among different studies, especially if published contextual descriptions are woolly or good sound recordings have not been made. I found this out when I studied pine squirrels in Colorado. In my field notes I describe three calls which I called 'tchip', 'tchuck' and 'tchrrr'. Christopher C. Smith (1978) has made a detailed analysis of pine and douglas squirrel calls and 'tchrrr' is clearly Smith's territorial rattle call. However, 'tchip' and 'tchuck' seem to be variants of Smith's 'chirp' call (Table 5.2). 'Tchuck' was a short aggressive call made by a squirrel when it was disturbed, 'tchip' was similar but a shorter, less intense call, which seemed to me to indicate anxiety. Koford

(1979) also found that 'chirp' calls were variable in douglas squirrels and appeared to reflect a wide range of excitement.

Squirrel calls have quite a wide range of frequency with harmonic structure and many consist of a series of individual notes which are repeated in short blocks with changes in frequency and amplitude (Viljoen, 1983). Emmons (1978) has made a detailed comparison of African and Holarctic squirrel vocalisations and notes similarities between them. Many, such as alarm and aggressive calls, have a low dominant or fundamental frequency with a moderately long duration which allows for good penetration and distance transmission in forests (Table 5.2; see Michelson, 1978). For example, C.C. Smith (1978) discusses in some detail the 'chirp' alarm calls of pine and douglas squirrels. Douglas squirrels emit a longer note than pine squirrels, but the fundamental (commonest and lowest) frequency in both is between 1 and 2 kHz. Different harmonics of the fundamental frequency were found within the same calls or in different calls and sometimes 'chirp' calls were initiated by a peep at higher frequencies. Fox, grey and abert squirrels have alarm calls with frequencies within the range 2 to 5 kHz (e.g. Table 5.2). Alarm calls of many forest birds tend to be at frequencies above 5 kHz and, therefore, do not travel far and are more difficult to locate. Interestingly, African squirrels have lower frequencies and longer calls than Holarctic squirrels which appears to be an adaptation to the thick, luxuriant vegetation of tropical forests (Emmons, 1978).

The elements of communication in Tables 5.1 and 5.2 will be further discussed below according to their function within different types of behaviour.

MAINTENANCE BEHAVIOUR

By maintenance behaviour I refer to activities which a squirrel uses to care for itself, other than foraging and feeding, and I include elimination, grooming and aspects of behaviour connected with thermoregulation, such as nest-building and sunbathing. Foraging and feeding were covered in some detail in Chapter 3, nest-building in Chapter 2 and thermoregulation in Chapter 4.

Not a great deal is known about eliminative behaviour in the wild. Captive adult squirrels tend to defaecate and urinate in set places within their cages but it is not known whether defaecation occurs indiscriminately in the wild most of the time except that Bakken (1959) has suggested that faeces may be placed at specific points during the autumn. (Young squirrels at first eliminate faeces and urine anywhere in captivity.) More often urine will be used as a form of odour communication and in these cases urine may be spread along branches or, and especially in breeding males and females, at specific marking points (see above). When urinating, squirrels adopt a crouched posture on all four legs with the body held slightly off of and parallel to the ground (Figure 5.2; Horwich, 1972; Laidler, 1980).

Squirrels spend quite a lot of time grooming but despite this they carry a number of different ectoparasites (Chapter 8). Russell Hampshire (1985) found that male grey squirrels in large enclosures spend, for reasons which are unclear, twice as long grooming as females when they were outside the nest. As in all rodents, grooming consists of a relatively fixed sequence of

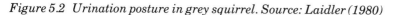

Figure 5.2 Urination posture in grey squirrel. Source: Laidler (1980)

actions which may stop at any stage during the sequence. This is described in some detail for the grey squirrel by Horwich (1972; also Laidler 1980), and, more formally, for the pine squirrel by Ferron and Lefebvre (1982). The latter workers recognised five groups of activities in the grooming repertoire: head and forepaw grooming, body grooming including the hindlegs but not the hindfeet, hindleg scratching, hindfoot licking and tail grooming. The sequence is as follows: the squirrel sits on its back-legs and starts the process by licking the forepaws and rubbing them down over its nose, effectively washing it. This may be repeated several times, with the movement of the paws progressively taking in more of the face and then the ears. After face washing the squirrel uses its mouth, by licking and combing with the teeth, to clean, the right and left sides of its body, its hindlimbs, rump, underside and finally its tail from base to tip. The squirrel may end up by cleaning its hindfeet and using them to scratch behind the ears and the nape of its neck. Variations in the order the actions are carried out within the sequence are not unusual and, for example, abbreviated parts of the sequence, such as face washing may occur at any time. Ferron and Lefebvre (1982) suggest that one act sequences are immediate responses to peripheral irritation, that longer sequences are controlled to a larger extent by internal, neural patterning of behaviour.

Young grey and pine squirrels start to groom at 30 to 40 days of age. This may occur first by the young animal separately washing different parts of its body such as hindlegs, rump, and tail. Laider (1980) states that the last technique to be mastered is face washing; eventually the actions are successfully combined into the characteristic sequence.

Another type of grooming is social grooming which is a form of cohesive behaviour helping to maintain close relationships between individuals, especially siblings. Horwich (1972) describes social grooming between immature squirrels which had been caged together since they were 10 weeks old. It includes one squirrel mouthing and biting the fur of another.

ALARM REACTIONS AND ESCAPE BEHAVIOUR

Squirrels are very alert and frequently pause during their normal activities to scan their surroundings for signs of possible enemies or other squirrels (Figure 5.3). If a squirrel is suddenly disturbed, there are several things it might do according to the nature of the disturbance. The commonest initial reaction to a moderate stimulus, such as a falling branch or another unusual sound, is to freeze. As all squirrel watchers will know, it is usually the movement of an animal which first attracts your attention to it, and the chances are high that you had missed seeing several animals because they 'spotted you first' and had instantly stopped moving.

In other situations such as the appearance of a predator the squirrel may make an alarm call. All squirrels make alarm calls which serve to alert other members of the population (Table 5.2). The particular characteristics of the calls depend upon the features of the habitats in which the squirrels live and in general there is a graded series of calls which vary according to the immediacy of the danger. Viljoen (1983) points out that many are short, staccato calls and other low calls which are louder and of longer duration carry information about position, that is squirrels and other animals can locate the origin of the call. This is unlike the calls of many forest birds (see above).

Alarm calls may be accompanied by visual signals. For example, the tail may be fluffed and held up, and flicked to one side or the other or backwards and forwards over the squirrel's back. The squirrel may also stamp with its fore or hindfeet. Farentinos (1974) has described a graded sequence of components in the alarm display of abert squirrels according to the severity of the disturbance. This sequence is tail fluffing, tail flicking, forefoot thumping and alarm calling. Farentinos observed mating chases (see below) disturbed by goshawks on two occasions and a coyote on another. All the squirrels involved in the chase ran to the nearest trees and turned towards the predator. Some sat quietly watching whereas the more excited ones performed the alarm display. Once the predator had gone the squirrels regrouped and continued the mating chase.

Thus, alarm calls can travel for quite some distance through the forest, and in general they carry information about position. Bouts of alarm calling are made in response to any disturbance and in particular to the presence of predators, such as goshawks. This behaviour, which might draw the predator's attention to the calling squirrel, appears to be altruistic in that the caller appears to risk its own life to the benefit of its close neighbours. Why then should squirrels draw attention to themselves by alarm calling? A well known study on Beldings ground squirrels has shown that alarm calling in this case is a form of nepotism (that is, favouring one's relatives) and is thus influenced by kin selection (Sherman, 1977). For example, adult females call more than adult males, and females with close female relatives nearby call more than females with distant female relatives nearby. The sex bias in calling is related to the fact that males disperse further away from their natal area than females. In other words the calling squirrel, though risking its own life, may save the lives of close relatives which share a high proportion of its genes. There is no evidence that tree squirrels call preferentially towards relatives (Emmons, 1978), but, on the other hand, it is possible that relatives are within hearing distance.

Figure 5.3 Head-up scan posture as squirrel pauses during descent of tree

Figure 5.4 Abert squirrel carrying young in mouth

It seems likely that the squirrel making the call is in fact in a relatively safe position and the risk to itself in making the alarm call is not very great. (C.C. Smith says that squirrels making alarm calls frequently get shot, but the gun is rather an unnatural predator.) There is some indication from bird studies that the caller may derive an advantage from doing so because it will not be the first bird to move and the first to move is more vulnerable. Further, Smith points out that another function of an alarm call may be to annoy or distract the predator, to tell it that it has been spotted, and that all the members of the population know it is there and that it is quite futile to stay around any longer. This seems to me to be quite plausible, especially since the alarm call may be made for some time, well after the initial alarm has been raised (e.g. Owings and Hennessy, 1984).

The other type of response a squirrel makes to danger is to escape and here their speed and agility through the trees is of paramount importance. Squirrels nearly always turn to the trees for escape even if they are on the ground when disturbed. This can be seen when watching squirrels; when disturbed on the ground a squirrel will dash to the nearest tree and run up the far side of the trunk so that you cannot see it. Squirrels may stay in one place when they reach the canopy, possibly watching quietly or making alarm calls, or they may move rapidly through the canopy to a safe den or drey site. Finally, a female which is nursing young will transfer the young to another nest if the first nest is disturbed in any way. She accomplishes this by carrying each one in her mouth (Figure 5.4).

BEHAVIOURAL INTERACTION

Most of the time, adult tree squirrels lead a fairly solitary existence and even when squirrels feed near to one another they still maintain an individual distance of at least 1 to 2 m between them. Characteristically, therefore, squirrels are called 'distance' species rather than 'contact' species.

An exception to the maintenance of individual distance occurs during cold weather when squirrels huddle together in small groups within nests to conserve heat (Chapter 4). In such cases the squirrels obviously tolerate one another, but the behaviour of the squirrels prior to huddling has not been recorded. Huddling may be possible because the participants are close relatives, such as a mother nesting with her young of the year (Shorten, 1954; Farentinos, 1974; also see Nixon et al, 1984). However, nesting groups of between two and five adults have been reported (Bruce Don, pers. comm.) but the familial relationships between the participants have not been known. In a large outdoor enclosure Russell Hampshire (pers. comm.) found that up to five adults would huddle together in one nest box in cold weather, whereas the maximum at other times would be three. It would be interesting to learn more about huddling behaviour in the wild. Huddling behaviour is unlikely to occur in territorial pine and douglas squirrels.

AGONISTIC BEHAVIOUR

Agonistic behaviour refers to all actions between two or more individuals which precede, involve or follow a fight, and thus includes aggressive, defensive and avoidance or escape behaviour. Before an encounter, a squirrel may respond to a squirrel call or the presence of another squirrel in the vicinity by exhibiting an attention posture. Here the squirrel sits or stands on its hindlegs with its forepaws against its chest and appears to be alert to sounds, smells, and movement. If the new squirrel is familiar then it will probably be ignored but if it is a stranger then it may be approached by the first squirrel and this is likely to result in an agonistic encounter.

Agonistic acts can be divided into those associated with threat, attack, chase, defence, avoidance and escape. Typical body postures are associated with these behaviours. A squirrel adopting a threat posture or making a threat or aggressive vocalisation will crouch on all fours with its body slightly of the ground. It may rise up onto its hindlegs from this position into an offensive threat or 'boxing' position. Its fur is raised along the mid-dorsal line of its back, its tail is held up over its back and its neck is stretched forwards with its ears up and pointing towards its opponent. Taylor (1966) has reported a narrowing of the eye, which is ringed by pale fur, in dominant animals. The focus of attention towards the opponent with an increase in apparent size is typical of many types of animal when they are aggressive. On the other hand, until attacked, a submissive squirrel will crouch down with its tail relaxed, its neck bent slightly up, its eyes wide open and its ears held back against its head. Aggressive grooming of a subordinate squirrel by a dominant squirrel sometimes occurs and this differs from social grooming by being particularly vigorous (Horwich, 1972). Submissive postures seem to inhibit the full aggression of the dominant animal.

Threat postures may turn into attack, or indeed a squirrel may attack without prior warning. An attack occurs when one animal rushes towards or leaps at an opponent. Dominant squirrels may indicate their readiness to attack by laying back their ears. An attack will normally result in the opponent turning and fleeing, being chased by the aggressor. In fact, dominant squirrels in encounters between two animals in the field were defined by Benson (1980) as animals which chased their opponent or held their ground. Submissive animals were ones which were chased or did not hold their ground. During the chase the squirrels make small leaps and they may go up and down and around trees as well as over the ground. When the pursuer gets near to the fleeing squirrel it may bite its tail. Tail bites are often seen and sometimes part of the tail will be lost altogether if the skin is torn completely away from the caudal bones. When this occurs, the caudal vertebrae dry and the distal part of the tail drops off (Layne, 1954).

Fights are rare but if they occur they involve wrestling or rolling over very quickly with the bodies of the two squirrels in close contact. The animals attempt to bite each other, mostly unsuccessfully (Ferron, 1979) but ears, for example, can be torn (Taylor, 1966) and cuts occur on head, shoulders and back (Horwich, 1972). Fighting usually takes place on the ground, but if it starts in the trees then the combatants can slip and fall to the ground, without any obvious damage to themselves. (I describe below a prolonged sequence of agonistic interaction involving fights between two pine squirrels which occurred during a territory takeover.) More frequently than intense fighting, sparring occurs. Here two squirrels square up to each other and slap at each other with their forepaws (Ferron, 1979). This often happens when one of the animals has taken refuge in a den or nest and is defending itself against its opponent. Fleeing is the usual outcome of these encounters.

Generally speaking, defensive acts are ambivalent, some components of both aggressive and defensive types of behaviour are seen (Ferron, 1979). When trying to get grey squirrels out of traps, I have noticed that sometimes they will turn on their backs, growling and squeaking, and make pushing movements with their fore and hindlegs. Aggressive vocalisations, tail movements and foot stomping by dominant squirrels accompany agonistic encounters. Similarly, defensive growls and alarm squeals are made by submissive squirrels during encounters and when chased.

Dominance Relationships

There is a considerable amount of evidence that a social pattern exists within squirrel populations at all times. Generally speaking this pattern is based on hierarchical relationships formed through agonistic encounters as described above. The outcome of encounters between squirrels is to some extent predictable because it is influenced by characteristics of the participants. For example, social rank is related to weight (Allen and Asprey, 1986; Wauters and Dhondt, 1985) and age. Thus adults dominate juveniles or subadults and dominant squirrels are normally heavier than subordinates. Furthermore, males tend to dominate females (although old females may dominate young males), and residents are aggressive towards immigrants. These relationships are continually modified as the composition of the population changes. For example, young squirrels grow and mature, residents may die and some immigrants may establish a position within the population. Hence, new dominance relationships will be formed from time to time (Thompson, 1978a). Encounters may be resolved with little aggression; running away in order to fight another day may be a better tactic than to indulge in an intense agonistic interaction, especially for young animals.

A consequence of dominant-subordinate relationships is that squirrels higher in the social hierarchy spend relatively more time out of the nest each day (Hampshire, 1985). This is not easy to measure in the wild but relationships among squirrels become clear when they congregate together for one reason or another. They are particularly evident at the time of mating (see below) or when feeding aggregations occur (e.g. Bakken, 1959; Sharp, 1959; Farentinos, 1972). Feeding aggregations refer to several squirrels congregating in a favoured feeding tree, or at an artificial feeding station. Pine and douglas squirrels are normally solitary and territorial but one or two instances of pairs of squirrels feeding on male cones (flowers) on the same tree during the spring have been reported (C.C. Smith, 1968). Some chasing was seen between the squirrels but generally they were more tolerant than normal. Two explanations for this rather unusual behaviour can be suggested. Firstly, territoriality is mainly associated with the storage of female cones during the autumn for the winter. Male cones on the trees in the spring are not likely to be economically defendable. Secondly, squirrels feeding on male cones are fairly exposed because they have to move to the end of slender branches to reach them. Some benefit may be gained by the two squirrels, therefore, from the increased chances of detecting a predator.

Pack et al (1967) described linear hierarchies between male and female grey squirrels at feeder hoppers. Although they did not find that subordinate squirrels were prevented access to the feeders, these squirrels were cautious and maintained constant vigilance which may have led to a reduction in feeding efficiency as has been described in feeding flocks of birds where subordinates, forced to feed towards the outside of the flock, have to be more vigilant for predators, and consequently feed less (e.g. Lazarus, 1978; Jennings and Evans, 1980). One could question the generality of the results obtained at feeder hoppers since these are artificial concentrations of food, but natural concentrations of food do occur (e.g. particular trees) and squirrels are known to aggregate in such areas.

There is an important point to be made here. When there is a shortage of a particular resource, dominance hierarchies among conspecifics result in individuals of a low rank having limited access to that resource. For example, where food is the resource, dominant squirrels will gain more food and be heavier and of a higher quality than subordinates. They may come into breeding condition earlier leading to early copulations and perhaps the chance for two litters during the breeding season for females living in temperate forests. Females in oestrus are another resource and the influence of dominance on the reproductive success of males is described in detail below. In fact, it is not really known whether subordinates have limited access to natural food supplies, although it is inferred and, as is suggested above, their feeding efficiency may be impaired when they are in the presence of dominant animals. Cached food is another important resource. Territorial *Tamiasciurus* squirrels defend a large central cache of cones all year against all conspecifics. Even when *Sciurus* squirrels scatterhoard food, there is the suggestion that stores close to nest trees will be defended (e.g. Nixon et al, 1984), or that favoured feeding areas will be defended (Kenward, 1985). In these cases, defence may be against all squirrels or, and perhaps more commonly, against unfamiliar squirrels. This brings us back to the question posed before as to how closely related are neighbouring squirrels within a forest.

A further point is that it is not really known over what area dominance relationships are maintained (Taylor, 1966). The evidence suggests that there will be a continuum of overlapping dominance relationships between a squirrel and its neighbours in different parts of its home range, and therefore, this is related to the spatial organisation of home ranges and territories. It is possible, therefore, that an individual may have a different social rank with its neighbours in a different part of its home range, and this may be one reason why males of similar rank may appear together during mating chases outside their home range (see below).

Although the social organisation within squirrel populations has been described as relatively permanent, there are times of the year when agonistic behaviour reaches high levels. Such times include the mating period and the establishment of territories in pine and douglas squirrels. These are discussed next, before a more general consideration of annual cycles in agonistic behaviour.

BREEDING BEHAVIOUR

The breeding season, that is the period between the time females enter oestrus and the weaning of offspring, is variable in duration lasting for 6 to 10 months of the year. Climate and food supply affect the length of the season and this is discussed in more detail in Chapter 7. Peaks in mating activity occur in the spring during a short season or in the winter and spring during a long season. The timing of mating is determined by the period of oestrus or heat in the female since it is only then that she is able to conceive and will receive the male. As we have seen urine and secretions from the female's vagina inform the males of her time of oestrus. However, recent evidence from work carried out on grey squirrels in England suggests that male odour may play a part in triggering the onset of oestrus in the female. Studies have shown that the presence of a breeding male, or simply the presence of male urine, is necessary for the onset of oestrus in female squirrels in large outdoor enclosures (Russell Hampshire, pers. comm). The role of male urine as a form of olfactory communication is supported by the fact that, at times of sexual activity, the hairs on the scrotum of male squirrels become stained dark brown, probably by urine. These hairs are moulted in April and July and replaced by clean white hairs (Taylor, 1968). Olfactory communication of this sort between males and females ensures coordination in breeding physiology and behaviour. Interestingly, male grey squirrels have no effect on breeding activity of females in small cages, and thus in some way 'space' is also necessary for the females to come into oestrus (Webley and Johnson, 1983). Further studies on different species may be rewarding.

Four main phases to mating behaviour have been identified. These are the prechase or preliminary following period, the mating chase, copulation, and post-coital behaviour (e.g. Taylor, 1966; Thompson, 1977b; Benson, 1980). The onset of oestrus in female squirrels occurs over a period of a few days and the timing of oestrus is evident from the external condition of the vulva which becomes pink and swollen (Farentinos, 1972; Koford, 1982). During these few days, males, usually one at a time, may approach and follow the female. This following behaviour may continue for anything up to 20 minutes, although the average time was found to be 5 minutes in one study on fox squirrels (Benson, 1980). Several different males may follow the same female at different times during the same day. In fox and grey squirrels, the female tends to tolerate this close attention of a male, although she still keeps him at a distance of 1 or 2 m for most of the time. The female rarely gets aggressive, but she may turn and adopt a defensive posture and briefly lunge at the male. In comparison, female abert squirrels apparently do not tolerate the advances of males during this prechase phase; they turn and attack the males. As we have seen above, the odour of the female is very important in informing the males that she is approaching oestrus. Occasionally during the prechase phase a female fox or grey squirrel may allow the male to sniff at her vagina and the frequency of sniffing increases as the day of oestrus approaches (Thompson, 1977b). Urine and vaginal secretions are also deposited by the female at marking points or generally throughout her home range, and males may be seen investigating the ground or branches over which a female has recently travelled. This particularly occurs in abert squirrels where the males do not appear to be able to get very close to the female. The prechase phase is obviously important in informing the males that the period of heat and hence receptivity in the female is imminent.

The home range areas of male *Sciurus* squirrels increase substantially during the spring and sumer breeding season, whereas those of female squirrels do not (Chapter 6). Conversely, during winter mating periods, the home ranges of males do not always increase in size (Don, 1981; Kenward, 1985 and pers. comm). For example, Robert Kenward did not find an increase in male grey squirrel winter breeding ranges in two out of three years. The adaptive significance of an enlarged home range is clear in that the males benefit from the increased number of contacts with females which will improve their chances of finding and mating with more oestrus females. However, there are additional costs related to the time and energy used by the males in these activities (Benson, 1980) which may explain the variable winter mating strategy of males. Thus the winter mating strategy of squirrels may be influenced by food supplies, weather conditions and the normally short daily active period (see Chapter 4). (Females may also be affected by these factors and not all will necessarily come into breeding condition.)

Olfactory communication by female *Tamiasciurus* squirrels attracts males from surrounding territories in a similar way to that for female *Sciurus*. Before heat, the unique coiled vagina of female *Tamiasciurus* becomes enlarged and swollen and it is possible that secretions from the vagina, or even the anal glands, produce the attracting smell (C.C. Smith, 1968). This odour is deposited by the female at certain points throughout her territory as a form of advertisement, and the nature and strength of this odour changes as oestrus approaches. It is not clear how often males of the territorial *Tamiasciurus* species enter the territories of females and indulge in prechase behaviour. Certainly males have been observed (C.C. Smith, 1968) sniffing through the territories of females and emitting calls when the females have not been in heat. Of course it could be a disadvantage to the males to leave their territories before it was absolutely necessary. However, it is of paramount importance to mate and pass on their genes to future generations, and so it would seem to be an acceptable risk for males to leave their territories and check on the stage of oestrus of neighbouring females during the mating period.

Some interesting observations on changes in spatial organisation of douglas squirrels in California have been reported by Rolf Koford (1982). In contrast to a rigid, year-round territorial system of pine and douglas squirrels at higher latitudes, he found that females would relax their territorial boundaries during the mating period and adjacent males would extend their activity into the female area. Here they would continue to exhibit normal territorial behaviour against other males with the result that territory sizes of males were greater in the breeding than the non-breeding season (reminiscent of the male *Sciurus*, discussed above). The males were not simply defending the female because neighbouring males would overlap with, and defend against other males, different portions of her territory. Male douglas squirrels were observed approaching females some three weeks before oestrus. The relaxation of the female territorial system, and the use of territoriality as a male mating strategy in Californian douglas squirrels, may be because cone caches have less significance for survival during the breeding season in California than elsewhere within their range (Koford, 1982).

The Mating Chase

Females come into heat on one day only, and on this day the behaviour of male squirrels changes dramatically. The pattern appears to be broadly similar in all squirrel species. Male squirrels turn up in large numbers, usually in the morning, and follow the female through the forest. Although this is called a mating chase, it is usually a less intensive affair, with the males simply following the female. Thompson (1977b) defined the mating chase as the behaviour acts which occur between the time two or more males group together at the location of the female, and the time of copulation. The number of males which are involved in mating chases varies considerably; Thompson gives mean numbers of grey squirrel males involved in mating chases as 5.5 during the winter and 9 during the summer. I have seen at least 12 grey squirrels engaged in a mating chase and C.C. Smith (1968) has seen more than 10 male *Tamiasciurus* with one female.

It seems likely that males which live near to the female, aided by regular reconnaissance explorations, are the first on the scene on the day when she comes into oestrus. As these males gather near the female then their activity appears to attract males from further afield. Thompson (1977b) has recorded average distances over which male grey squirrels have been attracted to females as 200 m with a longest distance of 626 m. Similarly, C.C. Smith has observed distances of 200 m in *Tamiasciurus*. Thus, the number of males participating in the mating chase increases. Males make calls during mating chases (e.g. 'buzz' calls in grey squirrels, 'bark' calls in abert squirrels) which may be agonistic or simply communicate to other squirrels that they are involved in the chase. Pine and douglas squirrel males give territorial or low aggressive calls (C.C. Smith, 1978). Other calls emitted by males are the same or similar to a form of contact call first used as young in the nest. These are called 'muk-muk' calls in grey squirrels, and similar calls, known as appeasement calls, have been described in pine and douglas squirrels (C.C. Smith, 1978). These probably function by encouraging the female to relax the maintenance of her personal, individual distance so that the male can get close to her. Finally, calls of a higher frequency have also been recorded from males during mating chases, including whines in fox squirrels

(Zelley, 1971) and screeches and screams in abert squirrels (Farentinos, 1974). At this stage of the chase, the female moves position periodically, either in response to the presence of the males or simply to continue foraging and feeding. The female can be aggressive towards males during a mating chase. Initially she repulses the advances of any other by making scream-type vocalisations, threats or by attacking them and chasing them for a short distance of 1 or 2 m. As the general level of activity increases the female seems to get more excited and may start running off, pursued by the males. Whether this is a deliberate tactic to goad the males into pursuit is not clear. However, when the time for copulation approaches, the female becomes less defensive. The approaches of the males towards the female do not appear to involve any elaborate soliciting or courtship behaviour apart from the appeasement calls described above. Rather, a male approaches a female cautiously, with many approach-withdrawal movements and flicking actions of the tail, to test whether the female is ready to accept him—a trial and error tactic (Horwich, 1972).

A mating chase brings together several male squirrels. The dominant males in the chase take up position closest to the female. This is necessary because the female usually copulates with the first male who approaches her when she is ready. Subordinate males make attempts to approach the female, but are chased away by the dominant sometimes for distances of 20 m or more. A dominant male so distracted may find another male has sneaked in and approached the female, and thus it has to reestablish its position. Benson (1980) points out that dominant males must expend a lot of energy in these chases, especially if they indulge in several mating chases within a period of a few days. The males lower down the hierarchy also interact with each other during mating chases. Thompson (1977b) reports a greater amount of agonistic behaviour between male grey squirrels during pauses within the mating chase than during the pursuit phase itself. Pauses occur whenever the female becomes cornered by the male following her, in which case she turns, wards off the male and eventually dashes past him. They also occur when the female holes up for a short time in a den or a drey.

Rolf Koford (1982) observed a different strategy in Californian douglas squirrels. He found that the male squirrels remained dispersed throughout the female's range and if the female approached one of these males, then the male sometimes started to follow her. Females were observed to mate with males which were known to be subordinate to others within her range. One reason for this appears that there was a spatial component to the males' dominance; a male that had exhibited territorial behaviour in the part of the female's range adjacent to its own would be dominant in that area but not elsewhere. Any male squirrel, therefore, might be dominant in some areas but subordinate in others.

The social standing of the males within a population seems to remain fixed for the duration of the breeding season in fox and grey squirrels. In comparison, Farentinos (1972) found that the male hierarchies in abert squirrels were not particularly stable between mating chases. This instability may explain why some triangular rather than linear hiearchies were observed. One factor influencing social position was, as in Californian douglas squirrels, the spatial relationship between the male and the female. A male was more likely to be dominant if the mating chase was with a female within or near his home range area.

Linear relationships among males appear to be the norm for fox squirrel males (Benson, 1980) but dominance hierarchies at the time of mating are not so clear-cut in grey squirrels as at other times. This seems to be because there may be two or three males of equal rank within the hierarchy (Thompson, 1977b). It is possible that this results from some sort of spatial component to dominance as in fox and douglas squirrels, but there is no evidence for this. On the other hand, it may result from the congregation of males of similar social standing from the different parts of the forest in which they normally live (see above).

Mating Behaviour

Thompson (1977b) describes the copulation phase in grey squirrels as follows: when the female is receptive, she quickly moves ahead of the males, stops and adopts the copulatory position. This involves crouching on the ground on all fours with the tail over the back and to one side (Figure 5.5). The first male to reach the female is allowed to mount immediately. After copulation, the female frees herself from the male and runs off to crouch and groom high up in a tree. The male grooms his genitalia, and then runs and sits as close to the female as he is allowed. The approaches of subordinate males are repulsed at this time. Thompson observed that a second copulation occurred with the same male on 30 per cent of occasions. This happened after another brief chase. Third copulations were not seen. Following all this, post-coital chasing occurred for several hours in a similar manner to the mating chase, but with declining intensity as males drifted away. Males ignored females the day after mating had occurred.

In abert squirrels, after the male has mounted the female, three distinct phases to copulation have been described (Farentinos, 1972). Firstly, there is a series of deep pelvic thrusts followed by a series of slower, deeper pelvic thrusts, and finally a phase of inactivity when the male remains mounted with his penis still inserted. The average duration of copulation was 72 seconds. C.C. Smith (1968) has seen a female *Tamiasciurus* mounted five times by the dominant male sometimes for several minutes at a time. Layne (1954) reports several instances where a female pine squirrel has carried a male on its back for some distance and Koford (1982) has observed mounting lasting for up to 25 minutes in douglas squirrels. C.C. Smith (1968) points out that, although the female controls the initiation of copulation, she may have some difficulty terminating it. In contrast with reports on fox, grey and pine squirrels, Farentinos (1972) observed that female abert squirrels would copulate several times with several males (on average up to 12 times), although the first and the highest frequency of copulations tended to be with the dominant male. There is no post-copulatory, male–female bond in tree squirrels.

Horwich (1972) observed that it was not the dominant male which mated with the female in grey squirrels, but the evidence from several field studies shows that this is misleading. In pine, douglas, fox and grey squirrels, it is usually the dominant male, or a male within the dominant group of males, which copulates most often with the female (Taylor, 1966; Pack *et al*, 1967; C.C. Smith, 1968; Thompson, 1977b; Benson, 1980; Koford, 1982). This does not preclude a lesser-ranking male sometimes copulating but, as one would expect, high-ranking males are responsible for most copulations and it is their genes which predominate in the next generation, that is they have a higher reproductive success. Even in abert

Figure 5.5 Squirrel mating postures. Top, normal position; bottom, extended position

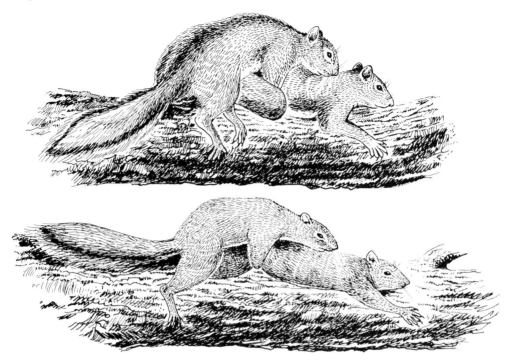

squirrels in which the females are more promiscuous, the first copulation and the highest frequency of copulations were associated with the dominant male.

One type of behaviour seen in squirrels which has not been fully explained is the so-called coy or bashful behaviour sometimes exhibited by females towards some males. In this way females may have some influence on which male they mate with. Bashful behaviour by females has not been reported very often in the literature but on occasions douglas and abert squirrel females appear to be less coy towards subordinate males than dominant males, almost as if they were soliciting mating behaviour (Farentinos, 1980; Koford, 1982). Why should females invite copulation with subordinate males? Koford believes that it may occur in territorial douglas squirrels because males are dominant in the part of their territory which overlaps with that of the female, and therefore the relationships among the males are not particularly significant. The selective advantage of mating with subordinates in abert squirrels is even more elusive. It is possible that subordinate males are less aggressive than dominant males and females are consequently less deterred by subordinates, or females may be attempting to provoke a reaction in the dominant animals (Farentinos, 1980). They may also avoid inbreeding by choosing a subordinate stranger.

The Mating System

From the description of the mating chase above, it is evident that tree squirrels are promiscuous. There is no lasting pair-bond between males and females, males will attempt to mate with more than one female, and females will sometimes mate with more than one male. There is no synchrony in the time of oestrus between females, and males have the opportunity to mate with several females during the breeding season. Odour signals between males and females coordinate physiological and behavioural breeding activity. The female's normal aggression towards other adult squirrels is overcome during the mating chase (and perhaps the preliminary following period) by contact and appeasement calls made by the males. Nevertheless there is no elaborate male courtship behaviour. The mating chase involves several males following the female prior to copulation.

It has been suggested that females may adopt bashful behaviour towards certain males influencing which male they mate with but there is little to suggest that this is common. Rather, during the chase the males contest the right to mate with the female. There is a dominance hierarchy among the males and the dominant male stays close to the female. Dominance is related to age, weight, experience and in some cases the proximity of the male and female home ranges or territories. High-ranking males mate significantly more often than low-ranking males, and therefore will have a greater reproductive success. High-ranking males probably remain dominant for most of their lives and high-rank does not seem to result in poor survival. Therefore, high-rank will result in a greater lifetime reproductive success. Clearly, dominant males are more fit than subordinate males. The female strategy appears to be to come into oestrus early if food and weather conditions permit, thus allowing the possibility of two litters within a season (Chapter 7), and to mate with a dominant male. The female investment in offspring is high and she can further her reproductive success by efficient care of the young so that they survive to become independent. Males contribute nothing to the parental care of offspring.

TERRITORY ESTABLISHMENT IN *TAMIASCIURUS*

Territorial disputes within pine or douglas squirrel populations have been described by several authors (e.g. Kilham, 1954; Streubel, 1968), but the sequence of behaviour exhibited by squirrels establishing territories has not been clearly documented. However, I had the good fortune of witnessing a squirrel establishing its claim to a territory during the autumn in a subalpine lodgepole pine forest in Colorado, and the following account is taken from my field notes (also see Gurnell, 1984).

Early on 23 September, 1982 I heard a great deal of noisy squirrel activity coming from one part of my study area. The reason for this became clear when I visited one of four small, adjacent middens belonging to one squirrel, illustrated in Figure 5.6. Midden J4 (the other three middens were J1–J3) was a large hollow log containing more than 500 cones. The remains of a squirrel skull and lower jaws, cleaned of flesh, and a lot of loose fur, were found near a hole under the log. The gut of the squirrel was found virtually intact on the pile of cones and no other remains were located. The stomach was full and contained 9 g of material. I concluded that the squirrel, the previous occupier of the territory centred on the J middens, had been killed at dusk the previous evening, probably by a red-tailed hawk (*Buteo jamaicensis*) which had been heard and seen in the

Figure 5.6 Territory establishment in pine squirrels. A, C, D, R, J₁ to J₄ = middens; solid lines = territory boundaries; x = position of former occupant's remains; y = initial position taken up by squirrel J; dotted line = movement of J to meet C; z = first encounter between J and C; arrows from z = change in this position during the first morning of J's takeover; dash-dot line = flee and return movements of J after initial encounters with C; dashed line = approximate position of squirrel J's circuit patrols; black square = vocalisations between J and A, and black triangles = initiation of chases by J of vagrant squirrels, in weeks after J's takeover; cross-hatch = unoccupied habitat. Source: J. Gurnell (unpubl.)

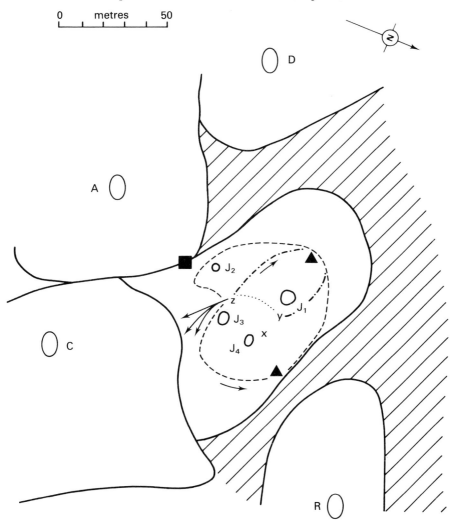

vicinity of the study area. The noise and activity going on was due to a squirrel (called J) making a takeover of this vacated territory.

Squirrel J was a young adult male (200 g in weight); young or vagrant squirrels are quick to determine that a territory is not occupied (C.C. Smith, 1968). By 9.00 a.m. that morning it appeared that squirrel J had taken up a position to the north-west of midden J4 near midden J1. It was from here that he made territorial 'rattle' or 'tchrrr' calls and initiated patrols around the J middens which later became defined as the defended boundary of his territory. During the morning I heard several encounters from all around J territory and it was clear that several squirrels had been attracted to the area. It should be noted that there was a considerable amount of unoccupied, low quality habitat (see Gurnell, 1984) around J territory which probably facilitated the approach of intruders. On one occasion I heard an encounter from the south-west which was probably between squirrels A and J. However, I saw most encounters between squirrel J and its neighbour, squirrel C, and these sequences provided the most interesting observations on the behaviour of the squirrels involved.

From his starting position (Figure 5.6) squirrel J would move to the south where he soon encountered squirrel C apparently well outside its normal range. C then chased J northwards, breaking off after 20 to 30 m and J would circle back to his start position. Squirrel C chased J eleven times during the first hour of observation. During this time J seldom managed to get past C but if he did he would circle around to the east and come back to J1. Chase-flee sequences were either very noisy, or, particularly later in the day, they could be silent. During noisy chases the chaser would make short high-pitched calls (probably the 'screech' call of C.C. Smith, 1978) as it ran along, and 'rattle' calls during brief stops. Because of the noise and speed of chases it was not possible to ascertain whether the squirrel being chased (J) was making screech or growl calls, but observations on other squirrels suggest that they do sometimes (see C.C. Smith, 1968). Chases between the squirrels involved running up and down trees with the pursuing animal never being more than a few metres behind its opponent.

Two further observations seem important; first, J's encounters with C started further to the south as the morning progressed, and second, J made his patrols by running, making loud screech calls as he did so, between tree stumps and low branches where he paused to make a rattle call. It was apparent that squirrel C was attempting to expand its range to include midden J3 but it became difficult to annex and defend this area within its normal home range. Areas circular in shape appear to be the most economical from which to harvest cones, and to defend (C.C. Smith, 1968 and below). Even so, squirrel C was found to have taken some cones from midden J3 some six weeks after squirrel J had become installed. During the first hour squirrel C initiated all the chases, but J was persistent and later, as the encounters approached the boundary to C's territory, the chases would quickly change direction, presumably, with the pursuing animal also changing. On one occasion it was clear that J chased C to the south and east, a short distance into C's territory.

By the end of the first day squirrel J seemed to have secured his newly won territory, even though some noisy encounters with other squirrels still occurred. Christopher C. Smith (1968) observed that squirrels were able to defend the boundaries of a new territory within 7 hours. In the following days, squirrel J regularly made silent patrols of his territory, sometimes completing the circuit quickly, whilst at other times spending several minutes in one part of the circuit. Other squirrels on the study area were observed to patrol their territory boundaries (also Kilham, 1954; Ferron, 1979). No further changes in territory ownership were observed by the end of the study in mid-November. Throughout the study the resident squirrels advertised their occupation of a territory with rattle calls although these

1. Kaibab squirrel (subspecies of abert squirrel); Grand Canyon National Park, Arizona, USA

2. A tropical tree squirrel, the five striped palm squirrel; India

3. Grey squirrel acrobatics at a bird table

4. Red squirrel; Isle of Wight, England

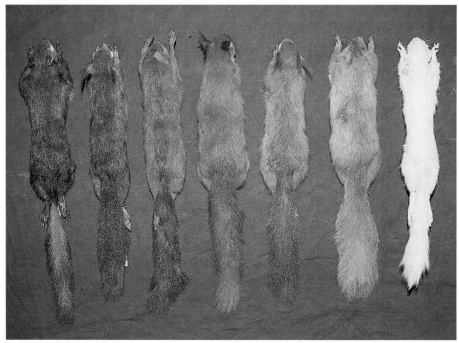

5. Coat colour variation in British red squirrels (museum skins)

6. Handling a red squirrel using gloves

7. A bemused grey squirrel in a handling cone

8. Grey squirrel drey; oak wood, England

9. Goshawk feeding on a grey squirrel

10. Grey squirrel drinking at forest fire tank; England

11. Grey squirrel debarking damage to silver birch; England

12. Grey squirrel debarking damage to beech; England

13. An 'urban' grey squirrel; Regent's Park, London

14. Pine squirrel midden in lodgepole pine forest; Colorado, USA

15. Typical squirrel feeding signs on fungi (*Russula erythropus*)

16. Fox squirrel; Illinois, USA

17. Douglas squirrel; Cascade Mountains, USA

18. Pine squirrel; Colorado, USA

19. Arizona grey squirrel; USA

20. Western grey squirrel; California, USA

calls were seldom answered by similar calls from neighbouring squirrels. Sometimes squirrels would take up positions either side of the territory boundary, about 3 to 20 m apart, and call at each other for many minutes, but chase-flee sequences were few.

In summary, squirrels attempting to establish their claim to a territory, first take up a position near the centre of an unoccupied or recently vacated area from where they make rattle calls and move out and circle round to ward off competitors. Squirrels may also take up positions on the edges of occupied territories and attempt to gradually make inroads into the territory and possibly take it over completely (C.C. Smith, 1968). The rattle-screech vocalisation sequence appears to be an important part of the behavioural repertoire of squirrels establishing a claim to a territory as well as in territorial defence. Lastly, regular boundary patrols may be critical for the maintenance and defence of a territory, especially during the autumn.

ANNUAL CYCLES IN AGONISTIC BEHAVIOUR

Seasonal peaks in agonistic behaviour have been reported many times in the literature but a close examination shows that these peaks do not always occur at the same time in different studies. This is partly the result of differences in the field techniques used to record behaviour, and partly results from differences in the interpretation of the data collected. Peaks in agonistic behaviour may occur during mating periods, when territories are being established in *Tamiasciurus* squirrels, when females are rearing young, and when squirrels disperse.

The problem is illustrated by Figure 5.7 which presents annual cycles of aggression from studies on fox, grey and pine squirrels. In the fox squirrel the seasonal peaks in aggression are related to the two seasonal peaks in breeding activity; here aggressive interactions occurred, particularly between males, during mating chases (Benson, 1980). Ferron's (1979) pine squirrel results also show a marked peak in male–male agonistic interaction at the time of mating, but this time there was only one mating period in March. On the other hand, the grey squirrel results show peaks in aggression at the time of spring and autumn movements of animals, notably young. Adults dominate young, and residents (overwintered adults) are aggressive towards intruders. Thompson (1978a) found that 61 per cent and 75 per cent of the agonistic interactions were between residents and immigrants during the spring and autumn periods respectively. The late, November, peak in agonistic behaviour in grey squirrels (Figure 5.7) was attributed to immigrants and a period of maximum home range expansion of summer young (Chapter 6). (The increased aggression during the winter and summer mating periods in the same grey squirrel study, previously described by Thompson (1977b), were not incorporated into his treatment of social behaviour and the annual cycle of aggression as shown in Figure 5.7.) Taylor (1966) has also reported that agonistic chases in grey squirrels in England reached a peak in autumn (eight times the minimum in June) at the time of the autumn dispersal of young and at the time that food was being cached.

The pine squirrel study also presents levels of interaction between males and females, and females and females. The peak in male–male aggression is coincident with a peak in male aggression directed at females. The peaks

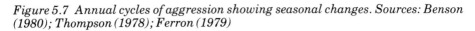

Figure 5.7 Annual cycles of aggression showing seasonal changes. Sources: Benson (1980); Thompson (1978); Ferron (1979)

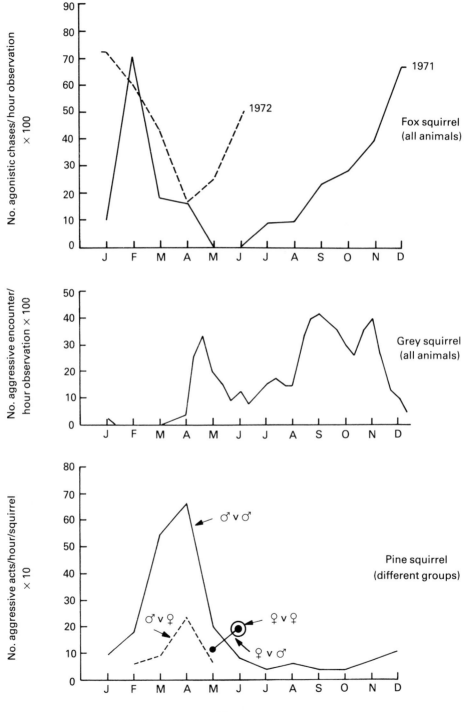

Month

in female–female and female–male interaction in June were mainly due to a mother raising her young; for example, she was very aggressive towards two other females. It should be emphasised that the pine squirrel study was carried out using 3 males and 3 females in a semi-field enclosure whereas the fox and grey squirrel studies were based on observations of squirrels in the wild. As we have seen, pine squirrels are territorial and solitary throughout most of their range, and it is very unlikely that 6 adult squirrels would occur naturally within such a small area (17 sq m). Nevertheless, many studies have shown that female *Sciurus* squirrels become aggressive before the birth of their young and remain aggressive afterwards until the young are weaned at about 10 weeks of age (Bakken, 1959). This aggression has frequently been reported to be directed against other females (Nixon and McClain, 1975; Berry *et al*, 1978) which may result in a tendency towards regular spacing in the breeding female population (Havera and Nixon, 1978a). Russell Hampshire (pers. comm.) observed in a large field enclosure that a lactating female greatly restricted the daily activity patterns of subordinate females until the young were old enough to leave the nest. This may indicate a temporal aspect to dominance. After the birth of the young the mother establishes a 'no-go area' around her nest tree. This can be interpreted as the establishment of a localised, temporary, nest (or nidal) territory which is maintained by the mother to prevent interference to the young and perhaps secure local food supplies for herself and her offspring (Chapter 6). Sometimes, when disturbed, the mother will move her young to another nest in another tree.

THE DEVELOPMENT OF BEHAVIOUR

In order to fully understand the behaviour of a species, it is necessary to know how the behaviour develops in the young animal (i.e. its ontogeny). Patterns of behaviour are, in part, genetically determined and moulded by natural selection. Learning also plays a part in the development of behaviour and thus individual variation in behaviour may result from genetic factors, environmental factors, or the interaction between both. Some important stages in the physical and behavioural development of pine, grey and red squirrels are shown in Table 5.3.

Squirrels produce altricial young, that is they are naked and blind at birth, and generally at an early stage of development. The young require an extensive period of maternal care since they are not weaned until they are about 10 weeks old. Two stages to the development of behaviour can be recognised: the emergence of behaviour patterns during early ontogeny and the integration into adult life during later ontogeny (Ferron, 1984).

The first actions of the young after birth are reflex reactions such as teat searching. Newly-born young, up to 10 days of age, are also unable to eliminate waste material without the stimulation of being licked by the female. The mother closely protects the young at this time. The first vocalisations of squirrels, squeaks, are made when they are 4 days old; thereafter a more extensive repertoire develops from about 2 to 3 weeks of age (Table 5.2). These first calls are contact seeking, hunger and distress calls and are responded to by the mother. Emmons (1978) remarks on a noticeable similarity in the structure of nestling calls in all tree squirrel species. Other comfort behaviours start to develop from a few days of age,

Table 5.3 Age (in days) at which some physical and behaviour patterns develop in the pine squirrel (Ferron 1981, 1984), grey squirrel (Horwich, 1972) and red squirrel (Eibl-Eibesfeldt, 1951). ?—unsure or possible error

Category	Pine Squirrel	Grey Squirrel	Red Squirrel
PHYSICAL DEVELOPMENT and EMERGENCE FROM NEST			
Hairs emerge to cover body	6→18?[1]	10→21[2]	8→19
Lower incisors cut	17–19	19–21	23
Upper incisors cut	26–29	31–42	41
Ears open	18–22	28(−35[2])	22
Eyes open	26–36	28–30	31–32
Out of nest (first sign)	33–34	29–46	36–42
Out of nest (at will)	37–39	54–58	45
COMFORT			
Self-groom to completion of sequence	30→51	29–65	36?
Social groom	36–39	42–46	54
Play fight	40–43	61–76	62
Sexual play	37–41	42–55	38
AGONISTIC			
Turning on back	16	—	—
Jump—directed	31–36	61–76	62
Crouch posture	34	21–24?	—
Bite	32–35	—	—
Foot stamping	35–41	—	44
Tooth chatter	32	37, 54[3]	—
OTHER			
Solid food	37–41	43–51	—
Digging	30–39	47–51	—
Nest building	36–39	48–57	92?
Inter-individual smelling	36–44	49–64	62
Cheek-rubbing	43–45	—	—

[1] Layne (1954)
[2] Shorten (1954)
[3] Lishak (1982)

such as reflex scratching, stretching, resting and sleeping postures (Ferron, 1981). The self-grooming sequence (see above) does not start until the young squirrels are 4 to 5 weeks old and it is not fully developed until they are 7 to 10 weeks old. Generally speaking, the early development of behaviour is geared to when the animals leave the nest, and the improvement of locomotion is of prime importance. As young squirrels are reared in arboreal nests, locomotion, coordination and all the sensory faculties, especially balance, must be at an advanced stage of development at the time they first leave the nest. The findings from a comparative study on two species of ground squirrel, a species of tree squirrel (the pine squirrel) and a species of flying squirrel emphasise the relationship between the complexity of locomotion and the speed of behavioural development (Ferron, 1984). Ground squirrels develop most quickly, followed by pine squirrels and then the flying squirrel. Table 5.3 shows that grey and red squirrels develop more slowly than pine squirrels, but it is unclear whether this is related to differences in adult body weight (see Chapter 2), or the solitary, territorial organisation of *Tamiasciurus* species. Emmons (1978) has found that some species of African tree squirrels are more advanced or precocial at birth than Holarctic tree squirrels; at birth their development is equivalent to an age of 3 to 4 weeks in the latter. A consequence of this is that these young need not stay for so long in the nest and it has been suggested that this is an adaptation to the increased risks of being taken by the many predators which occur in African rain forests.

The time when the ears and eyes open, and the sense of smell has developed, heralds a period of intense behavioural development for the young squirrel which ends when the young are weaned at about 10 weeks of age. The young squirrels become more alert and respond to an increasing array of stimuli. They exhibit their first signs of exploratory behaviour. Exploration, however, does not get under way in earnest until the young leave the nest. During the first few days after emergence from the nest the mother will retrieve the young by carrying them by the scruff of the neck. As time progresses the young venture further away from the nest and eventually come and go at will. They refine their innately programmed activities such as testing and manipulating food, which includes the opening of nuts and the burying of food (C.C. Smith, 1968).

The time when the young leave the nests starts a period of socialisation which does not really end until they become breeding adults at 12 to 15 months of age. From the time of their birth the mother and her offspring form a family unit and Horwich (1972) states that the development of sibling relationships is probably the most important factor in the development of social behaviour. The young learn how to greet each other, and engage in social grooming, play fighting and sexual play. Hence behavioural acts such as biting, chasing, mounting, threat, attack, and defence are practised and refined. Horwich (1972) gives detailed descriptions of these activities for grey squirrels and Bakken (1959) has observed young grey squirrels indulging in group play until 40 days after emergence from the nest. It is possible that solitary young are socially disadvantaged later in life because they cannot indulge in these behaviours. However, solitary play in the form of play-locomotion, object-play, and mock attacks on objects (and the squirrel's own tail) have been described in young squirrels. and these may generalise to other squirrels when they get older (see Ferron, 1975). Further, the mother will often tolerate the young playing with her. Joseph G. Hall (1981) described young Kaibab squirrels playing 'rough and tumble' with each other and attempting to do so with their mother, and Christopher C. Smith (1968) observed young pine squirrels engaged in sexual play and pseudo-copulation with each other, and the young males with their mother. Therefore, all may not be lost if you are the only squirrel in the litter!

Although the family unit may stay together for several weeks after the young first leave the nest, the general pattern is one of increasing independence as the mother–infant bonds are broken and the solitary existence of the mother is resumed. Christopher C. Smith (1968) observed that female pine squirrels in British Columbia moved their nestlings from the centre towards the periphery of their territories just before weaning, and here the young appeared to try and establish their own territories when they were abandoned by their mother. In contrast, Hélène Lair (1984) found that the position of suckling nests in pine squirrels in Quebec was related to habitat, and in fact there was a tendency for nests to be moved from the periphery towards the centre of the mothers' territories as the young approached weaning. In this case, the position of the nests did not minimise territorial conflicts between the mother and her young when they were weaned.

In *Sciurus* squirrels independence may be 'forced' on the young by maternal aggression, especially if the mother becomes pregnant for a second time during the breeding season. It is possible that young born in the summer stay within the same area of forest as their mother throughout the winter, if food supplies are reasonably good, and they may huddle together in the same nest as the mother in bad weather. There is some evidence that this is more likely to occur in young females than young males, which is similar to the situation in some ground squirrel species (Sherman, 1977). However, the closeness of the familial ties between neighbouring squirrels in a population is not really known and more information is required on the factors which influence independence of the young. The next critical time in the life of young squirrels is when they attempt to become established residents of a population (either their natal population or one to which they have moved). As they are socially subordinate at this age, many will be unsuccessful, and this, together with other aspects of their social organisation, will be discussed in Chapter 6.

6 Space-use and social organisation

All animals (and plants) require certain resources such as food, water, shelter, and, for breeding, mates. If a resource is in short supply (that is if there is not enough of it to satisfy all the individuals which require it), then individuals of different species (interspecific) or individuals of the same species (intraspecific) compete for the resource. These ideas were considered in earlier chapters in relation to food caching behaviour. In certain species and in certain situations, such as when caterpillars feed together on the same plant, all the individuals will get an approximately equal share of the resource (food), and this is called scramble competition. If the food runs out then all the individuals may die of starvation. In other species, individuals actively compete for the resource and this is called contest competition. Individuals which are better at competing for the resource will obtain more of it, and they benefit at some cost to the others. It is likely that good competitors will produce more offspring during their lifetime, and therefore may be said to be more fit, than poor competitors. Contest competition between members of the same species is mediated through social behaviour, particularly agonistic behaviour, as described for squirrels in the last chapter.

HOME RANGE AND TERRITORY

Resources vary in abundance through time and space, so an important characteristic of the resource is its predictability in time and space. To take a simple example, tree seeds occur in patches (trees or blocks of trees) and ripen in the autumn. Therefore, seed-eating animals and birds can benefit from this resource if they move to these patches at this time of the year.

Resources such as food, shelter and mates are distributed in space, so space itself becomes an important resource. How animals use space is closely linked to how they organise themselves socially, and species are characterised by the spacing patterns they adopt. The area over which an animal moves during the course of its normal daily activities is called its home range. Occasionally, the animal may make an exploratory excursion outside its normal range but usually these sorties are not included in calculations of the home range area. Within a population, the home range of individuals may overlap considerably. In contrast, a territory is defined as the defended part of a home range which means that a territory owner defends an area of habitat against members of the same species for its exclusive use. Sometimes individuals of different species are also excluded if they compete for the same resource. In fact, territories need not be held by just one animal and some species have group territories. Also, they may be held all the year or for only certain times of the year such as during the breeding season. A territory may vary in size from just the nest site to the whole of the home range. If the size of an animal's territory is smaller than its home range, then it is likely that there will still be some home range overlap within a population but the defended areas will be out of bounds to all individuals bar the owner.

For an animal to be territorial, the benefits to be gained from holding a territory must outweigh the costs of defending the territory (Figure 6.1).

Figure 6.1 Graphical model of economic defendability of a territory. Costs of defence increase as territory size increases, benefits increase at first then level off as resource becomes superabundant for the animal. Animal should only defend a territory between A and B where benefits > costs, and maximum net benefit is at territory size X

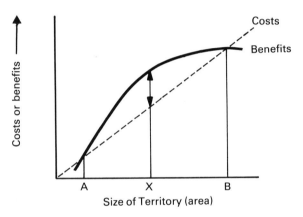

Figure 6.2 Types of spacing behaviour in relation to resource predictability and resource density. Source: Barash (1982)

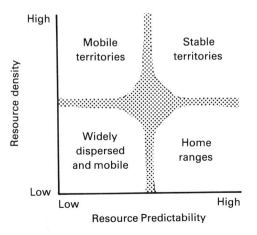

These are similar to the arguments examined in Chapter 3 in connection with squirrel caching strategies. In the case of territoriality, the costs can usually be expressed in terms of energy units and the benefits may also be expressed in energy units (food) but other currencies may be used, such as safe nesting sites or offspring. Figure 6.2 summarises the theoretical relationships between resource predictability (in time or space or both), resource density and animal spacing patterns. It is clear from this that animals utilising an unpredictable resource of low density tend not to be territorial, whereas those utilising a predictable, high density resource may well be territorial. Predictable and high density resources are most likely to be economically defendable.

These ideas are found throughout this book and are worth repeating here because resource distribution and predictability are fundamental to understanding the spatial and social organisation of animals. In this chapter I examine the affect of resource distribution and abundance on territory size and distribution in *Tamiasciurus* spp. and home range size and distribution in *Sciurus* spp. I shall also look at the phenomenon of dispersal which refers to animals moving in or out of a population. Some dispersing animals may find a permanent place in another population, many do not with the result that their chances of surviving without adequate food and shelter are slim. Lastly, I shall briefly review the relationship between the spatial organisation and the social organisation of tree squirrels. First, however, it is worth briefly considering the methods for studying and interpreting space-use patterns of squirrels.

Methods of Studying Space-use Patterns

One way of studying where squirrels go is to catch them in live traps placed throughout a forest, mark them (e.g. with a numbered ear-tag) and then recatch them on later trapping occasions. However, there are severe limitations to the study of movement using traps. Traps restrict the normal movement of individuals by the very fact that they capture and hold the individuals in one place, and temporary removal of an animal from the population when it is in a trap may affect the spatial organisation of neighbouring squirrels. In addition, squirrels may become trap-happy (captured frequently) or trap-shy (captured rarely) after first capture, which will also affect their normal movement patterns. Sometimes, such as during the autumn, squirrels are very difficult to catch when there is abundant natural food around (see Gurnell, 1983). Therefore, trapping has its uses but it is not particularly good for studying movement or home range.

Another method is to directly observe squirrels previously marked with fur dyes or topiarian tails (i.e. trimming the tail hairs to form recognisable shapes). However, squirrels can be difficult to see in many types of forest habitat, particularly when they are high in the canopy and to get a good set of observational data on several squirrels is therefore a lengthy and laborious, if not impossible, business. Even so, this method has been used (often in conjunction with other methods, e.g. Flyger, 1960; Doebel and McGinnis, 1974), and particularly with territorial pine and douglas squirrels. These squirrels are perhaps the most easy to observe in the wild, and territorial disputes between neighbours are good clues to the position of territorial boundaries. I was able to make use of another behaviour pattern of pine squirrels to map their territories (Gurnell, 1984). Squirrels

Figure 6.3 Red squirrel with radiocollar

harvest cones from within their territories and carry them back to their central middens. By placing piles of uniquely marked cones throughout my study area in Colorado, I was able to relocate the marked cones at the middens and estimate the size of the territories of the resident animals by mapping how far individuals went from their midden to retrieve the cones.

For most squirrel studies on movement, radiotracking is probably the best method (Figure 6.3). Individuals can be located, followed and their movements mapped. There are several ways of doing this, and one of the most popular methods is to take a fix of the position of the squirrel at regular intervals such as every few hours. As squirrels may move through their ranges in a standard manner and occupy the same parts of their range at different times of the day, fixes should either be made at reasonably short time intervals, or staggered throughout the day over a period of several days (Jessica Holm, pers. comm.; Connolley, 1979).

One last point concerns the way the data are treated to draw up the home range/territory boundaries. This is discussed in some detail by Bruce Don (1983) and the only point which needs to be made here is that drawing a line around all the locations plotted for an individual (sometimes called a minimum area polygon), or constructing in some way a circular or elipsoid home range shape, can give misleading ideas as to how that individual uses space. Certain parts of a home range (e.g. around a drey site, or a favoured feeding tree) will be heavily used, other parts will be lightly used (Figure 6.4; J.G. Hall, 1981). It is particularly important to know how much time each squirrel spends in different parts of its range (its space utilisation distribution) if information is required on the social organisation of the population.

THE TERRITORIAL SYSTEM OF *TAMIASCIURUS*

The spatial and social organisation of *Tamiasciurus* squirrels are dependent upon habitat. Both male and female *Tamiasciurus* squirrels defend exclusive territories year-round in mature coniferous forests throughout

Figure 6.4 Home range utilisation distribution of adult male grey squirrel in autumn in mixed deciduous woodland, southern England. (a) Three-dimensional presentation of data; x and y spatial coordinates are in metres, z coordinate represents relative intensity of space utilisation; (b) Two-dimensional presentation of same data; minimum convex polygon with filled circles = position of radio-fixes and small arrows = nest sites. Source: Don (1983)

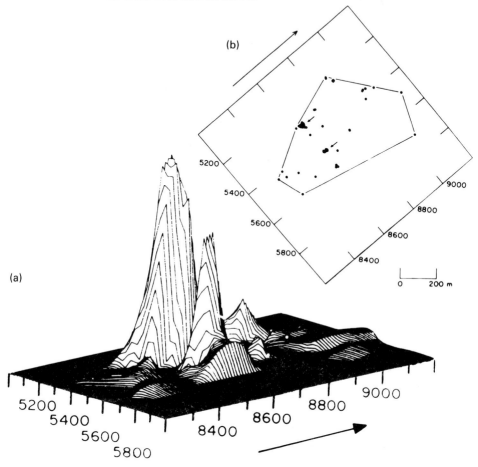

most of their range (Chapter 3). Where the distributions of the pine squirrel and the douglas squirrel overlap in the Cascade Mountains of British Columbia, the squirrels are territorial both within and between species (Figure 6.5; C.C. Smith, 1981). Each territory is centred on a large cache of cones and the territory owners have exclusive use of this important food resource. Males only leave their territories on those few days during the mating season when females come into oestrus (Chapter 5). On average, there is no difference in territory size between males and females—except male Californian douglas squirrels have larger territories during the mating season (see Chapter 5). Territorial activity is very evident in the autumn. At this time of the year two things occur. First, cone harvesting, which may have started in the summer, reaches a peak and the area of forest from which the cones are harvested around the cone cache(s) is secured and defended. Second, young squirrels born earlier in

Figure 6.5 Territories of pine and douglas squirrels. (a) Pine squirrels in lodgepole pine in Colorado; (b) pine (P), douglas (D) and possible hybrid (H) squirrels in lodgepole pine in British Columbia; (c) and (d) territories enclosing 75 per cent of observations of non-breeding douglas squirrels during September–December in California in 1976 (c) and 1977 (d). Sources: Gurnell (1984); C.C. Smith (1968); Koford (1982)

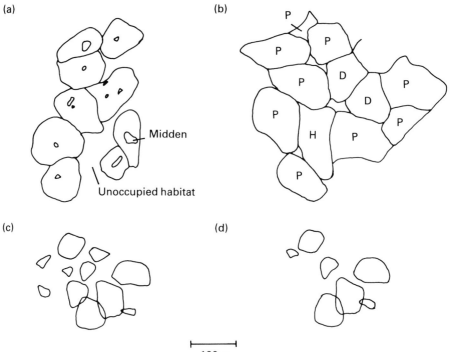

the year, and perhaps some adults which for one reason or another have vacated a previously-held territory, disperse in search of a territory of their own (Rusch and Reeder, 1978). Squirrels have been known to change territories within the same part of a forest from one year to the next (Rothwell, 1977). The sequence of events in the establishment of a territory has been described in Chapter 5.

Kemp and Keith (1970) studied pine squirrels in a patchy forest habitat consisting of aspen/balsam/hazel mixtures in some areas and black spruce in others. They found that the squirrels in the coniferous areas held all-year territories as described above; they called these 'prime territories'. They also observed some squirrels holding 'transient territories' for the duration of the winter only. As in prime territories, these transient territories were based on caches of food but they occurred only in the deciduous areas and the caches consisted mainly of hazel nuts. Transient territories were established in the autumn usually by juveniles. These squirrels would give up their sedentary existence at the beginning of the following summer as non-seed food supplies (e.g. fungi, berries) in the deciduous areas improved. They would then compete for prime territories.

In the autumn, squirrels in both the prime areas and the transient areas would once again become sedentary. Competition for prime territories was high, partly because the size of the hazel nut crop varied markedly between years which greatly influenced survival in the deciduous areas. When stored food runs out, the territory owner is likely to disperse in search of food and, unless another territory is found (which is unlikely), it will eventually starve to death. Cone caches provide a more stable food supply than caches of deciduous tree seeds (Chapter 3). In Chapter 3, I argued that large, central caches of deciduous tree seeds were not economically defendable on a permanent basis; other seed-eaters would be able to utilise this resource. Kemp and Keith (1970) state that they did not know how much competition for cached hazel nuts occurred although blue jays (*Cyanocitta cristata*) were known to take some. Undoubtedly, other bird species, and mice and voles, would also have taken them. Thus, stores of deciduous seeds should diminish in size more quickly than stores of cones.

It appears that the spatial pattern of prime and transient territories in Kemp and Keith's study occurred because of the patchy nature of the forest and the absence of other squirrel species which might compete with transient territory food caches (C.C. Smith, 1968). The squirrels which are able to survive the winter using hazel nut caches can be thought of as a floating reserve of squirrels which will take over prime territories should some become vacated in the spring (Rusch and Reeder, 1978). A third type of social organisation for pine squirrels has been described by Layne (1954) from mainly deciduous areas in New York State. Here he found that pine squirrels were not territorial and that they had overlapping home ranges similar to *Sciurus* squirrels (indeed, grey squirrels were also present on his study areas), although the pine squirrels did sometimes defend nest or feeding sites.

In summary, territoriality in *Tamiasciurus* is intimately tied up with economically defendable food supplies. These only occur in mature, boreal and temperate coniferous forests. When pine squirrels live in deciduous forests at the southern limits of their range, they are non-territorial adopting a social organisation similar to *Sciurus* squirrels.

Territory Shape and Distribution

Territorial *Tamiasciurus* not only defend the area directly around the cone cache but also the forest from which the cones are harvested. In theory, territories should be circular in shape with a central cache; this would minimise the distance that cones and fungi have to be carried, and this in turn would minimise the time and energy required for gathering the food (C.C. Smith, 1968, 1981). Several studies, based on observations of territorial boundaries, have shown that territories are indeed approximately circular (Figure 6.5; cf. Rothwell, 1977), although naturally they vary according to habitat heterogeneity, the distribution of food, and the influence of neighbouring squirrels. For example, territory boundaries are not necessarily as sharply demarcated as Figure 6.5 suggests. I found in lodgepole pine forests in Colorado that territory boundaries adjacent to unoccupied, low quality habitat were not clearly defined, and also squirrels occasionally entered or crossed other squirrels' territories (Gurnell, 1984). Other workers have found that some patches of habitat remain unoccupied (e.g. where the trees are sparse and small) and confirm that vegetation boundaries can serve as territorial boundaries (e.g. Rothwell, 1977; Fancy, 1979). Koford (1979) found home range overlap in Californian douglas squirrels but this overlap was confined to the outer parts of the ranges. The core areas (in his case, 75 per cent of all observation points) remained exclusive (Figure 6.5) except when females relaxed their boundaries towards males during the mating period (see Chapter 5).

Most large or primary middens remain in use from one year to the next and become well established features in prime habitat. Occasionally one finds abandoned, primary middens and, more often, small, temporary middens. The distribution of primary middens in an area is not random but tends towards uniformity (Figure 6.5; Streubel, 1968; Rothwell, 1977; Vahle, 1978; Fancy, 1979), and this effectively spaces animals out and influences population density. However, the area of forest defended around a midden may vary in size between years (Rothwell, 1977). Furthermore, in some years squirrels (notably transient squirrels) may take up positions between territories centred on primary middens. When there is little food around, some middens may be abandoned and temporarily become incorporated into adjacent territories. Therefore, the density of primary middens may not always give a clear picture of population density at all times, and, conversely, the density of squirrels is not necessarily the reciprocal of territory size, particularly since low quality habitat may not contain resident squirrels (Gurnell, 1984). Nevertheless, in the long-term, the distribution of primary middens, and hence all-year territories, may be related to food supply (Gurnell, 1984). I shall now turn to examine in more detail the relationship between territory size and food supply.

Territory Size and Food Supply

As the size of the territory increases so the costs in defending the territory increases (Figure 6.1), proportional to the circumference of a circular home range; and the costs of harvesting the cones increases, proportional to the radius of a circular home range (C.C. Smith, 1986). On the other hand, for a fixed density of food, the benefits (availability of cones for caching) would increase at first, but then level off as the squirrel becomes unable to take advantage of additional cone supplies on the trees. Where the benefits exceed the costs, the territory is said to be economically defendable with a maximum net gain where the two curves are furthest apart. For low food densities larger territories should be more energetically expensive to harvest and defend. This means that territory size is inversely proportional to food density (C.C. Smith, 1968). There will be an upper limit to territory size in that it will be physically impossible for a squirrel to defend very large territories and energetically very expensive to harvest a large number of cones (Chapter 3). Conversely, if squirrel numbers are high during the autumn, then competition will be high which may lead to smaller territories than necessary for overwinter survival. This is illustrated by the work carried out by Christopher C. Smith (1968). Competition for autumn territories was intense during 1962 and 1963 in western hemlock and lodgepole pine forests in British Columbia since food supplies in neighbouring forests were generally poor. Smith found that mean territory sizes for adult squirrels varied between the two forests-types and that on average they held little more than the squirrels' minimum annual food requirements (Table 6.1). In fact, he found that only

2 out of 13 squirrels remained on the larger territories over winter, whereas 5 out of 9 squirrels survived the winter on the smaller territories. This shows that squirrels do not necessarily defend areas of sufficient size to ensure their winter survival.

Table 6.1 shows territory sizes from three studies in a variety of habitat types. Most other published figures on territory size give average values of between 0.25 ha and 1 ha (e.g. Klugh, 1927, Hatt, 1929, 1943; Streubel, 1968; Searing, 1975; Fancy, 1979). An exception comes from a study of pine squirrels in white spruce forests in Alaska (M.C. Smith, 1986) which estimated an average territory size of 1.6 ha during the winter following a seed crop failure, and an average territory size of 4.8 ha the following winter after a second crop failure. This indicates a large territory size in poor food years which supports C.C. Smith (1968). It is also likely, of course, that the defended area will be restricted to just a small area around the midden in years of an acute food shortage since this is where most of the food will be found (Searing, 1975 in Koford, 1979). Other studies confirm that overwinter survival is largely determined, directly by the abundance of stored seed energy on a territory (Koford, 1979), or indirectly by the density of seed-bearing trees on a territory (Rothwell, 1977). Further complexities come when one considers whether territory size remains the same over winter once the cones have been harvested. The findings from a trapping study by Zirul and Fuller (1970) in Alberta strongly suggest that territory size decreased markedly during the winter and increased again in the spring prior to breeding. On energetic grounds, this makes sense, and I discussed in Chapter 3 the case of pine squirrels defending territories in serotinous lodgepole pine forests where most of the food for the squirrels remained on the trees over the winter period. Territorial defence and foraging for food may be very energetically expensive during the winter in these types of forest. In contrast to the above, Rush and Reeder (1978; Table 6.1) observed that territory size did not change over several years and they stated that territory size was related to cone supplies in poor seed years. Thus, territory sizes in white spruce were smallest, those in mixed spruce, larger and those in jack pine, largest in all years irrespective of seed crop size.

There are, therefore, two hypotheses concerning density regulation in territorial tree squirrels: one, that density is regulated by food supply and will vary between years, and two that density is regulated at levels below acute food shortage, which occurs in poor seed years, and density will remain stationary between years. Some information as to which (or both) of these hypotheses should be refuted may come from the experimental manipulation of food supplies. Thomas and Druscilla Sullivan (1982a) have carried out one such study by hand distributing sunflower seeds and whole oats to douglas squirrels in western red cedar/western hemlock/ douglas fir forests in British Columbia. They found that food-treated plots produced a 5 to 10 fold increase in density compared with control plots and they concluded that density was determined by food supply and, therefore, would fluctuate between years. After C.C. Smith (1968), they suggested that territorial behaviour spaces individuals within populations according to available food supply. However, they made no measurements of the spatial or social organisation of the squirrels and it is possible that, because the extra food was not a defendable resource, the normal territorial behaviour of the squirrels was overridden.

Species (Location)	Dominant tree species	n	Territory size (ha) Mean (st. dev.)	Range	Terr. size needed for annual food reqmt Territory size	Comments
Pine[1] (Alberta)	White spruce	6	.24 (.07)	—	.83 (1967); .25 (1968)	Territory size stable between years
Pine[1] (Alberta)	Mixed spruce	11	.35 (.07)	—	.83 (1967); .26 (1968)	Territory size stable between years
Pine[1] (Alberta)	Jack pine	7	.66 (.45)	—	.98 (1967); .94 (1968)	Territory size stable between years
Pine & Douglas[2] (British Columbia)	Western hemlock	4*	.51 (.18)	.35–.72	Av. = .63 (s.d. = .19)	Site 7; 1962
Pine & Douglas[2] (British Columbia)	Lodgepole pine	10*	.91 (.20)	.62–1.18	Av. = .76 (s.d. = .28)	Site 6; 1963
Pine[3] (Colorado)	Lodgepole pine	8*	.60 (.13)	.41–.80	Av. = .47 (s.d. = .12)	Median estimates of food supplies used
Pine[4] (Wyoming)	Mixed conifer	14	.28 (.09)	.16–.48	—	Winter of 2 years (1974–1975)
Pine[4] (Wyoming)	Lodgepole pine	10	.48 (.16)	.25–.66	—	Winter of 2 years (1974–1975)
Douglas[5] (California)	Cedar/fir	26	.31+(.32)	.03–1.1	—	Autumn of 4 years (1974–1977)

[1] Rusch and Reeder (1978) [2] C.C. Smith (1968) [3] Gurnell (1984) [4] Rothwell (1977) [5] Koford (1979)
* For adults only
+ territories enclose 75 per cent of all observation points

Table 6.1 Territory sizes of pine and douglas squirrels in North America. An indication of the relationship between an estimate of the size of territory needed to contain one year's food supply and observed territory size is given for three studies. The douglas squirrel territory sizes embrace 75 per cent of all observation points and are, therefore, smaller than the home range sizes

THE HOME RANGE SYSTEM OF *SCIURUS*

Bruce Don (1983) and Lawrence Heaney (1984) have recently reviewed much of the literature on home range size which varies greatly within and between species, and according to the method of study. For example, mean home ranges of 0.15 ha have been recorded for non-territorial pine squirrels in one woodland in New York State (Layne, 1954) and ranges of more than 16 ha for fox squirrels in Ohio (Donohoe and Beal, 1972, in Flyger and Gates, 1982a). Care must be exercised, therefore, when using values of home range size for comparative purposes (e.g. Damuth, 1981), and often it will be more informative to examine why there is variation among individuals rather than dwell too much on mean values (Don, 1983). As discussed above in relation to territoriality, range size is affected by population density, food supply and type of habitat. Range size also varies according to sex, age and season of the year.

Home ranges overlap whereas territories do not, and in general, the home ranges of male adult squirrels are large and overlap considerably, whereas the home ranges of adult females are smaller and overlap to a lesser extent. For example, in Belgian coniferous forests, Wauters and Dhondt (1985) recorded home range sizes over one year of 3.6 ha for adult male red squirrels, 2.6 ha for females and 2.4 ha for juveniles. They also found that there was much less overlap between animals of the same sex than between animals of the opposite sex (Table 6.2). This is an important distinction between the sexes which will be returned to below. However, before the factors which affect home range size are examined in more detail, it is worth noting that recently there has been a tendency in the literature to distinguish a core area within the home range of an animal relative to the total area over which an animal may range during a given period of time (Havera and Nixon, 1978; Don, 1981; Kenward, 1985; Koford, 1982). There are various ways of doing this, but in essence this approach goes part of the way to considering the spatial relationships between the detailed utilisation distributions of groups of individuals discussed in the introduction to this chapter. The approach focuses attention on the areas in which the squirrels spend most of their time (e.g. 60 to 75 per cent depending on the study) and are therefore most heavily used. The important point about this is that core areas are very much smaller than total range areas. For example, Kenward (1985) found mean sizes for 60 per cent core areas of male and female grey squirrels in England of 0.84 ha; this represented a 75 per cent reduction of the mean range area of 3.3 ha. Greater reductions were found in breeding, female fox squirrels in Illinois by Havera and Nixon (1978).

Home Range Size and Body Weight

The home range of an animal must satisfy its food and other biological requirements, and for animals which use similar types of food and similar

Table 6.2 Number of individuals overlapping per home range and mean percentage area overlaps for red squirrels in a coniferous forest in Belgium (from Wauters and Dhondt, 1985)

Group (Overlap with . . .)	Sample Size	Mean Number of Individuals Overlapping/Home Range (Stand. Dev.)	Mean % Overlap/Home Range (Stand. Dev.)
Female with females	11	2.2 (0.6)	32 (18)
Male with males	16	3.5 (0.7)	40 (9)
Female with males	11	5.6 (1.7)	44 (11)
Males with females	18	6.0 (1.9)	29 (12)
Female with males + females	11	7.7 (2.0)	76 (27)
Males with males + females	16	9.6 (2.6)	66 (25)

types of habitat one would expect that food consumption should increase with body size (body weight). In turn one would also expect that a larger range size should be necessary to provide for the increased energy requirement. In other words, there should be a predictable relationship between body weight and home range size. Such relationships have been found within groups of carnivores and herbivores covering a wide range of body size (McNab, 1963; Harestad and Bunnell, 1979) although the home range of carnivores, for example, tends to increase more rapidly with body size than it does for herbivores. These are only approximate relationships and there are many studies which do not fit in with the general pattern. There are several reasons for this including: different methods of measuring range size, habitat variability (e.g. productivity), and the fact that the amount of home range overlap varies within and between species. It follows from the last point that the number of individuals sharing the resources in any one area will vary, and this is related to population density and social organisation (Damuth, 1981).

There is no relationship between body size and home range size (Figure 6.6) for six temperate and boreal species of tree squirrel (cf Heaney, 1984). Notice, for example, that red squirrels tend to have similar mean ranges to abert squirrels which are much larger. This, I believe, partly reflects the

Figure 6.6 Relationship between home range size and body weight. Mean and standard error bars; number of studies in brackets. Source: modified from Don (1983)

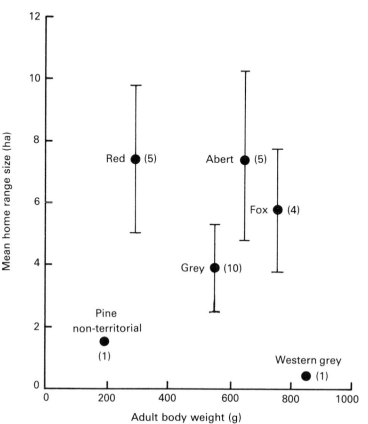

type of habitats these squirrels usually live in (i.e. coniferous habitats—Chapter 2) and the foods which they utilise (Chapter 3), although it should be pointed out that the red squirrel data are based on studies on a variety of different types of habitat, both coniferous and deciduous. Note also that Figure 6.6 includes just one data set for the Western grey squirrel and one for a non-territorial population of the pine squirrel (further studies on these species may produce completely different results), and that there is wide variation in home range size within the other species. As Bruce Don (1983) points out, body weight is a poor predictor of mean home range size in tree squirrels. We must, therefore, turn to other reasons for this variation in range size.

Home Range Size, Population Density and Food Supply

Unfortunately, there is little quantitative information on the relationship between food supply and home range size, although some workers have started to tackle this difficult topic. Robert Kenward (1985) suggests that the density of grey squirrels is the main factor affecting mean range size rather than food supply. However, as pointed out above and by Bruce Don (1983), the amount of food available to each individual and population density are closely linked, and it is difficult to separate the two without careful experimental investigations. This is explored in more detail below.

There is reasonable evidence that home range size is related to density. This evidence is derived mainly from comparisons among different population studies on the same species (Figure 6.7), although there is now some evidence from studies on the same population at different densities (Kenward, 1985). Figure 6.7 shows an inverse relationship between range size and population density, i.e. the more squirrels there are, the greater the level of interaction between them, and the more circumscribed becomes the average range area. If small ranges and high densities are tolerated by squirrels, food supplies would appear to be adequate. Broadly speaking, the data as presented in Figure 6.7 suggest differences in food productivity between the habitats in which the studies were carried out, although other factors such as nest site availability, could also be important. In the winter season with no breeding activity, large home ranges would suggest that the squirrels require this size of range to obtain sufficient food. Farentinos (1979) found that abert squirrels have larger winter ranges than summer ranges and that this was associated with increased foraging behaviour for the innerbark of pine twigs (Chapter 3). Robert Kenward (1985) similarly attributed large range sizes in a few non-breeding grey squirrels during winter to increased foraging movements, and increased spring ranges in grey squirrels have been related to food supplies in studies by Bland (1977) and Thompson (1978a). One last point about winter range areas should be made and, again, it shows how difficult it is to make broad generalisations. Lemnell (1970) found that a male red squirrel in Sweden had a much reduced active period (1 to 2 hours—Chapter 4) and a much reduced range area (down to 0.7 ha) in very severe weather in January. Therefore, weather can affect activity in space as well as time.

Ultimately food supply affects both population density and home range size. However, density results mainly from food supplies in the past whereas range size depends upon food supplies in the present. This may be one reason why it is difficult to separate cause and effect. It also

Figure 6.7 Relationship between home range size and squirrel density for grey squirrels based on 9 studies. Broken line is line of best fit to data by least squares regression. Solid line is the theoretical home range size if home ranges were defended as territories. Source: Don (1983)

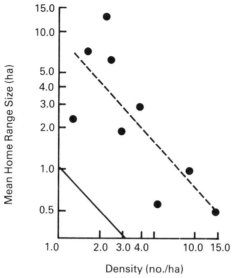

emphasises the problems of dealing with average range sizes calculated from several weeks of observation. We need to know detailed range movements and utilisation distributions based on short time periods, and to see how these change through time in relation to population density and food supplies. I shall return to range area and food resources in the next section where I consider variation in range size within populations.

Home Range Size, Sex, Age and Breeding Condition

Whichever species of *Sciurus* is considered, it seems to be the case that adult males have larger home ranges than adult females and young squirrels tend to have ranges similar in size to those of females. The main reason for the difference in range size between males and females is that there is an increase in male range size during the spring and summer, and sometimes the winter, relating to breeding activity (Figures 6.8, 6.9; Don 1983). At these times males wander well outside their normal range in search of females in heat (see Chapter 5). However, it may not be as clear-cut as this. First, winter and early spring mating is not always associated with an increase in male range size (Don, 1981; Kenward, 1985). It was suggested in Chapter 5 that energetic considerations relating to weather and food supply may influence the male winter-mating strategy in some years. Second, as Bruce Don (1983) points out, even when mating activity is taken into account, males still appear to have larger home ranges than females. There is no difference in body size between males and females which can account for this, and so the behaviour of females, particularly breeding females, must be further examined.

In general, range overlap between females is less than that between males which is to be expected if females occur at the same densities as males and have smaller ranges. Females tend to mate towards the centres of their ranges and there is no increase in female range size in relation to

Figure 6.8 Seasonal variation in mean home range size of grey squirrels in mixed deciduous woodland in southern England (studied by radiotelemetry). Source: Don (1981)

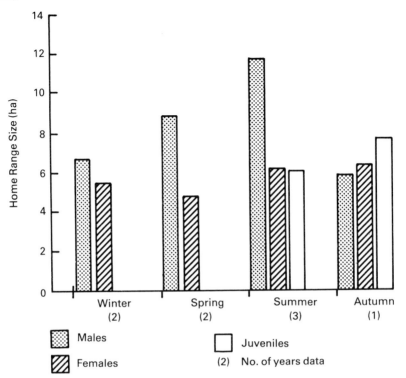

mating activity as seen in males. Once mated, females appear to select a breeding nest site which is well separated from other breeding females and perhaps other heavily used parts of the forest (e.g. Gull, 1977). Havera and Nixon (1978) found that breeding female fox squirrels in Illinois had den sites which tended to be uniformly distributed with at least 50 m between them (Figure 6.10). Thus the females were well spaced out which would tend to minimise interference between them. Gull found a similar spacing pattern in female grey squirrels and noted that intensively used areas of forest were not shared between members of different family groups (that is the mother and her offspring). For the first few days after giving birth, the range of movement of the female is greatly reduced as she stays close to, and frequently visits, the nest (Jessica Holm, pers. comm.). At this time, when the young are vulnerable to interference from other squirrels or predators, the female has to protect and suckle them as well as increase her overall activity to obtain sufficient food for the extra energy she requires for lactation (Chapter 4). In fact, throughout the period of lactation, the range of the female gradually increases. Robert Kenward (1985) gives a mean home range size of 1.6 ha for lactating grey squirrels, whereas females which failed to wean litters had a mean range size of 3.5 ha and females which did not breed, 4.7 ha. Therefore, on average, females rearing young have fairly small range areas. Lactation lasts for about 10 weeks and occurs in the spring and the summer, coincident with the time that males have enlarged home ranges.

Figure 6.9 Mean home range size in breeding and non-breeding abert squirrels in ponderosa pine forests in Colorado (studied by direct observation of marked individuals). Source: Farentinos (1979)

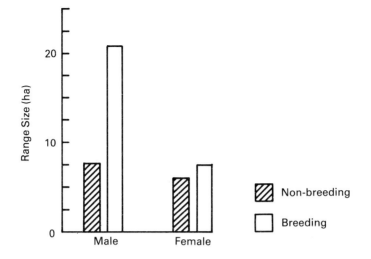

Figure 6.10 Distribution of home ranges and main den sites of adult female fox squirrels in a mixed deciduous woodland in Illinois (studied by radiotelemetry). The centres of the home ranges are the geographic centres of all radio-fixes for a particular animal, the circles are based on a standard diameter of 120 m calculated to include 68 per cent of all fixes of all squirrels around their centres of activities. Source: Havera and Nixon (1978)

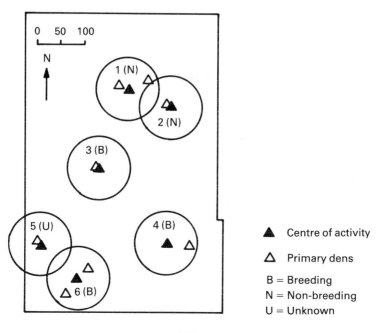

Thompson (1978a) found that female grey squirrels in his Ontario study area (a cemetery) had ranges which changed little in size during summer, autumn and winter but they increased slightly, along with a more marked increase in males, during the spring. He put this down to a shortage of food and an increase in foraging activity. Interestingly, Heaney (1984) suggested that males and females utilise different foods, particularly during the spring and summer. This is to say that food resources are partitioned between the sexes. It should be remembered that the spring and summer is the time when squirrels turn to a wide variety of foods since primary foods such as seeds and fungi are in short supply (Chapter 3). Particularly during the summer then, males may range widely in search of patches of preferred food whereas breeding females stay close to the nest and use local food supplies. In addition, breeding females are aggressive, and deter squirrels coming too close to their nest site—in other words they defend nest territories (Chapter 5). The enlarged ranges of males during the spring and summer, therefore, may result from three things: an avoidance of the territories of breeding females, an increase in foraging range, and mate-searching activities. As seen above, the explanation for variation in range size is complex and really requires further, more precise study.

Young squirrels leave the nest at about 2 months of age and slowly increase their range. Soon after they become independent, between 3 and 6 months of age, their home ranges expand rapidly (males more so than females) as the squirrels grow to the size of adult animals. Gull (1977) found that young Minnesota grey squirrels had range size of 0.45 ha during early summer and 4 ha by late summer. Range overlap between mother and young decreased from 91 per cent to 53 per cent during this time. Thompson (1978a) found that range sizes in young males and females were similar to adult males and females respectively when they were 12 months old, although males less than 15 months old were not sexually mature and did not expand their range during the mating periods. Kenward (1985) recorded home range sizes of 12.8 ha for yearling squirrels which left the population within 3 months during late winter and spring; the equivalent size for squirrels which remained in the population was 4.4 ha. This suggests squirrels expand their ranges prior to dispersal, I shall turn to this topic in the next section.

DISPERSAL

It is believed that once adult squirrels (whether *Tamiasciurus* or *Sciurus* species) have become established residents in a population, they remain in the same general area of the forest for life, unless a shortage of food forces them to leave; this is called site fidelity. Although this appears to be the general rule, adult squirrels may make exploratory excursions outside their normal range or shift their home sites or centres of activity within the area they are familiar with. In some instances squirrels may migrate between two separate ranges 1 km or more apart (Don, 1981). Such movement may particularly occur in forest habitats which consist of a mosaic of patches or small stands (e.g. <20 ha) of trees. Here squirrels may regularly visit several patches according to food availability. Clare Knee and I have found that more than 30 per cent of the grey squirrels captured in a 10 ha oak wood in southern England were regular visitors to neighbouring woods. In addition, linear habitats, such as trees along the sides of roads or rivers, are used by squirrels to move between larger blocks of trees. Heterogeneous habitats like these make it difficult to define the population of squirrels in time and space, and tend to complicate the study of movement.

The movement of animals out of a population (emigration) or into a population (immigration) is termed dispersal. Young squirrels (6 to 12 months of age) disperse much more than adults (e.g. Jordon, 1971; Thompson, 1978a), and there are two main types of dispersal which occur at different times of the year. Gull (1977) distinguished short-distance dispersal and long-distance dispersal in young grey squirrels from Minnesota. Short-distance dispersal referred to juveniles gradually shifting their centres of activity away from their natal area to a new area nearby. A consequence of this type of dispersal is that it results in neighbours being close relatives (see Chapter 4 in connection with overwinter huddling behaviour). Thompson (1978a) found that most young remained in their natal area, but this is unusual.

In Gull's study, long-distance dispersal referred to juveniles moving more than 1 km from their natal area. In fact, dispersing animals may move considerable distances. Allen (1943) found that several fox squirrels moved distances of over 16 km in Michigan, and one moved an incredible 64 km. Several studies indicate that more juvenile males than juvenile females make long-distance dispersal movements (Mosby, 1969; Gull, 1977; Don, 1981) but further data are required to see whether more females than males stay close to their natal area as occurs in ground squirrels. Such a sex-biased dispersal strategy would avoid close inbreeding. Few dispersing squirrels appear to become established in resident populations which means in the long-term they have a poor chance of survival (e.g. Thompson, 1978a).

Dispersal appears to occur most frequently in the spring/summer (the exact timing depending on the study) or during the autumn (e.g. Jordon, 1971; Thompson, 1978b; Don, 1981). Some of the spring/summer dispersal may be attributed to males increasing their ranges in relation to breeding activity, but many young of the previous year or early spring-born young of the same year disperse in the spring and summer. Bruce Don (1981) could find no relationship between the amount of summer dispersal and population density but he did find some last-year's young moving back into their natal area. This means they must have wintered elsewhere (perhaps in marginal habitats) but returned to try and establish themselves back in the population. Wauters and Dhondt (1985) found that immigration exceeded emigration in red squirrels during the spring period.

The autumn period of dispersal has been reported in the literature more frequently than the spring–summer period, and for fox and grey squirrels in North America it has been colloquially called the 'fall reshuffle'. I established earlier in the chapter that autumn is a most important time for territorial pine and douglas squirrels. Residents reaffirm their territories, juveniles seek to obtain territories and seed caching goes on in earnest. The timing of dispersal in *Sciurus* populations varies between August and mid-December (e.g. Flyger and Gates, 1982a) and mainly involves spring- and summer-born young, but some adults may also move and the amount of dispersal appears to depend to a large extent on food supplies, especially tree seeds. Indirect evidence for this comes from studies which report the number of individuals which do not survive in the population over the autumn and early winter periods (Chapter 7). Some of these individuals may have died or have been killed but probably most of them moved out of the population. When food supplies are good, few young (and adults) disappear from the population; when food supplies are poor many young and some adults disappear (Gurnell, 1983). Autumn dispersal can often be recognised by an increase in the number of road casualties at this time. I find many dead squirrels on the roads around my study areas in southern England during September and October.

Accounts of very large numbers of grey squirrels on the move during the autumn have turned up in the literature from North America during the last 200 years, and similar reports about red squirrels come from Russia (Ognev, 1940). Some descriptions are reminiscent of stories about lemming migrations with hundreds of thousands of animals all moving in the same direction at once, many drowning as they cross rivers and crops being destroyed in their wake (Seton, 1920). Although perhaps a little exaggerated, these stories are based on fact, and large numbers on the move are still reported from time to time. Mass migrations of fox squirrels have also been reported during the autumn, but these are on a much smaller scale than grey squirrels (Flyger and Gates, 1982a). The explanation for these autumn large scale movements probably lies in a combination of very large populations resulting from good seed crops the previous year, with very poor autumn food supplies; therefore, the squirrels move in search of food (e.g. Flyger, 1960; Formosov, 1936; Mikheeva, 1973). Similar mass movements occur in territorial pine squirrels when food runs out (M.C. Smith, 1968).

The association between autumn dispersal, food availability and population density suggests that squirrels space themselves out through contest competition in relation to food resources. This may occur by some sort of territorial defence of small areas around favoured food trees or food cache areas (Chapter 3; Kenward, 1985; Havera et al, 1984). This is not well documented and more work is needed on this very fundamental idea. In consequence, of course, young and subordinate animals would be the first to move out and certainly this seems to be true in the case of young. Thompson (1978b) believes that dispersal is the primary factor regulating the size of grey squirrel populations, and that this is mediated by food availability. Strictly speaking, for regulation to occur the food available per individual and the amount of dispersal should be proportionally related. This is a sound hypothesis which requires further study in both *Sciurus* and *Tamiasciurus* squirrels.

SPATIAL AND SOCIAL ORGANISATION

I have discussed in some detail in this chapter and in Chapter 5 the spatial and social organisation of tree squirrels and it should be clear that they are intimately linked. To end this section, therefore, I emphasise that, although apparently very different, *Tamiasciurus* and *Sciurus* squirrels in fact have much in common. *Tamiasciurus* squirrels are solitary and territorial all year round whereas *Sciurus* squirrels have an overlapping home range system. However, *Sciurus* squirrels are also solitary with a dispersed social organisation within the home range system based on inter-individual distance. Species of *Sciurus* may differ slightly in how much they space themselves out. For example, Armitage and Harris (1982) suggest that fox squirrels have a larger inter-individual distance than grey squirrels; this is to say they are less tolerant of close contact with one another than grey squirrels. Red squirrels are normally even more spread out and live at densities of about 1 squirrel/ha even in deciduous forests (e.g. the Isle of Wight; Jessica Holm, pers. comm.) where, for example, grey squirrels would probably exist at densities several times higher. It appears, therefore, that red squirrels may have large 'inter-individual distances' which result in low maximum densities irrespective of habitat. Therefore, in a similar way to a territorial system, a dispersed social system may influence the density of individuals in an area at any one time, and density can also affect territory and range size in the reverse manner. Furthermore, the size of both home ranges and territories (whether based on minimum food supplies which occur in poor food years or related to food supplies in any one year) are both influenced by food availability.

The use of space by *Sciurus* squirrels is very similar to *Tamiasciurus* squirrels in two further respects. Firstly, lactating female *Sciurus* squirrels defend nest territories in order to prevent interference to their young and to secure food supplies close to the nest for themselves and their offspring. This clearly resembles the territorial system of *Tamiasciurus*, although it should be pointed out that the territorial system in *Tamiasciurus* is based entirely on the defence of food supplies. During the summer and early autumn these food supplies (seed cones) occur both on the trees and in large central caches of food called middens. From late autumn and overwinter the defended food supplies are to be found entirely in the middens (with the exception of some types of lodgepole pine forest—see Chapter 3). However, there is evidence which needs further corroboration, that *Sciurus* squirrels also defend and have exclusive use of food supplies (for themselves or for closely related neighbours only), and that these are based on scatterhoarded food or food within favoured feeding areas (particularly during the autumn).

How animals use space is perhaps one of the most fascinating subject areas linking behaviour and ecology, and there is a great deal of scope for further studies on the spatial organisation of tree squirrels. I am sure that many such studies will benefit from using radiotracking techniques and the fine scale mapping of space-use patterns based on short time periods. Lastly, it is worth noting that in nearly all other aspects of their behaviour, *Tamiasciurus* and *Sciurus* are very much alike. The similarity between these two groups of squirrels is also evident in the next chapter where I consider their population ecology.

7 Population dynamics

Throughout most of their geographic range, Holarctic tree squirrels have long been important game animals, and have been harvested for fur, food or sport. More recently some species have become endangered and are subjects for conservation whereas others are pests and are controlled (Chapter 9). Consequently, many investigations have been conducted on what underlies the fluctuations in densities of squirrels living in particular habitats, and on the effects of management (e.g. Ognev, 1940; Kemp and Keith, 1970; Nixon, McClain and Donohoe, 1975; Rowe 1980, 1983). In the present chapter, I examine the first of these questions in relation to unexploited populations and at the outset we must remember the observations made in earlier chapters on movement and social organisation; these play an important part in understanding population dynamics. Once some knowledge of why squirrel numbers change through time and space has been acquired, it will be possible to discuss squirrels in the context of the communities of animals and plants to which they belong (Chapter 8) and the effects of management (Chapter 9). In the first sections of this chapter I consider the research techniques which have been used to study populations, and this will include methods giving an indication of relative habitat use as well as estimates of squirrel densities and dynamics. I do this partly because there is a certain fascination in the various methods used to study these rather elusive animals, and partly as a reminder that the quality of the information about squirrel populations is not always as good as it might be.

METHODS OF STUDY

Live-trapping is the method which has been most frequently employed to study the dynamics of a population through time and will be considered in more detail below. Information, not all of it necessarily quantitative, has also been derived from direct observation, nest counts, the use of nest boxes, feeding signs and radiotracking. Direct observation (e.g. in the case of territorial *Tamiasciurus* squirrels) and radiotracking have been considered in earlier chapters. Direct observation can be used to census *Sciurus* populations by surveying a forest in a standard manner and counting the number of squirrel sightings per unit time and or per unit area (Bouffard and Hein, 1978). Knowledge about the variability in activity patterns of squirrels (Chapters 4 and 5) indicates that this method is subject to considerable error.

Kill-trapping or shooting returns also provide information on population structure and density at specific moments in time (e.g. Uhlig, 1957; Nixon, McClain and Donohoe, 1975) but they are destructive sampling methods and not particularly suitable for long-term studies. However, fur returns, for example, may provide crude indices of year-to-year changes in population numbers (e.g. Mikheeva, 1974). Various types of snare or dead-fall traps have been used and some of these are described by Laidler (1980).

Live-trapping

Live-trapping, as with all field techniques, is an art as much as a science and experience is invaluable for obtaining good results. There are many designs of live-traps and they are made out of a variety of materials including wood, metal and wire-mesh; it is not possible to consider these in detail here (see Rowe, 1980; Laidler, 1980). I use multi-capture traps (i.e. traps which will capture several animals in one setting) for studying grey squirrels in southern England, but single-capture traps are perhaps more common. Traps are usually sited at the base of a good 'squirrel' tree which provides the animal with a clear view of the trap and a clear escape route. Some success has also been obtained, for example with red and grey squirrels, by placing traps on platforms 1 to 2 m up the side of a tree and this has the advantage that it tends to prevent interference by badgers or other large animals (Don, 1981; Tonkin 1983). For catching resident pine squirrels in a subalpine forest in Colorado, I placed the traps at the middens of the squirrels. Traps are baited with an appropriate bait which tends to vary among the species being studied and personal preference. Whole maize, wheat, peanuts, peanut butter, sunflower seeds, walnuts, acorns, and pine cones are just some of the baits which have been used. Food is also placed in the traps and it is good practice with an open, wire-mesh trap to completely cover the trap with a waterproof sheet to protect the captured animal from the elements and to keep the inside of the trap reasonably dark. This reduces the amount of activity by the captive animal. Some traps have a wooden nest box at the back of the trap into which the animal can retreat. Ideally live-traps should be visited at least twice a day, during mid-morning after the first active period (Chapter 4) and last thing at night. Leaving animals in traps for long periods, such as overnight, and especially in bad weather, can lead to mortalities resulting from exposure or shock (see Chapter 4) but this is rare if the above guidelines are adhered to. Handling squirrels has also to be done with care, both for the squirrel's sake and that of the handler! It is usual to use some sort of handling cone made of wire-mesh (e.g. Halvorson, 1972) so that the animal can be examined, weighed and tagged (e.g. with a numbered or coloured ear tag) in safety. If radiocollars or coloured marker collars are to be placed on the animals, it is good practice to anaesthetise the animals first so that the collars can be fitted correctly.

The main aim of live-trapping is to capture all the members of a population or at least a representative sample of the population. Most ecologists know that quantitative field methods, such as live-trapping small mammals, are bedevilled by many sources of error. For example, in a large stretch of forest, where does a population of squirrels begin or end and how can one find out whether all individuals within the population have been captured? There may be differences in trappability (i.e. the probability of trapping an individual) between sex or age classes of squirrels. I have found, for example, that male grey squirrels are easier to trap than females and that juveniles are easier than adults, but not all workers have had similar experiences. Furthermore, traps, particularly on the periphery of the defined study area, may attract squirrels from some distance away and thus indicate a greater number of resident animals than actually live there. This is part of a complex phenomenon related to the pattern of traps employed and known as the 'edge-effect'. Catching the animals is only the first step in estimating population numbers. Since in practice one is unlikely to capture all the individuals in the population, estimation methods are required. Many statistical methods for estimating population numbers have been applied to live-trapping results of squirrels. The methods are dependent on a number of assumptions which are never likely to be wholly true for any population (Don, 1984).

Some workers, especially those working on red squirrels living in coniferous plantations in Great Britain, have experienced great difficulties in catching any squirrels even though they are known to be present (e.g. Reynolds, 1981; Moller, 1986). This may be partly related to the animals spending most of their time in the canopy of the trees (Chapter 4) and to the unattractive nature of the bait used when favoured natural foods are present. The inverse relationship between the abundance of natural seed supplies and grey squirrel trappability has been demonstrated several times (Gurnell, 1983). Therefore, in the autumn and winter in England when, for example, there are good mast crops, it is very difficult if not impossible to catch squirrels. Perry et al (1977) have examined other factors which affect trappability; wind velocity, rain and cloud cover were significant climatic factors and site factors included the density and girth of various tree species. These factors probably operate by influencing the activity of squirrels in time and space respectively.

Nest Counts and Nest Boxes

The density of winter dreys in a woodland can give an approximate index of how many squirrels are present, particularly in deciduous woodland where dreys are more easily seen when there are no leaves on the trees (Uhlig, 1955; Shorten, 1951). This technique has the advantage that there is no need to catch or handle animals but its success to some extent depends upon whether squirrels are using tree dens, and how many dreys are being used by each squirrel (Chapter 2). Wauters and Dhondt (1985) have used drey counts to estimate numbers of red squirrels living in Belgian forests and Bruce Don (1985) has made a comparative study of drey density and grey squirrel density from many types of forest in England. Bruce Don found a reasonable relationship between drey density and squirrel density and believes the method has potential as a management tool (Figure 7.1). For areas where ten or more squirrels were captured, Don's data give a mean number of dreys per squirrel as 2 (based on estimates of squirrel numbers; n = 10, s.d. = 0.49). Wauters and Dohndt give figures of 2.7 to 3 dreys per red squirrel in coniferous habitats in Belgium and Mel Tonkin (1983) 3.8 dreys per red squirrel in deciduous woodland in northern England. The results of Moller (1986) and Tittensor

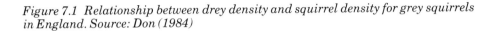

Figure 7.1 Relationship between drey density and squirrel density for grey squirrels in England. Source: Don (1984)

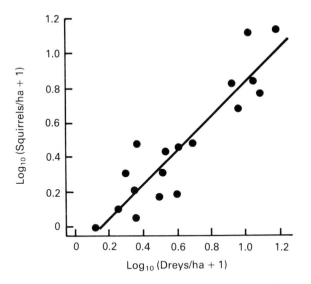

(1970) indicate that figures may be much higher than these in some Scottish coniferous forests. Even if information on the number of dreys per squirrel is not known, then drey counts can still be used effectively to assess relative habitat utilisation (e.g. Sanderson *et al*, 1976).

Wooden nest boxes, usually placed at heights of 5 m to 7 m in the trees, have been used in several studies, particularly with fox and grey squirrels in North America (e.g. Allen, 1943; Burger, 1969; Longley, 1963; Lustig and Flyger, 1975; Nixon and Donohoe, 1979). There are two main reasons for using nest boxes: (1) as a management tool to increase the number of animals living in an area on the assumption that the number of natural nest sites is limiting the number of squirrels living there, and (2) so that young nestlings born in the nest boxes can be counted and tagged at an early age.

Perhaps the most detailed study on the effects of nest boxes on squirrel demography has been carried out by Nixon, Havera and Hansen (1984). Subadults and adult males tended to make use of the boxes during winter and there appeared to be an increase in density and survival of adult males in the presence of boxes. On the other hand, females only used boxes from time to time during winter and pregnant females did not appear to favour boxes at all. Nixon and his colleagues propose that fox squirrels are adapted to living in open, or savanna forests with poor shelter. Tree cavities are not abundant in these sorts of habitat and squirrels make extensive use of leaf dreys so nest boxes are only used on a limited basis. In contrast, there is some evidence, although not from all studies, that nest boxes can increase grey squirrel densities as a result of enhanced reproduction and better overwinter survival (e.g. Burger, 1969). Grey squirrels are adapted to living in broadleaf forests where tree dens, from trunk cavities formed by broken limbs and woodpeckers, can be numerous, particularly in stands of old timber. These findings suggest that red squirrels, for example, which rather like fox squirrels predominantly use dreys, would not take to nest boxes very readily although they have been known to use and rear young in owl nest boxes (Steve Petty, pers. comm.).

Feeding Signs

Feeding signs and diet have been discussed in Chapter 3. In one or two instances feeding signs have been used to assess habitat utilisation. Abert squirrels feed a great deal on the inner bark of ponderosa pine trees in the south-west of the USA, particularly during winter. They cut subterminal twigs off the trees and consume about 10 per cent of the twigs in terms of weight (Patton, 1974). The twigs or needle clusters then fall to the ground and area counts of these have been used to estimate habitat use (Brown, 1982). Joseph G. Hall (1981), for example, describes the use and limitations of needle cluster indices for studying the distribution of feeding areas of the Kaibab squirrel (a subspecies of *Sciurus aberti*) in the Grand Canyon National Park. By itself this technique gives little indication of absolute squirrel densities. In a similar manner, I have recently been evaluating the use of cone feeding remains on permanent 50 m by 1 m transect lines for studying coniferous habitat utilisation in red and grey squirrels. Coupled with estimates on cone crop size, this technique may give a crude measure of squirrel densities in large tracts of forest.

DEMOGRAPHIC PROCESSES

Squirrels exhibit annual fluctuations in population size as well as year-to-year changes in overall numbers. For example, squirrel numbers are likely to be highest in the autumn/early winter and lowest in the spring/early summer. Further, peak numbers will vary considerably between years and, equally of interest, different squirrel species living in different types of forest will tend to fluctuate around different long-term average numbers (Gurnell, 1983).

The above points will be returned to later but fundamental to our understanding as to why numbers change through time we must consider the two basic population or demographic processes of reproduction and immigration which increase population size, and the two processes of death and emigration, which reduce population size. Rather than discuss deaths, it is common practice to consider its counterpart, the survival of individuals in the population. In addition, it is usual to refer these processes to some time interval such as a month, season or year, and sometimes (since populations do vary in size) to an 'average member' of the population. Therefore, for example, we may be dealing with rates of reproduction (e.g. the number of offspring born to the population during a specific time interval), or rates of reproduction per individual or per adult female in the population.

It is important to have a good understanding as to what is meant by the 'population of squirrels' being studied at a particular time. It is not too much of a problem, for example, to investigate the squirrels living in 10 ha of habitat if a 10 ha wood has been selected as the study area. This is not the case when considering large tracts of forest, for example, 100 ha in size. Where does the '10 ha population' begin and end? One has to hope that our findings from 10 ha of 'representative habitat' are applicable to the forest as a whole and to consider densities of squirrels, such as the number of animals per hectare, rather than simply numbers.

Male and Female Reproductive Cycles

Holarctic tree squirrels are seasonal breeders and mating may occur at any time between December and July. Female squirrels exhibit typical mammalian oestrous cycles involving physiological and anatomical changes to the ovaries and reproductive tract which prepare the female for pregnancy (Webley and Johnson, 1983). The female advertises to the males in the population, by her behaviour and the use of olfactory signals, that she is approaching oestrus (Chapter 5). Oestrus refers to the period of heat when ova (eggs) are released from the ovary and may be fertilised by the sperm of a male. Oestrus lasts for no more than one day, and the sequence of events (involving the mating chase) which leads up to copulations between the female and one (or more) of the males in the population has been described in Chapter 5. There is some evidence from work carried out on grey squirrels in England that the presence of a breeding male is necessary for ovulation to occur and it is speculated that the act of copulation is in fact necessary to trigger ovulation (Webley and Johnson, 1983). This so-called induced ovulation is a tactic which many mammal species adopt to ensure that the release of eggs from the ovary and sperm into the reproductive tract occur at the same time, and this minimises the risk of eggs remaining unfertilised.

The period of gestation varies from approximately 33 days in the pine squirrel, the smallest of the species, to about 38 days in the red squirrel, and to 44 to 46 days in the larger species, the grey, fox and abert squirrels (Ognev, 1940; Farentinos, 1972; Tittensor, 1977a; Flyger and Gates, 1982a, 1982b; Webley and Johnson, 1983; Lair, 1985a). In certain circumstances which will be outlined below, females may enter another oestrous cycle during a breeding season, and hence may become pregnant for a second time, and they are described, therefore, as polyoestrous (Figure 7.2). However, a second oestrus does not usually occur until they have nearly finished suckling their first litter of young (although see Ognev, 1940). In all species, weaning occurs when the young are about 9 to 10 weeks old, and the total period from conception to the independence of young is 14 to 16 weeks.

Male squirrels exhibit an annual cycle in the production of sperm by the testes and in the activity of associated glands (e.g. the prostate and Cowper's glands). This is reflected in the weight and size of these glands; for example, the testes of grey squirrels tend to be large in spring and summer before decreasing in size during July and August (Figure 7.2; for other species see Farentinos, 1972; Degn, 1973; Rusch and Reeder, 1978). The testes may incease in size again in November or, in certain circumstances (see below), this increase may be delayed for anything up to 4 months, for example, until the following March (Webley and Johnson, 1983). Therefore, it is possible to get some idea of the reproductive condition of male grey squirrels by examining the size of the testes as they appear in the scrotum of live animals, although this in itself does not indicate whether viable sperm are being produced. Degn (1973) states that the weight of the paired Cowper's glands is the best indicator of reproductive condition. However, in the case of grey squirrels, for example, reproductive condition is further indicated by the fact that the hair on the scrotum becomes darkly stained in actively breeding animals (Chapter 5). In fact it is not quite as simple as this because sometimes male grey

Figure 7.2 Reproductive cycles in fox and grey squirrels in Illinois. Source: Brown and Yeager (1945)

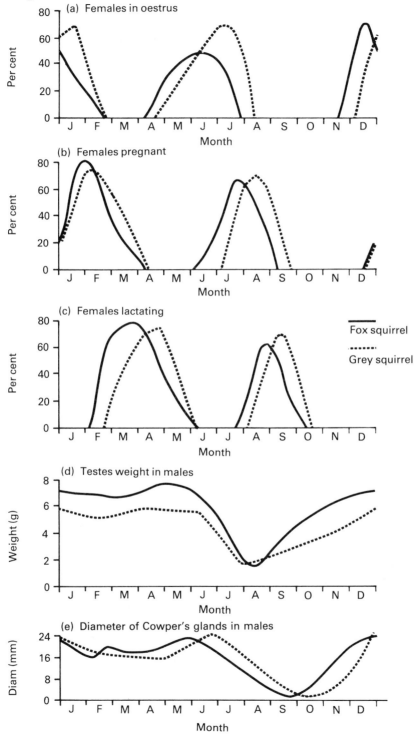

squirrels in England do not show such a marked seasonal cycle and fertile males have been found in all months of the year (Shorten, 1962).

The Breeding Season

Although squirrels are seasonal breeders, the length of the breeding season is variable and can have a marked effect on how many litters of young are produced during the year. The time of the start of the breeding season is affected by two main factors; weather (Heaney, 1984) and food supplies (Gurnell, 1983). Breeding activity in fox, grey and Western grey squirrels, which inhabit temperate forests, starts around December if food supplies, particularly tree seeds, are reasonably good (Figure 7.2; Ingles, 1947; Flyger and Gates, 1982a; Gurnell, 1983). However, if the tree seed crop fails, then the start of breeding is delayed until February or March. Pine squirrels inhabiting cold boreal forests in North America, generally have one litter during a breeding season which is born between March and May (Sullivan and Sullivan, 1982a; Flyger and Gates, 1982b), and our scanty knowledge concerning breeding in abert squirrels suggests that they also have one litter a year (Flyger and Gates, 1982a). On the other hand, when the winters are not so severe and there are sufficient food supplies, pine squirrels are quite capable of having two litters in the same way as fox and grey squirrels. Millar (1970b), for example, found that pine squirrels in southern British Columbia produced two litters in one year when reproduction started in February, but only one litter in another when breeding started in May. He attributed this to a difference in the weather conditions between the years. Rusch and Reeder (1978) have also associated delays in the start of breeding with the number of days of snow cover in pine squirrels in Alberta. I suggest that red squirrels living in similar cold boreal forests behave in a similar way to pine squirrels, but there are few data to go on. Certainly Ognev (1940) and Mikheeva (1974) show that two litters a year can be produced in coniferous forests in the USSR and red squirrels are known to do so in milder temperate forests (Tittensor, 1977a).

The breeding season in squirrels, therefore, can start in December during the winter if food supplies are good and the weather is amenable. If the weather is poor with cold temperatures and heavy snowfall, which of course depends to a great extent on the prevailing climate, then the start of breeding is deferred (Rusch and Reeder, 1978). Similarly, the start of breeding is delayed if food is in short supply. The end of the breeding season is usually around July or August, although litters of young are sometimes born well into the autumn, and lactation frequently continues in September and October (Figure 7.2; Ognev, 1940; Millar, 1970b). Since the period from conception to independence of young is in the order of 3 to 4 months, it can be seen that progressive delays in the start of the breeding period will make it increasingly unlikely that a female will have sufficient time to produce two litters during the breeding season.

Males come into reproductive condition at the start of the breeding season and remain so until at least the summer and perhaps later. The indications, therefore, are that they are capable of mating with a female during this time. This is an important tactic of the male because all the females in a population do not come into reproductive condition together and conceptions can occur at any time during this period; this is discussed in more detail below.

Breeding Success

Delays in the start of the breeding season resulting from poor weather conditions or food supplies can quite simply be explained on energetic grounds. The physiological and anatomical changes associated with reproductive condition, and reproductive behaviour (e.g. mating chases) require a considerable amount of energy above that needed for thermoregulation, body maintenance, foraging and feeding (Chapters 4 and 5). Squirrels will not enter reproductive condition unless they are in a positive energy balance and we have noted in Chapter 5 how competition among individuals, which is affected by age and body weight, can influence foraging behaviour. This is self-reinforcing in that heavier animals are dominant, forage more efficiently than subordinates, and this, of course, maintains their body weight and position in the hierarchy. Furthermore, reproductive success in both males and females has been related to age and body weight (Chapter 5). For example, subordinate females or light-weight females in poor condition will defer entering reproductive condition at the beginning of the season and perhaps skip breeding completely that year. As will be seen below, once squirrels reach adulthood, they may live for several years. Therefore, to postpone reproduction for a year may benefit the animals in the long-term since at least they may 'live to breed another year'.

Following on from the above, it is possible to understand why there is a considerable amount of variation between females in the time that they first enter oestrus during the breeding season. Juvenile females less than 9 months old virtually never enter breeding condition in the year of their birth (Ognev, 1940; Smith and Barkalow, 1967). Yearling females (9 to 15 months old) usually produce only one litter (if at all) with oestrus occurring 2 to 3 months after the start of the season, but dominant adult females (2 years old and older) reproduce at the beginning of the season, rear their offspring and may reproduce for a second time. Adult females lower down the social hierarchy may rear two litters or, like yearlings, produce only one litter (Gurnell, 1983). All-in-all, in a good seed year and with an early start to breeding, usually no more than 30 to 40 per cent of the females in a population produce two litters (e.g. Nixon and McClain, 1975), even though some 90 per cent or more of the females breed at some time. On the other hand, as we have mentioned, a few adults and some yearlings may not breed at all in a year (e.g. Taylor, 1969). If food crops are poor then fewer adults will breed and considerably fewer yearlings. For example, Curt Halvorson found that in a good seed year, 92 per cent adult and 88 per cent yearling pine squirrels produced litters, whereas in a poor–moderate seed year, 88 per cent adults and only 51 per cent yearlings did so (Halvorson, pers. comm.).

When viewed as a whole, a population of squirrels will often exhibit two peaks in litter production during a season. These peaks refer the periods of spring litter production, resulting from early conceptions, and summer litter production, resulting from late conceptions (e.g. yearlings) or second conceptions. Understandably, from what has been discussed above, there is quite a lot of variability around these peaks (Figure 7.2) and if the season is foreshortened then the spring peak is likely to be missed altogether. Only two instances are known where the summer period of litter production has been missed (Nixon and McClain, 1969; Tait, 1978 and

Gurnell, 1981). Both of these concerned grey squirrels, although one study was in the USA and the other in England, and both occurred when summer densities were high following a good overwinter survival and a high spring recruitment resulting from heavy seed crops the previous autumn. It has been suggested that high spring–summer densities, perhaps at a time of limited food availability, inhibited reproduction in these cases (Gurnell, 1983).

As well as the number of litters produced during a season, the size of individual litters will affect the total recruitment of young. Squirrels appear to be capable of having litters of 7 or more young (Ognev, 1940; Barkalow, 1967), but usually the litter size at weaning is within the range of 1 to 5 young (Tittensor, 1977a, 1977b; Flyger and Gates, 1982a; Gurnell, 1983). Heaney (1984) quotes litter sizes for five species of squirrel from 15 studies in North America; they range from 2.4 to 4.2. He suggests these data show an indication of a positive relationship between litter size and latitude. However, he points out that squirrel populations at higher latitudes have, on average, fewer litters per year so that the total reproductive output (i.e. number of litters multiplied by mean litter size) remains remarkably constant across the continent.

Losses of young can occur inside the female before they are born, or during the nestling stage. Pregnant females in poor physical condition resulting from a shortage of food, for example, may resorb embryos from the uterus (Ognev, 1940), and in general litter sizes in good food years tend to be larger than in poor food years (e.g. Brown and Yeager, 1945; C.C. Smith, 1968). Furthermore, adult females produce larger litters than yearling females. For example, Rusch and Reeder (1978) found that the mean number of young per female in a population of pine squirrels was 3.4 for adults and 0.7 for yearlings in a poor seed year, and 4.7 and 3.9 respectively in a good seed year. Losses from birth to weaning can also be considerable and may result from predation (Chapter 8), bad weather or the abandonment of the young by the mother if she cannot obtain sufficient energy to nourish them. Spring litters may be smaller than summer litters unless food is particularly abundant (Gurnell, 1983).

Throughout the above, it can be seen how food supplies influence each stage of the reproductive cycle, the length of the breeding season, the number of adults which produce two litters, the number of adults and yearlings which produce one litter, and the mean litter size at birth and weaning. Thus the total recruitment of young per year is much higher when food is abundant than when it is scarce. In a similar way, food supplies affect another population process, survival. This will be considered below.

Annual Survival

Losses of individuals from a population may result from animals dying, being taken by predators or emigrating and we have very little knowledge on the importance of each of these three loss factors. In the next chapter I shall be dealing in more detail with mortality factors such as predators, parasites and diseases. Demographers tend to concentrate on the survival of animals in populations which can be interpreted as the residency time of individuals since animals which disappear may not have died. Patterns of survival appear very similar between squirrel species. On average only about 15 to 25 per cent of young survive to the second year of life, thereafter year-to-year survival is 50 to 70 per cent. These figures increase substantially in good food years when 90 to 100 per cent of adults may survive from one year to the next and 50 to 60 per cent of juveniles (Gurnell, 1983); and, of course, in poor food years, and particularly if the weather is severe during the winter, then survival rates can be very low with few if any young surviving and 30 per cent or less of adults. Stephenson and Brown (1980) found a reasonable relationship ($r = 0.85$, $p < 0.01$) between annual mortality and the logarithm of the number of days of snow cover of 10 cm or greater depth for abert squirrels in Arizona. It appears that squirrels are often seen to be in poor physical condition in spring after winters of heavy snowfall and this probably results from the greater difficulty in foraging for foods.

There is one further influence of food supply on mortality which will be taken up in the next chapter. Squirrels of poor nutritional status appear to be more susceptible to disease which hastens their demise (e.g. Lampio, 1967). Occasionally epizootics (epidemics) of disease kill large numbers of squirrels. For example, Lampio (1967) estimated that the intestinal disease coccidiosis (Chapter 8) killed nearly one million red squirrels in Finland during the year 1943-4. Middleton (1931) reports heavy losses from the same disease in grey squirrels in England in 1931, which may have partly resulted from a lowered resistance to disease at a time of poor food supplies (Shorten, 1954).

There is very little good information about squirrels actually dying of cold or starvation. Bad weather in itself is probably not a direct cause of death (except in the case of abandoned litters) but, like disease, is probably associated with starvation or poor body condition (Allen, 1943; Lampio, 1967; see Chapter 4). Adult squirrels have occasionally been found frozen in dreys and this may occur more frequently than is known. Some unexplained mortalities were observed in grey squirrels in the New Forest in southern England during the early summer of 1985. Several dead squirrels were picked up without any signs of injury and one was actually seen dying and falling off a branch. All the animals were thin and no signs of disease were revealed. In this instance animal densities were high following good spring breeding and, although it is believed that food supplies were not good at the time, one can only speculate that these animals died of hunger or perhaps stress as a result of high levels of interaction.

Length of Life

In captivity, grey squirrels have been known to live for 20 years, fox squirrels for 13 years, Western grey squirrels for 11 years and pine squirrels for 9 years (Tittensor, 1977a; Flyger and Gates, 1982a, 1982b). Longevity in wild squirrels is generally less than this although grey and perhaps other species may survive until they are 8, 9 or 10 years old. Also, it is important to remember that very few animals will live to these sorts of ages, perhaps less than 1 per cent of individuals. Survivorship curves for pine squirrels in the USA and grey squirrels in southern England are shown in Figure 7.3. These 'age-specific' survivorship curves are based on data collected on individual squirrels from the time they were juveniles until they disappeared from the population, and, therefore, required studies spanning many years. There are few data sets collected in this way. Crude indices of survival from one age class to the next are sometimes

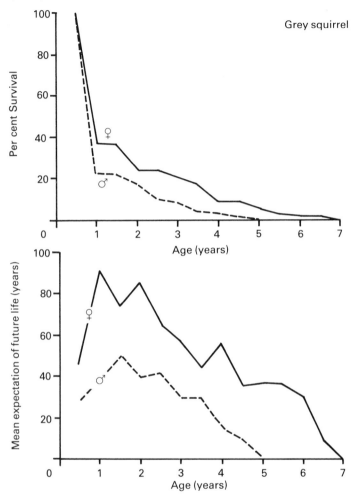

Figure 7.3 Survivorship and life expectancy curves for grey squirrels in England and pine squirrels in Montana. Sources: J. Gurnell (unpl.); Halvorson and Engeman (1983)

obtained from the shrinkage of successive age classes of animals collected at one sampling time; these are called 'time-specific' survivorship curves (e.g. Rusch and Reeder, 1978). They provide no information on past events which may have affected survival and they also require the determination of the age of the individuals. The various techniques which have been developed for this are listed in Table 7.1. For live animals they only distinguish one, two or three age classes (e.g. juveniles, yearlings and adults) whereas many of the more refined techniques can only be carried out after the animals have died.

A few grey and pine squirrels in the particular studies quoted in Figure 7.3 lived to 6 or 7 years old, although I have known some grey squirrels living to 9 years old in the wild. Overall, the maximum life span for all Holarctic species appears to be between 5 and 10 years although it should be pointed out that there is little good information on several species including fox, red, douglas, Western grey and abert squirrels. The grey

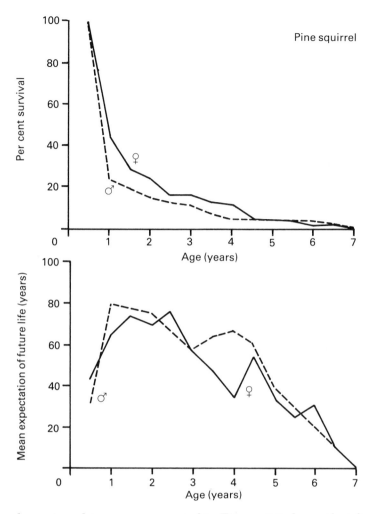

squirrel survivorship curve presented in Figure 7.3 shows that female grey squirrels from southern England survive better than males and although such a distinction is not quite so clear from the pine squirrel survivorship curve, similar differences in survival between the sexes have been found in other studies (e.g. Erlien and Tester, 1984). The survival data in Figure 7.3 are also expressed as age specific life expectancies. These show how long animals are expected to survive once they attain a particular age. The curves reflect the high losses of juvenile animals and the low expectation of future life as the animals approach the maximum life span. At all ages female grey squirrels have greater life expectancies than males but such clear differences between the sexes are not apparent from the pine squirrel curve.

Immigration and Emigration

Immigration and emigration have been discussed at some length in Chapter 6 under the heading of dispersal. From the point of view of demography these two processes represent gains and losses to and from the population, and the earlier chapter highlighted two times of the year when

Table 7.1 Squirrel age determination methods

Method	Comments	Species	References
A. LIVE ANIMALS			
Body weight/size	Of little use except when juveniles very small	Grey	Dubock (1979)
	Note: Standardisation of body weight for body size—good index of indiv. quality	Grey	Don (1981)
Sexual maturity	Only clearly distinguishes those adults breeding (also dead animals)	Red Grey	Shorten (1954) Kirkpatrick and Barnett (1960)
Pelage/tail hairs	Juvenile/adult	Grey Pine	Sharp (1958) Barrier and Barkalow (1967) Kemp and Keith (1970)
Ossification of epiphiseal cartilages using X-rays	3–4 age classes	Grey Fox/grey Red	Petrides (1951) Dubock (1979) Carson (1961) Degn (1973)

B. DEAD ANIMALS

Method	Notes	Species	References
Teeth—cementum annuli	Possible but not easy to distinguish year classes	Grey	Fogl and Mosby (1978)
			Knee and Gurnell (unpl.)
		Red	Lemnell (1973)
Teeth—eruption, replacement and wear	Juvenile, subadult and adult age classes	Red	Shengkan and Mingshu (1979)
			Shorten (1954)
		Grey	Hench et al (1984)
Cranial measures	Of little use	Grey	Hefner (1971)
Size of baculum in males	Too variable but may be used in conjunction with other methods	Red	Degn (1973)
		Grey	Kirkpatrick and Barnett (1957)
Eye lens weight	Best method, at least up to about 4 years of age	Red	Degn (1973)
			Beale (1962)
		Fox	Fisher and Perry (1970)
			Dubock (1979)
		Grey	Kemp and Keith (1970)
			Davis and Sealander (1971)
		Pine	Rusch et al (1982)

this is most likely to occur—during the spring/summer, and the autumn. I described how both food supplies and intraspecific behaviour can influence dispersal and all that needs to be reiterated here is that if food supplies are good (particularly during the autumn) then fewer animals (particularly juveniles) move out of the population and year-to-year survival is good. Furthermore, immigration may be high and so boost overwintering population densities, although it should be kept in mind that the territorial system of *Tamiasciurus* or the behaviour of resident *Sciurus* may limit recruitment and influence squirrel densities (Chapter 6). If the food supply is not good, then many juveniles and some adults leave the population, year-to-year survival is poor, and immigration is low (Gurnell, 1983). One further point is that the movements of squirrels are greatly affected by the patchiness of the forests in which they live. In large uniform tracts of forests dispersing squirrels may not be able to find a suitable patch of forest in which to stay (either because of resident animals or lack of food). This may result in many animals leaving the forest at around the same time and in the extreme case may lead to mass migrations (Chapter 5). Where forests consist of small blocks (patches) of different tree species, then dispersing squirrels may find some habitats where resident squirrels are few or there are sufficient food supplies which allow them to survive.

Sex Ratios

Most animal species produce offspring with a 1:1 sex ratio; that is, on average, there are an equal number of sons and daughters. This can be readily explained in terms of a self-correcting system preventing surpluses of sons or daughters based on natural selection acting on the individual. There is not room to explain this here but it has been elegantly described in many modern textbooks (e.g. Krebs and Davies, 1982; Barash, 1982). Of course, the sex ratio of offspring at birth is not so interesting (unless it differs from 1:1) as the 'functional sex ratio' at the time the offspring become breeding adults. If the sex ratio changes during the time of parental care then it may be because parents invest differently in sons and daughters thus affecting their survival and subsequent reproductive prowess. There are data from several species of mammal, including deer and human beings, which suggest that parents can manipulate the functional sex-ratio. There is little information on sex ratios at birth in squirrels and for the time being it must be assumed that they approximate a 1:1 ratio. Further, sex ratios of juveniles and adults fluctuate quite considerably and often without any discernable pattern. On the available evidence, therefore, there appears to be no parental manipulation of sex ratios in squirrels and variations in sex ratios after weaning must be examined in terms of differential mortality resulting from, for example, reproductive effort, or biases due to sampling.

Squirrel densities do not appear to have any influence on sex ratios (Uhlig 1957; Lampio, 1967) but some studies have shown that males predominate in samples collected by shooting or trapping, possibly because they are more wide-ranging than females and encounter hunters (or sampling devices) more frequently (Brown and Yeager, 1945; Farentinos, 1972). Kemp and Keith (1970) suggest that more male than female pine squirrels (which, remember, are territorial) are sampled in the spring because, whereas the females are sedentary, males tend to move about in pursuit of females. However, not all studies using traps or shooting produce male biased sex ratios (e.g. Uhlig, 1957).

There is some evidence, although not universal, that juvenile age classes contain slightly more males than adult age classes. For example, Lampio (1967) found that the overall sex ratio from large samples of red squirrels in Finland was almost 1:1 (Table 7.2) but juvenile animals from several samples gave ratios well in favour of males. Consequently, sex ratios in adults tended to be biased towards females. In this study no sampling bias was believed to have occurred and the results suggest that female juveniles survived better than males. In fact Lampio showed that males were more prone to disperse (Chapter 5) and were more susceptible to disease. He also stated that predation took a heavier toll on males.

Different sex ratios between juvenile and adult age classes may result in an annual cycle in overall sex ratios, with a preponderance of males at the end of the breeding season in the autumn, and an equal sex ratio, or a female bias by the spring when natural mortalities have taken their toll (Lampio, 1967). In addition, if males have poorer survival than females, there will be a tendency for more males to survive in good food years than poor food years and thus winter or spring sex ratios will vary between years. Despite Lampio's detailed study we cannot generalise his findings to other populations. Andy Tittensor (1970), for example, found in Scotland that more female than male young red squirrels were recruited at the end of the breeding season which led to female-biased sex ratios in the autumn. On the other hand, Rusch and Reeder (1978) reported that sex ratios in pine squirrels in Alberta during the summer were 1:1 but female losses occurred during the autumn leaving a preponderance of males through to the following spring. In the spring, males suffered heavy mortalities returning the sex ratio to 1:1. There is some evidence from other studies that adult females have a slightly better survival and life expectancy than males (e.g. Halvorson, 1984; see above). This in part may result from more males dispersing or males ranging over larger areas than females, and it may, therefore, reflect differences in residency time rather than mortality.

From the above it can be seen that it is almost impossible to draw any unifying conclusions as to the most important factors which affect observed sex ratios in tree squirrels. In the case of individual studies, it is possible to explain a changing annual pattern in sex ratios in terms of differential survival. In a similar way I shall now turn to examine annual and year-to-year fluctuations in numbers.

ANNUAL CYCLES AND FOOD SUPPLIES

In certain cases squirrel populations exhibit marked seasonal changes in numbers leading to clear annual cycles whereas in other cases seasonal changes may be less dramatic (Figure 7.4). The changes in numbers result from the net effects of the demographic processes described above. Some gains to and losses from populations, resulting from, for example, animals moving in or out of the area, happen all the time but there appear to be four important phases to the annual cycle. These are: (1) an increase in numbers during the late spring/early summer resulting from the recruitment of young from spring litters, and/or more animals moving into a population than animals moving out (i.e. net immigration); (2) a peak phase in summer or early autumn; (3) an autumn decrease in numbers

Table 7.2 Sex ratios. S = shooting; T = trapping (usually live-trapping); N = nest sampling

Species	Age Group	Sampling Method	n	M:F	Authority (Comments)
Grey	Spring juvs.	S	3486	0.89:1	Uhlig (1957) West Virginia, USA
	Summer juvs.	S	4291	0.93:1	
	Adults	S	4618	0.98:1	
	Spring juvs.	T	75	0.96:1	Thompson (1978) Ontario, USA
	Summer juvs.	T	75	1.41:1	(Cementary)
	Adults	T	102	0.96:1	
	Nestlings	N	87	1.07:1	Shorten (1954) England
	Juveniles	S	152	0.81:1	
	Adults	S	570	0.85:1	
	Nestlings	N	1023	0.93:1	Barkalow et al (1970) North Carolina, USA
	Juveniles	S	866	1.03:1	Nixon et al (1975) Ohio, USA
	Yearlings	S	281	1.13:1	
	Adults	S	638	0.91:1	
	Juveniles	T	147	1.16:1	Gurnell (unpublished) England
	Adults	T	360	1.14:1	(From 10 years of trapping)
	All	T	685	0.95:1	Jones (1970) Delaware, USA (Semi-urban population)

			Sample	Ratio	Reference
	All	S	1211	1.54:1	Brown and Yeager (1945) Illinois, USA
	All	Kill-T	171	1.09:1	
	All	T	61	0.97:1	
Fox	Juveniles	S	115	1.13:1	Nixon et al (1975) Ohio, USA
	Adults	S	131	1.14:1	
	Nestlings	N	43	1.05:1	Brown and Yeager (1945) Illinois, USA
	All	S	2749	1.46:1	
	All	Kill-T	341	1.49:1	
	All	T	64	0.78:1	
Abert	All	S & T	729	1.33:1	Farentinos (1972) Colorado, USA
Pine	Juveniles	S & T		1.13:1	Davies and Sealander (1971) Saskatchewan, Canada
	Adults	S & T		1.08:1	
	Juveniles	S & T	589	1.08:1	Kemp and Keith (1970) Alberta, Canada
	Adults	S & T		1.08:1	In Erlien and Tester (1984) (No difference between S & T samples)
	Juveniles	T	293	1.06:1	Rusch and Reeder (1978) Alberta, Canada
	Adults	T	436	1.33:1	
Red	Juveniles	S	1849	1.33:1	Lampio (1967) Finland
	Adults	S	196366	1.03:1	

Figure 7.4 Annual population cycles. Sources: Rusch and Reeder (1978); Don (1981); Tonkin (1983)

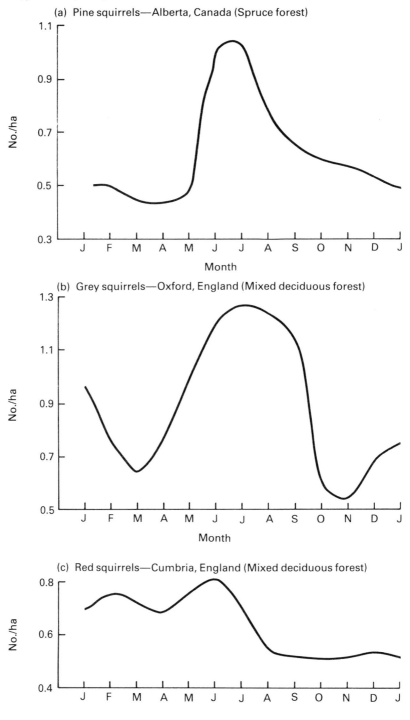

(a) Pine squirrels—Alberta, Canada (Spruce forest)

(b) Grey squirrels—Oxford, England (Mixed deciduous forest)

(c) Red squirrels—Cumbria, England (Mixed deciduous forest)

resulting from squirrels, particularly juveniles, dispersing away from the population; and (4) a drop in numbers overwinter resulting from animals dying or possibly emigrating. Young from summer-born litters do not as a rule result in a further observed increase in numbers in the autumn. This is probably because the young appear in the population at a time when numbers are already falling, and in fact many may not stay around for long enough to be sampled. For example, Mel Tonkin (1983) found that young red squirrels were born in late July in her study in northern England but none were captured in her traps (Figure 7.4).

Food supplies, and to a smaller extent weather, are the main factors affecting the size of these changes in numbers. As we have discussed several times, good tree seed supplies can enhance reproduction, improve survival and reduce dispersal (Figure 7.5), and of course the reverse is also true. This will be further discussed in the next section where I consider year-to-year changes in numbers.

YEAR-TO-YEAR CHANGES IN NUMBER

Unexploited populations of squirrels living in an area can change dramatically in density between years, as much as ten-fold or more (Figure 7.6). There may be times, therefore, when squirrels appear to be very abundant (e.g. Pulliainen, 1982) whereas at other times sightings of squirrels may be very few and far between. As mentioned above, the reasons for this to a large extent come back to the abundance of food supplies and the prevailing weather conditions. This can be illustrated by considering summer densities in two years, 1977 and 1982, from my own work on grey squirrels in an oak wood in southern England.

In 1977 numbers were very high with densities of more than 16 squirrels/ha. Conversely, 1982 showed very low densities for my particular study area with about 2 squirrels/ha (in fact, this is still a high density compared with many populations of grey or other species of squirrel—see

Figure 7.5 Schematic relationship between food supplies and squirrel numbers showing feedback links and indicating the importance of competition for food from other birds and animals. Source: Gurnell (1983)

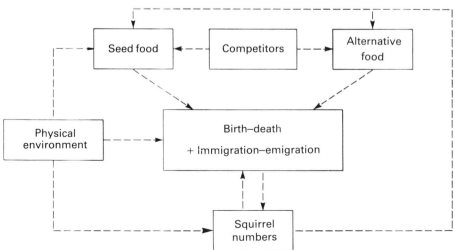

below). The very high 1977 summer population density resulted from a very good acorn crop in 1976; intact acorns were still to be found on the forest floor in May and June 1977. The survival of adults from summer 1976 to summer 1977 was well over 90 per cent, more than 50 adults moved into the population between 1976 and 1977 and spring breeding was very successful with more than 50 young present in the summer of 1977 (Gurnell, 1981, 1983). The events leading to the all-time-low, 1982, population numbers were the opposite. The 1981 acorn crop failed, the autumn and early winter of 1981–2 was very wet and cold (mean December temperatures were 3.5°C lower than the long-term average). Of all the squirrels present in the summer of 1981 80 per cent failed to survive to the summer of 1982. Only seven adults entered the population between 1981 and 1982, there was no spring breeding in 1982 and no 1982 summer young were captured. I believe the very poor year-to-year survival resulted from a shortage of food and bad weather conditions during the winter. As discussed before, undernourished squirrels not only appear to have a lowered resistance to disease but also more easily succumb in persistently bad weather.

LONG-TERM AVERAGE DENSITIES

There are only two detailed studies that I know of which have been carried out for more than ten years and from which it is possible to establish long-term average densities for a particular species in a specific habitat. From twelve years work on a grey squirrel population in an oak wood in southern England I found that the mean peak summer density was 8.1 squirrels/ha (Figure 7.6), and the mean mid-winter density was 4.5 squirrels/ha; the overall mean was 6.3 squirrels/ha. In the second study, of pine squirrels in the USA over 13 years, Curt Halvorson (pers. comm.) found a mean density of 1.3 squirrels/ha on two islands in Montana.

In another article (Gurnell, 1983) I attempted to assess densities of different species in different habitats by drawing on average figures from several short-term studies. The main findings from this are that grey squirrels are essentially a high-density species in mixed deciduous forests, density values ranged from 2 to 16 squirrels/ha. Fox squirrels could also attain densities of 2 to 4 or more squirrels/ha in riverine forests or open, deciduous woodland along forest edges, or in blocks of trees interspersed with farmland or prairie (Flyger and Gates, 1982a; Hansen and Nixon, 1985). For all species, densities can be considerably lower in marginal or less-preferred habitats.

Squirrels living in coniferous forests have significantly lower densities. Abert squirrels in ponderosa pine have densities ranging from about 0.1 to 1.1 squirrels/ha (Nash and Seaman, 1977). Densities of douglas and pine squirrels range from about 0.3 to 2 squirrels/ha but occasionally densities may be higher. Densities of their Old World counterpart, the red squirrels, appear to be similar. For example, densities in British coniferous forests ranged from 0.3 to 1.1 squirrels/ha (Shorten, 1962; Tittensor, 1977b; Reynolds, 1981; Moller, 1986), and densities from coniferous forests in the USSR, Belgium and Spain have been recorded as 0.8 (Bobyr, 1978), 1.3 (Wauters and Dhondt, 1985) and 0.1 (Purroy and Rey, 1974) squirrels/ha respectively. Interestingly, studies on red squirrels in deciduous forests in England, Spain and Belgium give a similar range of densities of 0.3 to 1

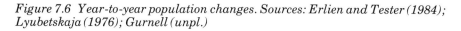

Figure 7.6 Year-to-year population changes. Sources: Erlien and Tester (1984); Lyubetskaja (1976); Gurnell (unpl.)

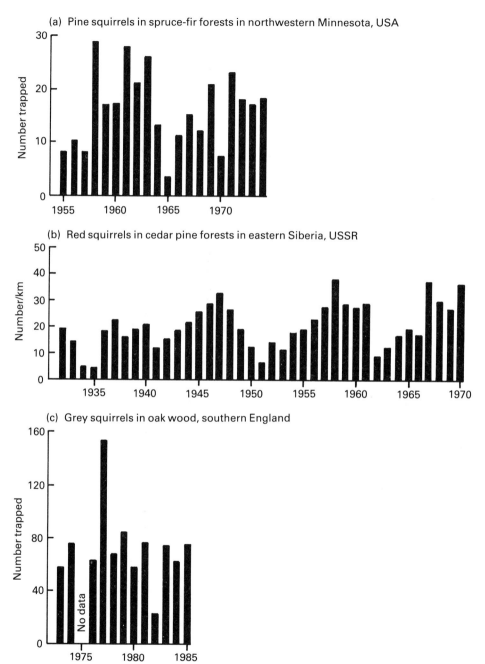

squirrels/ha (Purroy and Rey, 1974; Tonkin, 1984; Wauters and Dhondt, 1985; Jessica Holm, pers. comm.). I am of the opinion that densities of the larger grey squirrel would be considerably higher in these habitats.

Therefore, it appears that red squirrels characteristically exhibit densities of 0.3 to 1.5 squirrels/ha irrespective of whether they live in a deciduous or a coniferous forest. One theory which would explain this is that red squirrels have evolved a stable solitary form of social organisation, probably in boreal coniferous forests, which is based on large individual distances and results in low densities (Chapter 6). The question which follows is why has not a new form of squirrel evolved with a more flexible social structure which can achieve higher densities in deciduous forests? It is possible that differences in diet or other aspects of habitat utilisation may also account for density differences between red and grey squirrels in deciduous habitats. One such difference was noted in Chapter 4 in that red squirrels, irrespective of the time of the year, appear to spend a much greater proportion of their time in the canopy than grey squirrels (Kenward and Tonkin, 1986).

Are Squirrel Populations Regulated?

A question which some biologists may ask is whether squirrel population densities are regulated. Population regulation may be occurring when it appears that the density of animals or plants is continuously being adjusted to some sort of equilibrium level. This results from stabilising factors which tend to reduce, if too high, or increase, if too low, numbers back to the equilibrium level. For this reason, stabilising factors are usually described as being density-dependent, that is they vary proportionally in their effect according to population density. Such factors may influence any of the demographic processes of birth, death, immigration or emigration. Intraspecific competition is an obvious candidate as a possible regulatory factor. Other factors, which are unrelated to population density are termed density-independent and tend to be non-stabilising. Weather often falls into this category (see Begon and Mortimer, 1981).

It has been established that squirrel population densities are very variable both within and between years and this does not favour the idea of regulation over long periods of time, unless regulation is very finely tuned to food supply. Secondly, food supplies and weather are known to be important factors influencing population size and they are interrelated in that, for example, bad weather has a greater impact on mortalities when food supplies are poor. The autumn period appears to be a likely time of the year when regulation could occur. Intraspecific competition has been discussed in Chapters 4 and 5. The establishment of territories in *Tamiasciurus* during the autumn tends to limit the density of squirrels according to seed supplies. Similarly, the amount of autumn dispersal away from populations in *Sciurus* squirrels, especially juveniles, appears to depend on seed supplies (Thompson, 1978b). In both cases intraspecific behaviour tends to adjust densities to food availability during the autumn, and argues in favour of regulation occurring at that time. It would be unwise to state categorically that density-dependent regulation occurs during the autumn, or indeed at any other time of the year, until further quantitative studies have been carried out, but without doubt, both density-related and density-unrelated factors determine changes in squirrel abundance at different times.

8 Community ecology

A group of species, including both animals and plants, which share the same habitat is called a community, and these species, to a lesser or greater extent, interact with each other. In some cases, interactions will be virtually non-existent, in others they may be quite subtle and pass unnoticed or again they may be dramatic and obvious. Some of the relationships between forest animals and squirrels are explored in this chapter. I leave consideration of the relationship between man and squirrels to the next chapter since it has an important bearing on how forests and their squirrel populations are managed.

Populations of different species may adversely affect one another by competing for a resource which both require but is in short supply (e.g. food), or by one species directly exploiting another, by eating it or by living in or on it. The former case refers to interspecific competition and I shall particularly consider competition between different species of squirrel which live in the same habitat. In the Nearctic, there are several areas where the geographic ranges of squirrel species overlap (i.e. they are sympatric), and within these areas they are frequently found in the same or neighbouring habitats (i.e. they are syntopic). In the Palaearctic this is not the case since the red squirrel has the virtual monopoly from Europe in the east to China in the west (Chapter 1). The exception is Great Britain where introduction of the grey squirrel from North America has had profound repercussions for the native red squirrel in these islands. Because of this and the fact that much of my own research has been carried out on British squirrels, I discuss the red/grey problem in the British Isles at some length. First, however, I shall turn to the groups of animals which have an obvious and direct affect on squirrels: predators, parasites and disease organisms.

PREDATORS

Squirrels are a food source for almost any opportunistic predator which hunts in or over forests. Consequently from time to time squirrels have been recorded in the diet of a variety of animals including stoats, weasels, wildcats, foxes, lynx, eagles, owls and snakes. Some of these predators, such as stoats, may take young from the nest, but in all cases, with the possible exception of the wildcat (*Felis sylvestris*) in European forests and some species of owl, squirrels only constitute a very small portion of their diet (seldom more than 5 per cent, often less than 1 per cent). However, there are two groups of predators which hunt squirrels more frequently. These are hawks, such as the red-tailed and red-shouldered hawks (*Buteo* spp.) from North America and the Goshawk (*Accipeter gentilis*) from North America and Europe, and the martens (*Martes* spp.) which include the American pine marten, the European and Western Asian pine marten, the European beech marten, the Siberian sable, the yellow-throated marten from Eastern Asia and the Japanese marten.

While I was studying squirrels in a subalpine forest in Colorado, I encountered the fresh remains of a pine squirrel on a log (see Chapter 5). These remains consisted mainly of the lower jaws cleaned of flesh, the entrails and some fur which is typical of the remains left by hawks. The squirrel could have fallen prey to a red-tailed hawk which had been seen and heard in the vicinity during the previous few days. It is not clear how important squirrels are in the diet of these raptors. In a 4-year study of red-tailed hawks in Alberta, Luttich and his colleagues (1970) found that only 2 per cent of the prey items fed to young birds in the nests by their parents were pine squirrels. Ground squirrels, hares and grouse were the most important prey in this study. In a 15-year study of goshawks in Sweden, red squirrels on average constituted 9 per cent of the food brought to young in the nest. In one year this figure rose to 34 per cent and there appeared to be a positive relationship between the abundance of squirrels and the number preyed upon each year (Sulkova, 1964). One of the problems with some of the studies carried out on the diet of hawks is that they have been confined to the birds' breeding season because of the ease of assessing prey items brought to the nest. Few records have been available from the winter months until recently when biologists using radiotracking equipment have been able to follow goshawks throughout the year. Robert Kenward and his colleagues (Kenward *et al*, 1981) found that red squirrels were the most frequently taken prey during the winter months in areas of central Sweden with mixed forest and farmland. Squirrels were 33 per cent

Table 8.1 Composition of goshawk diet during the breeding season (March to July) and the winter in boreal forests in central Sweden (P. Widen, 1985). %n = per cent of prey numbers; %w = per cent of prey weight

Prey	Late March–July Males + Females		Winter Males		Females	
	%n	%w	%n	%w	%n	%w
Ground-nesting birds (tetraonids)	26	60	15	40	4	3
Other birds	60	31	12	8	4	1
Squirrels	14	} 9	73	52	86	60
Mountain hares	<1		0	0	7	36
Sample size	904		33		28	

of the prey, and provided 15 per cent of the biomass for male goshawks and 10 per cent for females. Per Widen (1985) showed that red squirrels were even more important for goshawks in Swedish taiga (Table 8.1). In contrast to Sulkova's breeding season records, the proportion of squirrels in the winter diet were similar in both 1978–9 and 1979–80 (83 per cent and 76 per cent) despite squirrels densities being three times higher in 1978–9 than in 1979–80. Widen found a marked difference in the diet of goshawks between the winter and the breeding season with, on average, 79 per cent of the prey taken being squirrels in the winter but only 14 per cent in the spring and summer. This difference was only partly attributable to the presence of migratory birds during the breeding season. It appears that squirrels were much more vulnerable to predation in winter than in spring and summer and they are taken by goshawks during their restricted but intensive bouts of foraging activity. The reverse was apparently true for ground-nesting grouse and capercaillie. Prey catchability as well as abundance, therefore, are important influences on the seasonal diet of hawks. The landscape also affects the diet of hawks. For example, a study carried out on the Dutch–German frontier found no squirrels in the diet of goshawks. The bulk of the hawks' prey consisted of wood pigeon, domestic pigeon, jay, pheasant and fieldfare (Opdam *et al*, 1977). Although 35 per cent of the land consisted of forests, red squirrels were apparently rare at the time of the study and the goshawks took most of their prey from the forest-edge and farmland. Similar factors affect the diet of terrestrial carnivores as we shall see below. Robert Kenward (pers. comm.) has made some interesting observations on goshawks and the larger grey squirrel in England. A female goshawk took 7 grey squirrels in 10 days shortly after she was released in Oxfordshire and she was feeding almost exclusively on squirrels. Male goshawks are smaller than females (average 850 g as opposed to 1,300 g) and tend to take smaller prey. Robert Kenward found that, despite male goshawks making several attacks on grey squirrels, none were successful. In general, full grown grey squirrels appear to be too strong for male goshawks.

Martens are small-to-medium sized carnivores belonging to the mustelid family which are equally at home hunting in the trees as on the ground (Figure 8.1). They are found in coniferous and mixed forests, less often in

Figure 8.1 Pine marten with dead squirrel

deciduous forests. Martens are active all year round, mainly at dusk and during the night, and eat a variety of prey including voles, lemmings, squirrels, shrews, and ground-nesting birds such as grouse. They also eat berries, mushrooms and the remains of large animals such as reindeer. The composition of their diet varies from season to season and from year to year according to prey availability. In open forests with a well developed grass and field layers or grass clearings, their diet depends a great deal on the availability of voles and lemmings. In northern forests, voles and lemmings exhibit 3 to 4 year cycles in numbers so that in some years they are very abundant and in other years they are very scarce. In peak years voles and lemmings may constitute the bulk of the marten's diet whereas in years of low vole and lemming numbers, squirrels and other foods are included in their diet. Pine squirrels were the second most important food of martens in a study carried out in Alaska, particularly in the spring when they constituted 12 per cent of the diet (Figure 8.2). On the other hand, red squirrels were taken most often in the winter by martens in Finnish Lapland (Figure 8.2). In neither of these studies did squirrels contribute more than 16 per cent of the diet of martens. However, they have been reported to occur more frequently in the diet of martens in other studies. For example, the diet of martens in a Swedish forest during one winter was 51 per cent squirrels, 21 per cent mice and voles, and 13 per cent birds (Hoglund, 1964).

Martens hunt by following the tracks and trails of prey animals and after detecting a squirrel, the ensuing chase can be fast and spectacular. Fuente (1972) describes one such chase where a squirrel tried to make its escape by running and leaping through the trees on the thinnest of branches. The marten, equally adept at leaping through the trees, counteracted this by outflanking the squirrel and forcing it to a lower level in a tree, thus trapping it. The squirrel leapt away but the marten caught it in mid-air with its sharp claws and pulled it to the ground. As the two animals rolled over, the marten finished the job by biting the squirrel in the neck. Martens have also been known to attack sleeping squirrels in their nests at night, with again both predator and prey frequently falling to the ground before the squirrel is killed (Ognev, 1940). Martens have also been observed following large numbers of migrating squirrels in Russia. Squirrels are too large for martens to eat entirely in one go and so the remains are hidden in snow or under a fallen log for later consumption. Martens live at low densities of between one animal per 80 ha and one animal per 10 sq km and there is no evidence that martens, or other natural predators, have any impact on squirrel populations.

PARASITES AND DISEASE

Like all wild animals, squirrels suffer from various parasites and diseases. The numbers of parasitic species, for example, which have been identified from squirrels are quite large (Table 8.2). For the most part squirrels tolerate these unwelcome guests without any apparent discomfort, although it should be made clear that, considering how common squirrels are, sick or dying animals are seldom found in the wild. (One example, concerning grey squirrels was described in Chapter 7.) This may be because animals die in nests or places where they are not found and that scavengers quickly remove the evidence. Many squirrels disappear each

Figure 8.2 Diet of pine martens in Alaska and Finland. Sources: Busrick and MacDonald (1984); Pulliainen (1982)

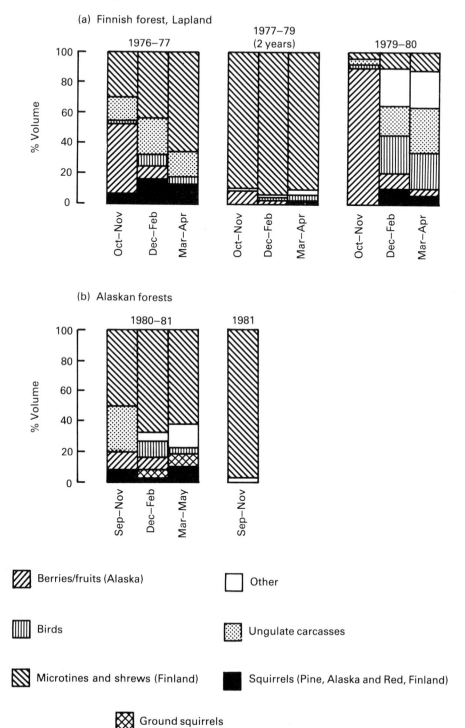

Table 8.2 The numbers of species of parasites identified from fox, grey and pine squirrels in North America. (Source: from Flyger and Gates, 1982a, b)

Parasite	Fox	Grey	Pine
INTERNAL PARASITES			
Protozoa (e.g. coccidia)	1	5	3
Cestodes (tapeworms)	12	9	9
Nematodes (threadworms)	11	18	6
EXTERNAL PARASITES			
Acari (mites, ticks)	13	28	22
Anoplura (lice)	3	7	6
Siphonaptera (fleas)	7	15	12
Diptera (bot flies)	1	1	1

year (Chapter 7) and it is not clear where they all go. Certainly many move out of the population but eventually they must die or be taken by predators. As we have seen, there is little evidence that predators have any impact on squirrel populations, and it is therefore possible that we underestimate the importance of parasites and disease.

The above said, sick squirrels are found occasionally but, unless the bodies are examined by a veterinary pathologist experienced in wildlife disease, descriptions of the disease are often inaccurate and misleading. For example, red squirrels in Britain have been said to suffer from distemper, diphtheria, consumption, scab disease and myxomatosis. People have been misled into thinking that red squirrels suffer from myxoma virus because they show similar signs with swelling of the eyelids and ocular discharge. Sometimes the animals are blind and lethargic with a loss of hair on the face and ears and perhaps elsewhere on the body (this is called alopecia), and they have stomatitis and nasal discharge. These squirrels are now believed to have been suffering from another type of virus called parapoxvirus but little is known about the nature of the disease (Keymer, 1983). There is no evidence that parapoxvirus occurs in grey squirrels in Britain but similar types of viruses (called leporipoxviruses) have been associated with skin tumours and lesions in grey and Western grey squirrels in North America. Other viral and bacterial infections which have been reported from squirrels in North America include California encephalitis virus in pine, fox and grey squirrels from Ohio and Wisconsin, western equine encephalitis in fox squirrels from Colorado, plague in fox squirrels from Colorado and California, leptospirosis in fox and grey squirrels from Florida, tularemia in fox, grey and pine squirrels from various parts of North America and tetanus in grey squirrels from Ontario (Flyger and Gates, 1982a, 1982b). Ian Keymer (1983) has identified pasteurellosis in a red squirrel and yersiniosis in a grey squirrel in Britain. Fungal infections are not common but turn up from time to time, including ringworm. These pathogenic microorganisms may be transmitted from squirrel to squirrel by direct contact (e.g. ringworm) or by blood-sucking ectoparasites such as fleas and ticks. Squirrels are not important in the transmission of human disease although some of the organisms with which they are infected are human pathogens (e.g. plague, yersiniosis).

Figure 8.3 Life cycle of Eimeria, *an important endoparasite of squirrels*

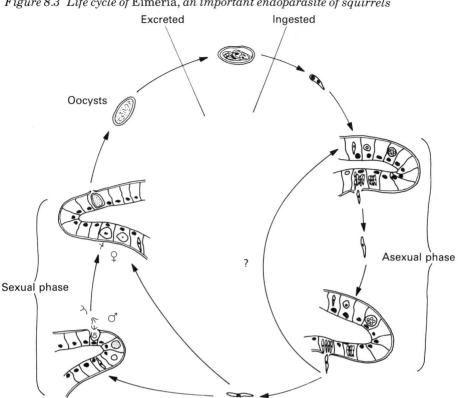

Very little is known about the pathogenicity of most squirrel parasite and disease organisms although it is possible that squirrels which are undernourished may build up heavy parasite burdens or become sick with disease such as parapoxvirus which eventually may prove fatal. A good example is that of coccidiosis which is said to have caused deaths in squirrels in epidemic proportions, particularly red squirrels in Finland and Scandinavia (Chapter 7). Coccidiosis is caused by parasitic protozoa (known as coccidia), most pathogenic species of which belong to the genus *Eimeria* and are found in many types of animal; several species have been described from squirrels. A typical life cycle of *Eimeria* is shown in Figure 8.3. The parasite, which appears to be endemic in individuals in many populations (Frank Nowell, pers. comm.), attacks the epithelial lining of the intestine. There are one or more asexual generations followed by a sexual generation which results in the formation of an encysted stage called an oocyst. The oocyst, protected from environmental influences by a highly resistant coat, passes out of the body in the faeces. Further reproduction occurs inside the oocyst with the development of four sporozoites inside each of two sporocysts. This process takes perhaps two to four days after which the oocyst is infective. It may remain infective for many months. After being ingested by another (or the same) host the wall of the oocyst ruptures in the small intestine releasing the activated sporozoites and the cycle starts again. It is not known for sure how the squirrels ingest the oocysts in the first place. It seems most likely that they

155

are either picked up directly from contaminated nesting material, or via the body by grooming. They may also be picked up as squirrels dig and cache seeds in contaminated soil. Oocysts may appear within seven days of infection and be passed out of the host for several days. It appears that many squirrels are continuously being reinfected since many have coccidia in them. Serious infections may cause bloody diarrhoea as pieces of the intestinal wall become sloughed off, and the host becomes debilitated. It can be conjectured that squirrels already weakened by a shortage of food may become severely infected as they remain for long periods in the nest. In such situations the disease could be progressive and eventually result in death.

Eimeria is an example of a parasite with a direct life cycle, and there is no intermediate host. Perhaps we should not expect the largely herbivorous–granivorous squirrel to have parasites which require inter-mediate hosts to complete their life cycle. However, they do have such parasites (e.g. cestodes) and this is for two possible reasons. Firstly, ectoparasites such as fleas may act as intermediate hosts (e.g. this is known to occur in the tapeworms *Hymenolepis nana* and *H. diminuta*, which occur in squirrels, and other definitive hosts). Secondly, squirrels do eat animal food, particularly when seeds and fungi are in short supply. Consequently, it can be speculated that more parasites may be picked up by hungry squirrels as they turn to a wider range of foods. It is worth pointing out that many of the parasites which require intermediate hosts are not specific to one species of mammal host (and some ectoparasites such as ticks are not host specific either). This will improve the chances of parasites being transmitted to squirrels since there will be a reservoir of infected intermediate hosts within the habitat. However, little is known about the life cycle of these internal parasites in squirrels and there is little evidence that they are pathogenic.

Ectoparasites are common, as anyone who handles squirrels will know. Fleas are the most obvious of these and they are not averse to jumping off the squirrel and onto the handler, as I often find to my cost several hours later. Fleas are wingless, laterally compressed blood-sucking insects which roam around between the hairs of the host. They are closely associated with nests because the egg, larval and pupal stages in the life cycle of the flea are not spent on the host but usually in its home. The nest, drey or den, therefore, is the site where fleas are picked up or transferred from squirrel to squirrel. (Nests containing lots of parasites may be one reason why squirrels build or move to new nests from time to time.) One study showed that 64 per cent of breeding grey squirrels carried fleas compared with only 31 per cent of non-breeding animals. This difference was attributed to less time spent in the nest by the latter group (Blackmore and Owen, 1968). It seems to me that nearly all the squirrels I handle carry fleas! Fleas are not particularly host specific. In Britain, for example, red and grey squirrels share the same species of flea, including the flea *Orchopeas howardi* which was introduced into this country with the grey squirrel.

Ticks are another prominent group of blood-sucking animals. Details of the life cycles of ticks vary slightly between species but in general, after mating and engorging themselves with blood, the adult ticks drop off the host and the female lays eggs on vegetation or possibly in the nest of the host. After the eggs hatch there is a larval and one or more nymphal stages, each of which attaches to a host, feeds and then drops off again to moult into the next stage. Each of these life stages can survive for many months without feeding and the complete life cycle may take two or three years.

Other types of ectoparasites are mites and lice, flightless, dorso-ventrally flattened insects which bite or suck blood from their host. Many of these animals spend their entire life cycle on the host and can cause skin irritations that must be uncomfortable (if human afflictions are anything to go by). The harvest mite (*Neotrombicula autumnalis*) is common on many species of mammal including squirrels. Only the larval stages are parasitic here and there is a distinctive seasonal incidence of infection peaking in the autumn. The larvae attach themselves firmly with their chelicerae to the host's skin where it is thin, and feed on lymph and cell debris aided by the digestive actions of salivary secretions. The mange mites (e.g. *Sarcoptes* spp.) are another group of mites which burrow into the surface layers of the skin, the cornified epithelium. Eggs are laid in skin burrows and, after hatching, the larvae wander over the surface before entering hair follicles where they change into nymphs. The whole life cycle may take one to two weeks. Along with poor food supplies and severe winter weather, they are reported to have contributed to population declines of fox squirrels in Michigan (Flyger and Gates, 1982a). Squirrels may lose hair for several reasons (e.g. because they are moulting or because of heavy infestations of fleas and lice) and since mange results in hair loss it probably has been reported more frequently than it occurs. Ian Keymer (1983) found no convincing evidence that mange mites occur (at least in any numbers) on British squirrels, despite statements to the contrary (e.g. Laidler, 1980).

The last parasite to mention is the bot or warble fly (*Cuterebra* sp.; this genus is only found in North America). These flies lay eggs in the nests of squirrels (e.g. fox, grey and pine squirrels) and, after hatching, the larvae attach themselves to a host and proceed to burrow into the skin. They form cyst-like pockets in the sub-dermal layers which communicate with the outside via a small pore. The appearance of the infection, often called myiasis, is conspicuous and unpleasant, but the larvae eventually drop out and pupate in the ground. Population infestation levels vary between 7 per cent and 50 per cent in North America, and many squirrels which are shot in the autumn before mid-October when the larvae have gone, may be discarded as seemingly unfit for human consumption (Jacobsen *et al*, 1979).

COMPETITION AMONG SPECIES OF TREE SQUIRREL

It can be seen from Chapter 1 that the geographic ranges of fox and grey squirrels overlap to a large extent with each other but this is an exception for Holarctic squirrels. Even so, different species may occur together at the edges of their respective ranges or where one species has been introduced within the range of another. I shall consider a detailed example of the latter below where the interaction between the introduced grey squirrel with the red squirrel in the British Isles will be examined. Examples of the former mainly come from North America where, for example, pine squirrels overlap with abert squirrels in the Rocky Mountains in Colorado, with the douglas squirrel in the Cascade Mountains, and with the grey squirrel in eastern Canada and the USA. It should also be clear from the previous chapters that all Holarctic squirrels live in a very similar way, and so it is interesting to examine these areas of overlap to see whether the different species compete with each other which in turn could influence population demography and community structure.

Unfortunately, there has been little research carried out on competition among sympatric Holarctic squirrels but the basic idea of how similar species can survive within the same habitat was discussed in Chapter 1 in relation to tropical squirrels. In warm climates many species of tree squirrel live within the same piece of forest but each species is adapted to a particular set of environmental factors or niche. For example, species differ according to body size, which layer of the forest they live in and what foods they eat. If there are enough resources, such as food and nest sites, to go round then there is no reason why two similar species should not live together in the same habitat. As in the case of competition within a population (Chapter 6), the problems for the squirrels begin when one of the key resources starts to run out. Of course, a first consideration is whether two (or more) species are actually living within the same habitat. Squirrels appear to be habitat generalists since they are found in all types of forest habitat within their range (with the exception of the abert squirrel), but they have evolved characteristics which are more 'finely tuned' to some habitats as opposed to others. (This can be seen by the existence of large numbers of squirrel subspecies.) Areas of overlap between species usually occur where one type of habitat intergrades with another. As an illustration of this, abert squirrels are found almost exclusively in ponderosa pine forests, but pine squirrels only live in these forests outside the range of the abert squirrel (e.g. Wyoming). In Colorado,

Figure 8.4 Habitat expressed as proportion of ponderosa pine in ponderosa pine/douglas fir forests, and associated distribution of pine and abert squirrels in Colorado. Source: Ferner (1974)

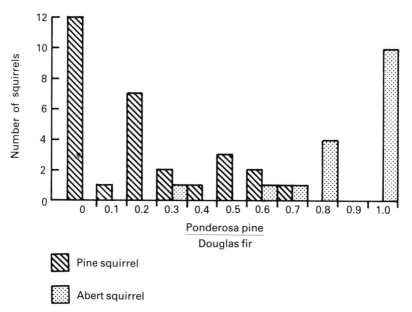

Ferner (1974) found that abert and pine squirrels only overlapped in the transition zone between ponderosa pine and douglas fir (Figure 8.4). It appears that abert squirrels in some way exclude pine squirrels from ponderosa pine. This type of phenomenon is usually referred to as the competitive exclusion of one species from a habitat by another.

Anecdotal evidence often suggests that squirrels physically chase individuals of other species and there are even stories that males may be castrated during such interspecific combat. However, there are also plenty of observations of squirrels of different species feeding apparently amicably together in the same or nearby trees. It is possible that occasionally one individual may chase another individual, of the same or another species. However, there is no good evidence that abert squirrels exclude pine squirrels by overt aggression. Other studies, such as that by Ackerman and Weigl (1970) on pine and grey squirrels, support the idea that different species are not particularly aggressive towards each other. Therefore, the apparent superiority of abert squirrel within ponderosa pine points to a more subtle form of competition, perhaps involving avoidance rather than confrontation and a more efficient utilisation of the habitat. This idea can be illustrated by considering the closely related pine and douglas squirrels. A detailed analysis of the two species in their narrow band of overlap in the Cascade Mountains of North America by Christopher C. Smith (1981) has shown that pine and douglas squirrels differ in at least five characters which make them competitively superior within their respective ranges. Two of the characters (alarm calls, and coat colour) relate to the avoidance of predation, and the remaining three (jaw strength, body size, and reproductive rate) relate to a more efficient exploitation of the resources (e.g. food) within the habitats typical of their ranges. In the region of overlap, individuals are territorial both within and between species.

Areas of overlap between species occur, therefore, where one type of forest habitat is replaced by another. Squirrels which through evolution have become adapted to particular habitats, generally tolerate the presence of other species in the zone of overlap. The numerical relationship between the two species depends upon the mix of forest types in any one part of the overlap zone. These arguments are not so easy to apply to fox and grey squirrels which live in sympatry over very extensive areas in the eastern USA, even though, as before, aggressive competitive interaction does not usually occur. There is one report that the signals transmitted by a female grey squirrel that she was on heat were too much for a male fox squirrel who pursued her in a mating chase (Moore, 1968). Mating was not seen and, indeed, hybrids are not known. The literature strongly suggests that the larger fox squirrel and the smaller grey squirrel coexist because they prefer slightly different types of habitat. For example, grey squirrels prefer dense, mature woodland with large amounts of understory and fox squirrels prefer open woodland with sparse understory (Chapter 1). Even so, there have been few detailed studies looking at this and in fact one study on habitat selection in a wood in Illinois found that the amount of understory could not explain the distribution of trapped fox and grey squirrels (Brown and Batzli, 1984). It may be that trapping was not a good method to study habitat selection in this case or that habitat variables other than those measured were important. It is sensible to suggest that fox and grey squirrels have slightly different habitat requirements and use space differently. For example, even though neither of the species appears to exclude the other from any part of the habitat in which they occur together, there is some evidence of a tendency to segregate into species groupings locally in space and time (Armitage and Harris, 1982). Furthermore, although the social organisation of both species is based on individual distance and neither can be considered a social species (Chapter 6), fox squirrels seem to be more solitary than grey squirrels. Clearly, there are some exciting possibilities here for further research but differential habitat utilisation appears to hold the key to coexistence. The temperate, mixed deciduous forests in eastern North America in which fox and grey squirrels are found, vary considerably from place to place in community structure and composition. As a consequence, the relative numbers of fox and grey squirrels also varies from place to place (Chapter 1).

RED AND GREY SQUIRRELS IN THE BRITISH ISLES

The introduction of the grey squirrel from eastern North America into the British Isles, its subsequent spread throughout much of England and parts of Wales and Scotland, and the coincidental decline in the range of the native red squirrel, have been documented several times and consequently they will only briefly be outlined here (e.g. Middleton, 1931; Shorten, 1962; Lloyd, 1983; Reynolds, 1985b). The sequence of events is important, and scientists have been, and still are, fascinated if not puzzled by the recent replacement of one species by another.

Grey squirrels were first introduced into England and Wales from the eastern USA in 1876 and introductions continued to 1915 or later. It is believed that they were originally introduced as exotic animals in country-house parks and gardens. (It is not clear why only the grey squirrel and not other species from North America were introduced.) They were also introduced into Scotland from Canada between 1892 and 1920, and into Ireland from England in 1913 (Lloyd, 1983; Tittensor, 1977a). Between 1906 and 1937 grey squirrels were translocated to different places within Britain. (Grey squirrels were also introduced into Australia and South Africa—see Chapter 1).

At first, the grey did not spread very far from its major points of introduction but between 1930 and 1945 it dramatically extended its range (Figure 8.5). Since then, the range of the grey squirrel has continued to spread but in a more patchy fashion. Now it is found almost everywhere in central and southern England, Wales, the central lowlands of Scotland and the mid-eastern parts of Ireland.

To outline the recent history of the red squirrel in the British Isles, one must go back further in time, perhaps to when the last great ice-sheets covered much of the land, the last so-called Ice Age. The red squirrel did not survive on the British Isles during the last Ice Age since the ice-sheets

Figure 8.5 Distribution of red and grey squirrels in Forestry Commission forests in Britain in 1985 (based on F.C. land in 10 km squares; distribution of private forests are not included). Graphs show proportion of 10 km squares in Scotland, England and Wales with red, grey or both squirrels present between 1974 and 1985. Source: Forestry Commission Annual Squirrel Questionnaires

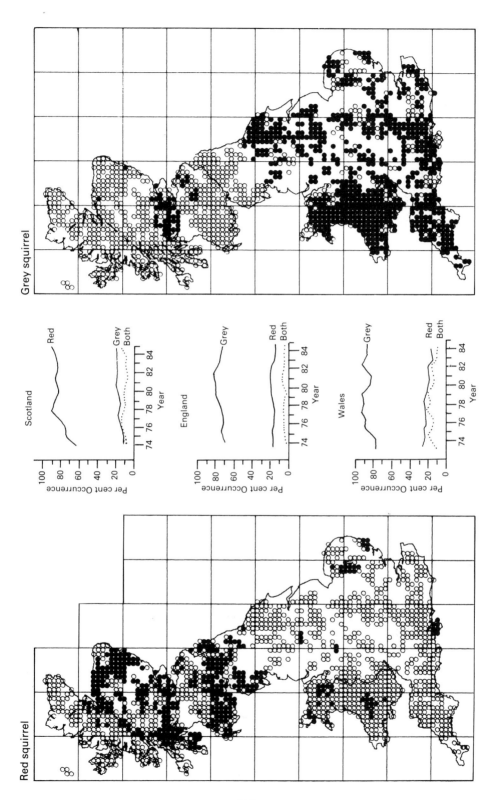

reached a line as far south as the Bristol Channel and the Thames Estuary, leaving only arctic tundra further south. It seems, therefore, that the red squirrel repopulated the islands from the mainland of Europe across the land bridge which existed between about 12,000 to 7,000 years ago. Some time after the ice sheets had retreated due to the warming of the climate, boreal coniferous forests came to cover much of the country. As the climate continued to improve these forests were replaced in central and southern England, Wales and Ireland by broadleaved forests of oak, beech and other hardwood trees. Although thought of as principally an inhabitant of coniferous forests, red squirrels were, and are, perfectly able to survive in broadleaved forests. Today they are found in broadleaved and mixed coniferous/broadleaved forests where they occur throughout Europe, and they live in broadleaved forests in the British Isles where the grey squirrel is absent.

From what we know about red squirrel populations today, it seems likely that numbers must have fluctuated quite widely during the last few thousand years but not much more is known of the red squirrel until about 500 years ago. Thereafter, there were periods where squirrels became very scarce variously in Ireland, and parts of Scotland, England and Wales. As outlined in Chapter 1, this probably occurred because of widespread forest destruction as well as severe winter weather in some years and perhaps disease. It also resulted in squirrels being imported from the Continent and translocated about the islands. This uncertain period ended between 1890 and 1910 when numbers became very abundant almost everywhere. Damage to trees (and to garden produce) occurred such that measures were taken to control the animals with, for example, the formation of the Highland Squirrel Shooting Club in 1903 and the Cornwall Squirrel Shooting Club in 1910 (Shorten, 1954).

After the high, numbers began to fall quite dramatically in different parts of the country and by the 1920s squirrels were again hard to find in many places. In 1927 control measures were stopped in the New Forest and by 1929 they were very scarce (Shorten, 1954). This decline seems to have been associated with disease but surprisingly little is known about which disease or diseases may have been responsible or whether other factors also played a part. For example, disease, as discussed in Chapter 7 and above, frequently becomes apparent in undernourished animals and disease may simply act as the 'coup de grace'. The important thing is that the decline occurred before the grey squirrel began to spread throughout the country and, in time and in the absence of the grey squirrel, there is no reason why the red squirrel should not have returned to at least the major afforested areas within its former distribution (cf. MacKinnon, 1978). However, by the time red squirrels began to recover in the 1930s the grey had begun to stake its claim to many areas of broadleaved or mixed woodland.

The story now enters the world of conjecture since the reasons for the decline in the distribution of the red (Figure 8.5) and spread of the grey are still unresolved. Two theories can be dismissed straight away. Firstly, there is no evidence that grey squirrels have brought with them a disease which is causing the downfall of the red. Secondly, although grey squirrels are considerably larger than red squirrels and have been known to kill red squirrel nestlings and occasionally to chase and fight red squirrels, direct aggression is not believed to have caused the demise of the native squirrel.

As discussed in connection with North American squirrels, it is now believed that some sort of subtle competition is occurring between the species based on habitat exploitation.

In earlier chapters, it was established that the small and lightly built red squirrel is a very arboreal, 'low-density' squirrel, principally adapted to living in coniferous forests. The much larger and stockier grey squirrel is a 'high-density' squirrel principally adapted to living in hardwood forests and tends to be more terrestrial than the red squirrel. Body size seems to be important, and not necessarily because it could influence the outcome of encounters between the two species. In fact, it does not hold true that grey squirrels always chase off red squirrels in the infrequent aggressive interactions. Body size, in the same way as other attributes of animals, has evolved so that animals are able to survive, forage, feed and reproduce efficiently, in their native habitat. The agile, light-weight red squirrels can move well out on the thin branches of coniferous trees where they search for cones, buds and flowers, and they tend to forage a great deal more in the trees than grey squirrels, even in the winter. The chunky grey squirrel, on the other hand, spends most of the winter in deciduous forests foraging on the ground for fallen or buried seed. This may also be the reason that red squirrels only increase their body weight by 8 to 12 per cent during the autumn as they lay down abdominal fat reserves for the winter. This is despite the obvious advantages of laying down more reserves for the winter months, especially in the cold boreal forests of northern Europe and the USSR. Grey squirrels, on the other hand, may increase their body weight by as much as 20 per cent or more in the autumn (Kenward and Tonkin, 1986).

Of course, the question arises as to what happens to grey squirrels when they move into coniferous forests, and what happens to red squirrels when they move into deciduous forests. It has been emphasised that red squirrels quite naturally live in deciduous forests, but they still tend to be more arboreal than grey squirrels and they do not build up high densities like grey squirrels. Little is known about the foraging efficiency of grey squirrels in coniferous forests. They may not be able to exploit large areas of pure conifer and their ability to survive will depend upon the size of the coniferous forest and whether deciduous trees or other sources of food are present. They certainly move into and use conifer forests but they may require alternative sources of food to be prosperous. Grey squirrels may also find it difficult to survive very cold winters without the use of tree dens (Chapter 2), and those of sufficient size would be few and far between in coniferous forests. (Red squirrels survive the coldest winters in dreys.)

Interestingly, it is on record that red and grey squirrels can live side by side for 20 years or more, for example in areas such as Thetford Forest in East Anglia, although how much direct contact there is between the species is not known but is currently being studied. Recently, red squirrels have been seen in parts of Thetford Forest where at one time it was thought they had been replaced by the grey squirrel (Mike Jordan, pers. comm.). Whether they have moved back into these areas or whether they have always been there but at low densities remains to be seen. Following the ideas discussed above in relation to sympatric squirrels in North America, coexistence for 20 years would appear to be possible because there was a sufficient mix of habitat-types which were suitable for both species. Nevertheless, the 'low-density' red squirrel appears to be vulnerable if mature, coniferous forests become fragmented and interspersed with belts of deciduous trees. These ideas need further study and will be returned to in relation to forest management in the next chapter.

Finally, it has been suggested that the grey squirrel is able to adapt more readily than the red squirrel to parks, gardens, hedgerows, copses, and other habitats with trees, which are characteristic of our present day landscape. This is debatable. Certainly grey squirrels are found in all types of habitat including urban areas. Red squirrels are also found in towns and gardens on the Continent, and, with reference to red squirrels in England in 1892, H. Poland wrote: 'Where it is abundant, and if left undisturbed, it becomes almost tame, and will approach the dwellings of man, and even enter the windows, more especially in the winter-time.'

Red squirrels were present in Regent's Park in the heart of London as recently as 1942. In 1984 David Moltu reintroduced ten red squirrels into the Park, to be alongside the present occupants, the grey squirrels. The red squirrels, which were originally young animals from Scotland, appear to be surviving very well despite two road casualties and one being taken by a cat (things which can happen to any urban squirrel!). These squirrels use grey squirrel dreys and even alternate with grey squirrels in the same drey. The two species appear to get on quite amicably with each other most of the time, but where a disagreement occurs, red squirrels chase away greys as much as the other way around. The red squirrels' only privilege is that they can obtain food from special hoppers which are 'out-of-bounds' to grey squirrels. Specific studies such as this one should greatly aid our understanding of competition and coexistence among squirrel species.

FOREST COMMUNITIES

With respect to squirrels, many of the components of forest communities have been covered in the preceding sections of this book. In particular these have been discussed in relation to where squirrels live, which other species of squirrel may be encountered, what squirrels eat, and which animals in turn eat them. There are, of course, many other forest plants and animals which have not been mentioned and, although they all contribute to the organisation and functioning of the communities to which they belong, few have an important influence on the lives of squirrels as far as is known. Some invertebrates, such as defoliating caterpillars, may be valuable sources of food during the spring and summer, others may indirectly compete with squirrels by consuming fungi, fruits and seeds which are a staple item in the squirrel's diet. Smith and Balda (1979) discuss groups of beetles, plant bugs, flies, wasps and moths which attack conifer seeds, mainly as larvae. Many birds and mammals also feed on conifer seed: the birds include woodpeckers, corvids (jays, nutcrackers and magpies), chickadees (titmice), nuthatches, crossbills and siskins. Not surprisingly, most of the mammals which eat conifer seed are rodents, in particular mice, voles, chipmunks, ground-dwelling squirrels and flying squirrels, although shrews may forage for single seeds. Seed crop size varies greatly between years and an important question is what happens to all these seed-eating species in years when seed supplies are poor? There are two main strategies adopted by animals in such situations. Many species stay put and turn to alternative sources of food and survive as best they can; other species, and notably pine seed specialists such as crossbills, siskins and nutcrackers, emigrate in search of forests with better seed supplies. It was seen in Chapter 5 that squirrels occasionally use similar tactics in response to seed crop failures, although of course they are not as mobile as birds. Formosov (1933) noted an association between the extent of the westerly migrations of Siberian nutcrackers (*Nucifrage caryocaractes*) into eastern Europe and the numbers of squirrels taken by hunters in the USSR. Both in turn were associated with fluctuations in the cone crops of the Siberian pine (*Pinus cembra*). As with emigrating squirrels, many (if not most) emigrating birds are not successful in finding better conditions and die. Of the diverse groups of conifer seed-eating invertebrates and vertebrates, many are limited in numbers by different predators, and the availability of alternative foods when seed crops fail (Smith and Balda, 1979); a few species, however, may suffer heavy mortalities as a direct result of the shortage of food. It is worth remarking on the fact that some conifers have evolved very close relationships with certain seed-eaters. White pines (*Pinus albicaulis*) in California, for example, only partly open up their cone scales in the autumn. Clarke's nutcrackers (*Nucifraga columbiana*) remove the seed and carry several at a time (in a special pouch in the mouth) and bury them throughout the forest. Some of these seeds germinate and Clarke's nutcrackers are important dispersers of white pine seed.

It is clear that seed specialists are more vulnerable to fluctuations in the seed crop than animals and birds which can use other sources of food. Deciduous forests provide a greater variety of foods than coniferous forests, both in terms of the variety of different tree seeds available, and in the abundance and variety of alternative food supplies. Similar taxonomic groups of seed-eaters are found in deciduous forests to those found in coniferous forests but the conifer seed specialists are replaced by birds and animals, such as pigeons, pheasants, and dormice which are able to feed on the larger deciduous tree seeds. Like squirrels, mice (including deermice), and to a lesser extent voles, show a strong numerical response to deciduous tree seed abundance. Deer will also eat considerable quantities of seeds such as acorns during the autumn. Some seed-eaters must wait for the seeds to fall to the ground before they can exploit them, others including birds, flying squirrels and tree squirrels have the advantage of being able to utilise the seeds before they disperse. (The influence of seed competitors on seed caching strategies of squirrels has been discussed in Chapter 3.) However, it appears that it is unusual for more than one or two seed-eating species, which share similar ecological requirements in other respects, to occur together in the same forest habitat (Gurnell, 1985). For example, marked seasonal changes in climate, cover and food supply are characteristic of temperate and boreal forests and some seed-eating mammals such as chipmunks, ground-dwelling squirrels and dormice hibernate during the critical winter months. Thus, partly because of their size and arboreal habitats, and excluding predators and man, there appear to be no forest animals which have any influence on tree squirrel numbers, with the possible exception of flying squirrels. Flying squirrels could compete with tree squirrels for both food and nesting sites. Of the three Holarctic species, two live in North America; the northern tree squirrel (*Glaucomys sabrinus*) from northern boreal forests and the southern flying squirrel (*G. volans*) from eastern hardwood forests, and the other, the Russian flying squirrel (*Pteromys volans*), is found in boreal forests from Eastern Europe across to China. They eat similar foods to tree squirrels but their nocturnal habits reduce the possibility of direct contact between them. This is not so with nesting sites. Nancy Wells-Gosling (1985) describes how pine squirrels are the chief competitors to flying squirrels for nesting sites in her study area in Michigan. It appears that a flying squirrel may repel a pine squirrel (which is larger in size) which is simply exploring its nest entrance, but if a pine squirrel is persistent, the flying squirrel has to abandon its nest.

9 Squirrels and man

With reference to the introduced grey squirrel, a recent article in a well known British magazine stated: 'People still think of the grey as cuddly, delighting children in the park with his fluffy tail, bright little eyes and entrancing ways. He is nothing more than a vicious tree pest, with his ratty nose, protruding teeth and vile temper' (Drummond, 1984).

Here we have two very different images of the grey squirrel in Britain, on the one hand an attractive, mischievous animal, on the other hand, a tree rat. Without doubt, describing the grey squirrel as a tree rat is misguided and misleading. Today the general public have a more enlightened attitude towards wildlife. Squirrels are a delight to see and hear in our city parks, gardens and woods. Park squirrels can become very tame and will take food from the hand, although it should be pointed out that they seldom make good pets (a licence is required to keep grey squirrels in Britain). It is true, of course, that sometimes they can be a nuisance. Very rarely, park squirrels start to attack pedestrians for no apparent reason and they have to be removed. Occasionally squirrels damage thatched or shingle roofs or enter lofts and buildings (especially outhouses and holiday cabins). Apart from blocking up the entrance holes (e.g. with wire netting), placing large quantities of naphthalene or paradichlorobenzene (both normally used for killing moths) in the entrance to a building or in a nest can act as a repellant. A useful repellant for keeping squirrels off of wood shingles is a solution of copper naphthenate in linseed oil (Marsh and Howard, 1977).

Squirrels have also been known to use power lines to travel from one place to another and they sometimes gnaw through the insulation on electricity cables. This damage can be prevented by protecting the cable with metal sheaths or coating the cable with small glass beads or sand, though it makes the cable a lot more expensive. Squirrels can be prevented from gaining access to cable or telegraph poles (or individual trees such as walnut trees) by wrapping about 1 m of sheet metal around the pole 2 to 3 m from the ground.

Squirrels are opportunists and readily take fruit and nuts put out for birds, even if the food is placed on a table. To prevent this, bird tables should be sited well away from trees or cables which would give them aerial access and, again, sheet metal should be wrapped around the table

167

support (or a metal pole used for the support). If bird tables have to be sited near trees, then metal 'umbrellas' can be effective in keeping the squirrels at bay. Squirrels may also take eggs and young from bird nests, such as those of pigeons, tits or pheasants, during the spring and it is possible that particular individuals gain a taste for these foods. However, squirrels are probably of minor importance compared with other bird predators, and there is no reason why they should be singled out in this respect. Squirrels can be a nuisance to keepers during the winter because they take the grain feed put out for pheasants.

More importantly, squirrels from time to time cause economic damage to arable crops, orchards and market garden produce (e.g. soft fruits). This sort of damage usually occurs at the local level in areas adjacent to mature woodland and when squirrel densities are high. Squirrels may dig up bulbs, corms and newly sown seed, eat ripe fruit or damage plastic bird netting. It is known that the corn crops of early settlers in North America particularly suffered from the attention of tree squirrels (Kenward, 1983). In severe cases, the farmer may turn to some form of local control, such as trapping or shooting, during the damage period.

Damage to forestry is of increasing importance and will be considered in detail below. Squirrels, however, can also help the forester. Pine squirrel caches in North America have provided foresters with an economic source of conifer seed. Because pine squirrels collect the best cones for their caches, germination rates are higher from seeds collected from caches than those collected from trees. Further, by their digging and seed burying activities, squirrels may aid the germination process (Alexander and Olsen, 1980); in contrast, squirrels, along with other seed predators, have been accused of preventing the natural regeneration of forests by consuming all the available seed. Certainly all the seed will be eaten in some years, but this is most unlikely to occur in years when trees produce very large crops (Gurnell, 1983). Historically, squirrels have been very important to mankind for another reason, and that is as game animals and this will be examined later under the general heading of squirrel hunting. I consider the management of squirrel populations at the end of the chapter.

SQUIRREL DAMAGE

Many types of mammal remove bark from live trees. Some, such as hares, rabbit, deer and cattle eat the bark, others such as bears, dormice and squirrels, leave the bark but scrape off and eat the exposed unlignified tissue under the bark. These are the conducting tissues of the tree; water and dissolved nutrients pass up the plant from the roots and organic materials down from the leaves. A limited amount of bark removal does little harm, the damaged part scars over (called callus growth) and sometimes the trunk grows round it leaving few outward signs that it had occurred. However, this degrades the value of the timber and bark removal makes the tree more susceptible to attack by microorganisms. One example is the spread of sooty bark disease caused by a fungus (*Cryptostroma cortocale*) on sycamore in Devon, which has been attributed to grey squirrels debarking the trees or eating terminal shoots (e.g. Abbott *et al*, 1977). If the tree is ring-barked or girdled (removal of bark right round the stem) then the consequences are more serious; the conducting system can no longer work and the upper part of the trunk or branch dies. This sort of damage to the base of the tree trunk effectively kills the tree, whilst damage higher up the trunk or in the canopy stunts the tree's growth and may result in the top being blown out of the tree (called wind-snap).

How squirrels remove the bark from the trees depends whether it is basal damage (up to 1 to 2 m from the ground), stem damage (higher up the tree), or damage to the branches in the canopy. This is partly related to the thickness of the bark which varies with size, age and species of tree. Young trees (e.g. between 10 and 40 years old) which are growing rapidly appear to be particularly vulnerable to squirrel damage. Grey squirrels cause basal damage by gnawing off the bark in small pieces, leaving the pieces on the ground and tooth marks on the tree. Where the bark is thinner higher up the main stem squirrels pull off the bark in strips 1 to 2 cm wide and several centimetres long. The unlignified tissue is eaten either from the inner part of the bark strip or off of the exposed part of the tree. In the latter instance, the tooth marks fade after a few weeks as the remains of the unlignified tissue dry, and so teeth marks are not left on the underlying woody tissue. The bark strips either fall to the ground or are left hanging on the tree. Squirrels remove stem bark in different ways. Red squirrels in Finland, for example, tear the bark upwards in a spiral fashion, the spirals going either to the left or to the right of the stem. Western grey squirrels start the stripping with their teeth and then use their forefeet to pull away the bark, again often in a spiral manner. In this case claw marks are left on exposed surfaces of the tree. Grey squirrels in Britain tend to strip the bark downwards and not usually in a spiral fashion.

Commercial foresters are particularly interested in the damage to their crops by squirrels (and other animals), and this may be one reason why the number of reports of squirrel damage has increased in recent years as more and more forests are intensively managed. Damage can vary considerably among species, size classes, individual trees and years. Tree spacing can also influence the amount of damage inflicted (Figure 9.1). It is clear that most squirrel species debark trees but in many cases this damage is insignificant. For example, red squirrels in Britain rarely reach densities whereby the damage becomes economically important. On the other hand, red squirrels are not totally innocent and damage to Scots pine, Norway spruce and European larch can be severe when densities approach two animals per hectare (Shorten, 1962). Damage can be particularly serious at the local level. A forester who loses a large proportion of his crop because of squirrel damage will not look kindly on squirrels. Reports of serious damage reach the scientific literature from time to time. For instance, a considerable amount of red squirrel ring-barking damage to young Scots pine trees was reported from different areas in Finland in 1954 and 1962 (Pulliainen and Salonen, 1963). In 1980 pine squirrels damaged more than a quarter of young lodgepole pine trees in one study in British Columbia (Sullivan and Sullivan, 1982b, c) and Western grey squirrels have recently caused serious losses to timber production in Jackson County, Oregon (Baldwin *et al*, 1986).

Since the grey squirrel was introduced into Britain and began to spread throughout the country (Chapter 2), it has been the centre of a great deal of attention because of its bark stripping habit. This was somewhat puzzling

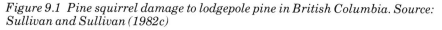

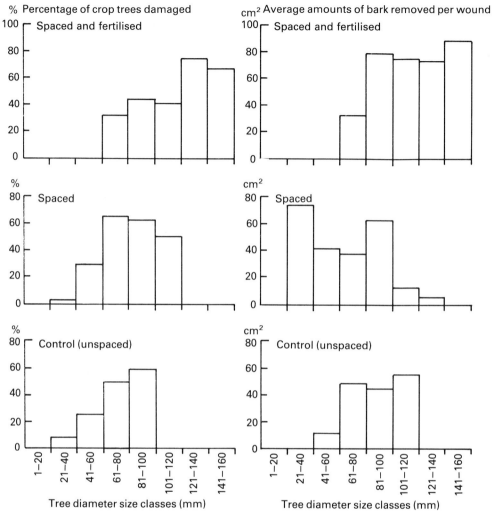

Figure 9.1 Pine squirrel damage to lodgepole pine in British Columbia. Source: Sullivan and Sullivan (1982c)

because there have been very few reports of grey squirrel damage in the USA (Don, 1981). An early report of damage was to American chestnut in West Virginia (Brooks, 1922), and damage to sugar maple (from which maple syrup is obtained) has been reported from Connecticut (Britton, 1933), Michigan (Brenneman, 1954) and Minnesota (Irving and Beer, 1963). The study by Irving and Beer was carried out in a mixed oak-maple stand and they found no direct relationship between squirrel density and bark stripping frequency or between acorn crops and bark stripping. Two possible reasons why more extensive damage has not been reported from the USA are that there have been no large plantations of vulnerable crops within the range of the grey squirrel (at least until recently) and that hunting has kept the numbers of squirrels below levels at which damage might have occurred. Although the grey squirrel poses a serious problem to commercial foresters in Britain, it is not easy to quantify the loss in timber production. In one area of England (the Chilterns) it was estimated that grey squirrel damage caused losses of up to 10 per cent of the timber from 15 per cent of the commercially grown oak and beech trees (H. Pepper, pers. comm.). Beech and sycamore are favoured by grey squirrels in England but maple, ash, larch, hemlock, hornbeam, poplar, birch and pine are other species which are attacked from time to time (Rowe, 1984; Rowe and Gill, 1985).

Why do squirrels debark trees? This may seem a curious question to ask but it has been a rich area of debate, particularly in relation to the damage caused by grey squirrels in Britain. The theories have been many, including a 'need to gnaw' to prevent excessive tooth growth (this can be dismissed), to obtain trace nutrients (unlikely), to obtain moisture during dry periods (possibly occasionally but damage occurs near forest fire tanks and water courses), to line nests (this certainly occurs and usually involves dead or soft bark but it is not significant), as a form of displaced agonistic behaviour and to obtain food (Kenward, 1983). The last two theories are the most promising. In the case of the agonistic behaviour theory, most squirrels appear to cause serious damage in the spring and summer, peaking between May and July. This is a time of high breeding activity and the dispersal of spring-born young (if breeding started early in the year). Many agonistic encounters may occur within the population (Chapter 5) and it is suggested that somehow (as yet unexplained) some of the aggressive behaviour is channelled into debarking behaviour, perhaps by juvenile or subordinate animals. This is not a very satisfactory explanation since, as Robert Kenward points out, the squirrels eat the sap rather than just attack the trees. They could be marking their home range or territory but marking with scent would seem to be a much more efficient method of doing this and removing large pieces of bark from, for example, the base of many adjacent trees in a block would similarly argue against this. There is support for the agonistic theory in the general sense in that the amount of damage is considerably more serious when the density of spring-born juveniles is high. This suggests some sort of triggering of debarking by agonistic interaction or possibly exploratory feeding. However, this is not a straightforward linear relationship as damage appears to level off when the density of juveniles in the population reaches about 0.25 juveniles/ha (Kenward and Parish, 1986).

Robert Kenward's recent research suggests that it may simply be a liking for sap which is responsible for a lot of debarking behaviour. The main damage period (May to July) is at a time when favoured foods such as tree seed and fungi are scarce (Chapter 3) and sap flow is highest, and in species such as the pine and the red squirrel it may be that squirrels debark the trees to get at this energy rich source of food. It should also be remembered that the inner bark of ponderosa pine trees is one of the staple foods of abert squirrels, but during the winter rather than the summer (Chapter 3). However, it is not as simple as this. For instance, there is not a great deal of food value in the sap in the amounts which are eaten (Kenward, 1982); abert squirrels lose weight if fed only on inner bark and grey squirrels lose weight in the most seriously damaged areas. Also captive grey squirrels cause damage to trees in large outside enclosures in the presence of excess food (including peanuts which they favour). Also putting out baited traps or poison hoppers in vulnerable crops can be counterproductive in that the damage to the nearby trees increases.

However, the thickness of the unlignified tissues varies considerably from tree to tree, from region to region and from year to year and the squirrels seem to attack those trees with the most sap (Figure 9.2). These trees would be growing vigorously and, as we noted above, lodgepole pine trees which had been spaced or thinned out (and presumably were growing more quickly) received more damage from pine squirrels than trees which had not been thinned (Figure 9.1). A liking for sap, therefore, would explain the wide variation in tree damage. In this case it may be quantity of sap rather than quality but that both may be important is suggested by the pine squirrel and lodgepole pine study in British Columbia. The damage was significantly more serious on trees which had been fertilised than those which had not (Figure 9.1). Finally, Robert Kenward is finding some evidence that the amount of damage in one year is related to the amount of damage in the previous year. That is, some squirrels resident in a forest may learn to debark trees.

The mystery of why squirrel damage occurs is compounded by the fact that damage does not always occur between May and July, even in Britain. Occasionally damage may be reported earlier or later in the year. Damage by grey squirrels in North America has been reported to occur between October and December (Don, 1981), and Western grey squirrels in Oregon debark conifer trees between mid-February and April (Baldwin *et al*, 1986). In summary, as yet there is no universal explanation for squirrel damage but since most detailed studies show that squirrels eat the unlignified tissues and select those trees which are fastest growing or have the most sap, some form of nutritional benefit remains a strong candidate. However, in some circumstances bark removal may be triggered by agonistic behaviour; clearly more work is necessary, so that appropriate control programmes can be formulated and used only when necessary.

Figure 9.2 Relationship between grey squirrel tree damage to beech and sycamore (expressed as a bark stripping index) and average phloem volume per unit area at 30 woodland sites in England over 3 years. Source: Kenward and Parish (1986)

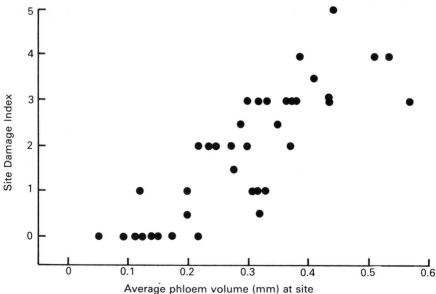

SQUIRREL HUNTING

As far back as the records show, squirrels have been a favourite game animal, hunted for their fur, as food and more recently as a sport. During the Middle Ages, luxury furs of sable, ermine, fox, marten and otter were highly prized, but squirrel furs were also much sought after. As one might expect, squirrels do not command the same price as some of the larger, rarer fur-bearers. (A Siberian hunter today will get about 15 roubles for a squirrel fur, but more than 200 roubles for a sable). In many countries, such as Finland, furs were at one time used to pay taxes and in fact the Finnish word for money, *raha*, originally meant the pelt of a red squirrel. Squirrel furs have been used by rich and poor alike. Wealthy people used them to line fine cloaks or gloves, or made them into collars, felt hats or boas (coils of fur worn round the neck by ladies). The poor used them, along with other cheaper furs, to make much needed warm clothing. Interestingly, the manufacture of boas from squirrel skins was a flourishing business in Britain at one time. In 1839 over 2,700,000 skins were imported into Britain largely for this purpose. Later Germany took over as the experts in dressing and preparing squirrel skins. Squirrel tails, at one time sold by weight, have also been used as fringes to cloaks or in the manufacture of the so-called camels' hair paint-brush (Poland, 1892).

By the fifteenth century in Western Europe, the demand for furs was so high that the supply of native furs was insufficient (Phillips, 1961). Europeans began to buy furs in large quantities, including squirrel pelts (then known commercially as calabars) from Scandinavia, Russia and Eastern Europe. The Russians greatly increased their trade in furs after they conquered Siberia, a vast country rich in fur-bearing animals. Towards the end of the sixteenth century, Holland, for example, regularly bought large quantities of squirrel, rabbit and weasel skins, as well as many luxury furs, from Arkhangelsk on the edge of the White Sea. All the early squirrel trade throughout the Old World was of course concerned with the red squirrel, but there were many colour varieties according to where they came from. For example, dark 'blue' skins came from Tobolsky in the Ural mountains and from further east in Yakutsk, Okhotsk and Sakaminoi, light 'blue' skins came from Yeniseisk, and red skins from Kazan in Russia. The sixteenth century was also a time when North American indians were catching many types of fur-bearing animal, which they used as barter with early fishermen and traders from Europe (particularly the French) in return for weapons, textiles and trinkets.

The fur trade lost some impetus in Europe after the sixteenth century as prices rose and fashions changed from furs to manufactured textiles, but trading was still high between North America, Russia, Scandinavia and China. The famous Hudson Bay Company in Western Canada traded in pine squirrel skins at one time. In 1886 it is reported that over 8,000 skins were imported by the Company, but numbers quickly declined over the next few years as their commercial value went down. Pine squirrels are still hunted in Canada today, for their fur rather than as a sport (Flyger and Gates, 1982b). Squirrels in the northern coniferous forests of the Palaearctic are also hunted for their fur. In contrast, squirrel furs have a very limited market value in the USA but squirrels are important as hunting recreation and as such can produce a considerable turnover of money in relation to licence fees, ammunition and travel.

Squirrels also make good eating, particularly the larger species. For those interested, young squirrels may be fried or broiled like rabbit but older and tougher animals may require par-boiling to make them tender. Some recipes for cooking squirrels are given by Ashbrook (1951). Squirrels would have been a valuable source of protein to poor people in days gone by, and are still eaten throughout North America and in many other places. Siberian hunters may also feed the carcasses to their dogs or use the flesh as carnivore bait, but this is discouraged in North America. Insecticide residues were found in fox squirrel meat in Illinois, but the concentrations were too low to be of any danger to the squirrels or to the people who ate them (Havera and Duzan, 1977).

Squirrels have been hunted in various ways, most of them based on shooting, snaring or trapping, but not all. One exception is the method

Figure 9.3 Dead-fall traps (top) and snares (bottom). Source: Petrides (1946)

Attached to bent sapling

carried out by the Tarahumara Indians of the Sierra Madre in North America. Once they had located a squirrel, they cut down the tree it was hiding in and set a hunting dog on the hapless animal (see Brown, 1984). Another method, not quite so dramatic and still in use, is to flush squirrels from nests by poking the dreys out of the trees with long extendable poles. Drey-poking is one method used to control grey squirrels in Britain (see below). Once flushed, the squirrel is shot. Today, shotguns or rifles (e.g. 0.22 calibre) are the standard weapons for shooting squirrels. This can be done by either flushing the squirrels in some way, such as above or by using dogs, and shooting them before they escape, or by using stealth and quietly stalking them. The latter technique is apparently more successful (Brown, 1984). Various types of traps are also used to catch squirrels including single-catch and multi-catch live traps, and kill traps such as dead-fall (Figure 9.3), Fenn and Imbra traps (Rowe, 1980; Bateman, 1979). Snares may be used (e.g. in Siberia) but they are not particularly easy to set to catch squirrels (Figure 9.3). In fact a certain amount of fieldcraft is necessary if snaring or trapping is to be efficient and successful.

It is not possible to make any broad generalisations about how many squirrels are taken each year. Flyger and Gates (1982a) quote figures for the number of fox and grey squirrels harvested in different parts of their range in the eastern USA. They suggest that about 40,000,000 grey squirrels are harvested annually. In Canada, one to three million pine squirrels are harvested each year (Flyger and Gates, 1982b). Obviously numbers taken vary according to the species, the region, the number of hunters and squirrel densities. It was established in Chapter 7 that squirrel numbers vary considerably between years and hunting returns have been used as indicators of population trends. Uhlig (1957), for example, stated that the number of grey squirrels killed per 1,000 acres during the first 1,000 gun-hours in West Virginia gave a 'reasonable estimate of population level'. Such a measure of population size must be used cautiously since it is difficult to disentangle the effects of pre-season density and hunting effort on squirrel returns. Either or both can be important. Charles Nixon and his colleagues (Nixon et al, 1974) found that the number of fox squirrels harvested in Ohio was associated with pre-season density but not hunting pressure. Brown (1984), on the other hand, reports the reverse for squirrels (mainly abert squirrels) in Arizona (Figure 9.4). Figure 9.4 also demonstrates how squirrel hunting has gained in popularity in Arizona over the last 20 years. In northern coniferous forests the numbers killed varies more directly in relation to pre-season densities. Some 30 to 40 years ago in Finland, where red squirrels are shot only for their fur, the annual kill sometimes reached almost 2.5 million animals (most of which were exported) but in other years no more than a few thousand were killed or hunting was stopped altogether. More recently, only 1,000 animals were killed in 1976 and in 1977, and 3,300 in 1983. Squirrels were totally protected between 1978 and 1982 (Paavo Voipio and Harto Linden, pers. comm.).

Mikheeva (1973) indicates that squirrel hunting in the Ural Mountains effectively regulates itself. For example, the method of hunting, whether or not dogs can be used, and the harsh climatic conditions all influence numbers captured. Consequently, catches are low when squirrel densities are low. Overharvesting squirrels apparently does not occur. Elsewhere, countries regulate hunting by having an open season which, in theory at

Figure 9.4 Squirrel hunting records for Arizona, 1962–1982. Source: Brown (1984)

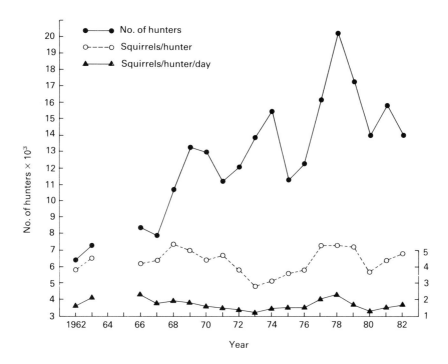

least, can be adjusted in duration according to squirrel stocks. Thus, there was no hunting season between 1978 and 1982 in Finland, while in 1983 the open season was from 1 December to 15 January. Open seasons are generally in the autumn and early winter when the squirrels have their new winter coat and, as a rule, are not breeding. Even so, the dates of the open season tend to vary from place to place (Figure 9.5). Some North American hunters apparently would prefer an earlier opening to the shooting season because hunting is easier when the squirrels are feeding on seed in the trees rather than on fallen seed on the ground. The objection to this is that many females will be nursing litters of young during early autumn, and more juveniles will be present later in the year to swell the numbers. As well as regulating the duration of the open season, local authorities may stipulate hunting hours and set bag limits and possession limits. As an example, in 1982 the Colorado Division of Wildlife stipulated an open season from 11 September to 28 February, hunting hours from half an hour before sunrise to sunset, and issued individual daily bag limits of 5 fox and 5 pine squirrels, and a possession limit of 10 of each species. Abert squirrels were protected in most parts of the State in order to allow numbers to recover from low levels.

What is the impact of hunting on squirrel populations? Regular hunting can affect population structure as well as numbers but in the long-term, hunting does not appear to seriously affect population numbers except in a few special circumstances. Squirrel populations are remarkably resilient

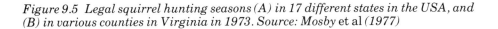

Figure 9.5 Legal squirrel hunting seasons (A) in 17 different states in the USA, and (B) in various counties in Virginia in 1973. Source: Mosby et al (1977)

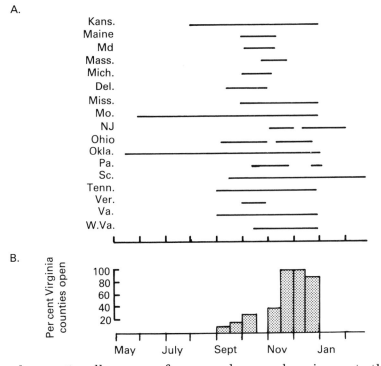

and can naturally recover from very low numbers in one to three years if food and weather conditions are favourable. Generally, hunted populations have proportionally lower numbers in the older age groups than unexploited populations, probably because they are more susceptible to being captured or shot, and there is a tendency towards a lower average age in the population (Lampio, 1967). It should be remembered that many of the older squirrels and most of the juveniles which are killed would normally be lost from the population even without hunting since, on average, the year-to-year survival for these groups is low (Chapter 7). The view of many wildlife managers in the USA is that hunting has only a minor impact on fox and grey squirrel populations and that differences in the length of the open season and individual bag limits have little effect. Fox and grey squirrels live at quite high densities and have a high turnover of individuals; natural mortality is often two to four time that of hunting mortality (e.g. Flyger and Gates, 1982a). However, overharvesting can occur from time to time, especially at a local level such as in small, isolated woods which cannot be quickly recolonised. The length of the open season is likely to be more important for squirrels which live in northern coniferous forests at lower densities than fox and grey squirrels. Therefore, natural mortality resulting from poor food and weather is probably more important than hunting mortality in affecting squirrel population levels, but at the same time, recovery from low numbers, particularly in northern coniferous forests, may be encouraged by adjusting the duration of the open shooting season.

SQUIRREL MANAGEMENT

It follows from the above that there are two main reasons why squirrel populations are managed. Firstly, squirrels are cropped or culled and used by man. This category includes squirrels which are killed for food, for their fur or as a sport. The aims of management, therefore, are directed towards maintaining populations of squirrels in good health and at densities approaching those which can be sustained by the habitat. These densities vary considerably according to the species and the type of forest. Secondly, squirrels cause damage to man's crops or artifacts, that is they can be a pest. In this case management is concerned with reducing population numbers by various control methods to levels which minimise damage. It is worth pointing out that the long-term eradication of a population of squirrels from an area is, in practical terms, very difficult if not impossible to achieve and it is not normally considered as a viable management strategy. In addition, squirrels are not considered important vectors of human disease and are unlikely to be controlled for this reason. There is a third reason why some sub-species or populations of squirrels require managing. This relates to management for recreation or because they are in danger of dying out. Measures are taken, therefore to conserve them. Such is the case with the abert squirrel in some states in the USA, the Delmarva fox squirrel (a subspecies of fox squirrel) in Maryland, and the red squirrel in England.

Judy Rowe (1983) has reviewed management strategies in relation to Holarctic *Sciurus* species and has pointed out that the objectives of management vary, not only in different parts of the range of a species, but also within a country. Consequently, conflicts in management objectives can occur. For example, the red squirrel is managed as a game animal in Switzerland but in 1969 in the Bernese Oberland debarking damage was sufficiently high to warrant financial compensation to landowners. The different management tactics which have been or are currently adopted are shown in Table 9.1 and will be discussed in more detail below. Whatever the management strategy, the primary objective is either to increase or to decrease numbers. In order to fully understand how these should be accomplished within the context of a management programme, it is essential to understand the natural demography and spatial dynamics of squirrel populations in relation to different types of forest habitat, and to the communities of plants and animals to which they belong. These have been discussed in earlier chapters of this book.

Squirrel Densities and Habitat Quality

It is not easy to define what is meant by habitat quality but I consider that it reflects in some way the total requirements of a particular species in terms of, for example, food availability, cover, and nest sites, as well as predator pressure and competition from other species. Predation and competition are not normally considered in habitat assessment since they are very difficult things to quantify. In practice, habitat assessment is based mainly on measuring characteristics of the vegetation and food supply. For squirrels, such vegetation characteristics include tree species, age and density, cover, nest sites, seed crops and alternative food supplies. A straightforward approach, therefore, to assessing habitat quality would be to use squirrel population census techniques to survey a number of

Table 9.1 Squirrel management strategies and tactics. D = damage prevention/control, U = hunting/utilisation, C = conservation, ? = no clear evidence. (Modified from Rowe, 1983)

Strategy			Tactic
			Habitat management
D			Change to single species (monocultures)
	U	C	Provide mixture of species (to stabilise seed food)
	U	C	Plant native species, plant exotic species
	U	C	Modify age class of tree
	U	C	Clear-cut (clear-fell), leave islands of nest/feed trees
	U	C	Selective cut (thin), leave nest/feed trees
	U	C	Leave tree corridors between blocks
	U	C	Use nest boxes
D			Protect individual trees, telegraph poles, bird tables
D			Chemical repellants (buildings and trees)
	U?	C	Supplementary food
	U	C	Supplementary water
D	U		Shooting (+/− drey poking)
D	U	C	Trapping (snare/cage/kill)
D			Poison
—	—	—	Manipulate disease/natural predation
D?			Reproductive inhibitors
D?	U?		Improve hunter access
D?			Bounty schemes
	U	C	Damage compensation
D	U	C	Legislation
		C?	Reduce competition from other squirrel species
	U	C?	Introduce/translocate
D?	U	C	Non-intervention

types of habitat and infer habitat quality from estimated squirrel densities. Then, using the results from the survey, any number of other habitats can be indirectly evaluated. Lastly, it is theoretically possible, although seldom done, to put together habitat quality assessments for a number of different species (e.g. forest animals) to formulate assessments for entire communities (Figure 9.6). In fact, sometimes a primary objective in managing communities is taken simply as maximising the number of species of plants and animals by maximising habitat diversity (Van Horne, 1983).

This 'blanket' strategy has its merits in many situations but by no means all, especially when particular species are named within the management plan. It depends, for example, upon the size of the area to be managed, the spatial dynamics of the animals in question and whether they are habitat generalists or habitat specialists. One example will illustrate this point. In England, red squirrels are in danger of disappearing completely from both deciduous and coniferous forests (Chapter 8). It has been suggested that their best chance of survival is within large tracts of mature coniferous forest but such areas are becoming increasingly

Figure 9.6 Three levels of habitat quality assessment. Source: Van Horne (1983)

Decreasing resolution ━━━━━━━━▶

LEVEL 1	LEVEL 2	LEVEL 3
Direct evaluation of habitat quality for a single species using on-site data	Indirect evaluation of habitat quality for a single species using on-site data	Indirect evaluation of habitat quality for a wildlife community

scarce. One reason for this is that habitat diversity within these forests is increased for reasons of forest management or for its amenity value. This is accomplished by cutting rides and clearings within stands of conifer, or by planting blocks or strips of hardwood trees. The problem is that this type of habitat management encourages the infiltration and establishment of grey squirrels which, in turn, could hinder the long term conservation of the red squirrel. Further work on habitat management as a conservation strategy for the red squirrel in England is required.

There are two further points worth making in relation to the application of the above approach to the assessment of habitat quality for squirrels. First, density in itself may not be a good measure of habitat quality. For example, young squirrels may occur at quite high densities in marginal habitats during early winter (Chapter 7). However, they may not survive through to the following spring, or, if they do, they may not reproduce very successfully. Therefore, it is necessary to consider carefully the time of the year when the populations are sampled. Also, an estimation of the success of a population should include measures of survival and reproductive success, as well as density. Second, it is labour intensive and time consuming to census squirrel populations in several habitats at the same time. Also, because squirrel population numbers vary widely, sampling should be carried out in different years. Actually, the best indication of good quality habitats can probably be obtained with the minimum of effort in years of overall low densities. Figures taken from the literature can be helpful and I used this source of information to find out the average densities which different species were able to achieve in different habitats (Gurnell, 1983). However, density figures so obtained are not directly comparable because of the different methods used to obtain them, and detailed habitat measures are not as a rule presented. Because of the practical problems of studying squirrels' populations in many areas, indices of habitat utilisation have been developed and include nest counts and the assessment of feeding remains. These methods, discussed more fully in Chapter 7, are promising but have not been fully tested for many species.

In conclusion, broad surveys of habitat quality are of little use without good baseline data obtained from intensive field studies. Furthermore, the effectiveness of habitat manipulation as a management tactic can only be assessed by subsequently monitoring the squirrel populations over several years.

Habitat Management

Squirrel stocks can be maintained or increased by providing the essential requirements of a good food supply and nest sites (Ffolliott and Patton,

1975). These requirements have to be considered in conjunction with timber production, and tactics may differ depending upon whether coniferous or deciduous forests are being managed. In fact, the success of particular species of squirrel depends upon the restocking programme. For example, in the north-east of the USA felling deciduous trees and replanting with conifers resulted in a decrease in numbers of grey squirrels and an increase in the number of pine squirrels. (This is of obvious interest to red squirrel conservationists in England.) Den (hollow) tree management for grey squirrels has been discussed by Sanderson (1975) and the potential usefulness of nest boxes has been considered in Chapter 7.

Tree seed crops (the main food of squirrels) vary markedly in size from one year to the next and planting a mix of different species (e.g. pine with spruce) can provide a more stable food supply in the long term. In a large commercial forest, timber rotation ages can also influence squirrel densities. Squirrels disperse after clear-cutting (Table 9.2) and do not re-enter the clear-cuts for many years; 15 in the case of grey squirrels in Ohio (Nixon *et al*, 1980). Squirrel densities in border habitats may temporarily increase after clear-cutting. Three further considerations for the forest manager are: the size of clear-cuts in relation to total forest area, the provision of travel corridors between uncut stands, and the provision of islands of good seed trees and nest or hollow trees within clear-cuts. In order to maintain grey squirrel densities, Charles Nixon and his colleagues (1980) recommended the use of small (<8 ha), narrow (<160 m) clear-cuts within forests where 40 to 60 per cent of stands were maintained at seed-producing age. Leaving islands of trees within clear-cuts is a long-term tactic since the islands may not be particularly effective until the rotation is 15 to 25 years old.

Selective cutting, that is thinning or harvesting only some of the trees within a stand, does not have such a marked impact on squirrel populations (Nixon *et al*, 1980). However, numbers may be reduced following selective cutting. Densities of Kaibab squirrels declined and home ranges increased in cut areas of ponderosa pine compared to control areas (Patton *et al*, 1985). Therefore, the same decisions in relation to cut area, and the number and diameter of remaining trees must be made by

Table 9.2 Pine squirrel densities before and after logging in June 1972 in Alaska (from Wolff, 1975)

Treatment	Total area (ha)	No. squirrels/ha	
		Before logging (1972)	After logging (1974)
Clear cut blocks	3.6	1.2	0
Thinned blocks (83 per cent trees removed)	7.2	1.5	0.5
Uncut forest adjacent to cut area	14.6	1.6	1.3
Uncut forest 3 km from cut area	21.0	1.3	1.5

the forester interested in maintaining squirrel populations. Again, leaving nest and feed trees can reduce the effects of selected timber harvest on squirrel populations. Groups of trees with one or more large conifers or logs are also important for providing the right environment for food caching by pine and douglas squirrels (Vahle and Patton, 1983).

In Maryland the Delmarva fox squirrel is in danger of dying out and Lustig and Flyger (1976) recommended habitat manipulation as a conservation tactic. To provide fox squirrels with a more open forest which they prefer, they suggested the removal of shrub and sub-canopy vegetation by light burning or cattle grazing. They also considered reducing the grey squirrel populations in the same forests to minimise possible interspecific competitive effects. However, they judged that this was practically impossible.

Apart from manipulating the tree species and age structure of a forest, it is more difficult to apply habitat management tactics which result in lower squirrel densities. Of course, removing den and feed trees could discourage the build-up of dense populations and this approach may be useful in certain situations. William C. McComb (1984) has made several recommendations for increasing and decreasing grey squirrel populations in urban forests in the USA. These are listed below and, following the above discussion, it is possible to see how the general tenor of some of these recommendations can be applied to many programmes of small woodland management.

A. Procedures to increase squirrel populations:

(1) Protect large mast-trees with wide-spreading crowns and further encourage them by thinning.
(2) Remove exotic instead of native tree species where there is a choice of tree removal. Plant a variety of native trees (e.g. red oaks, white oaks, hickories and walnuts in the United States) to ensure stable food conditions.
(3) Protect den trees and erect nest boxes (using nest boxes resulted in higher squirrel populations in Washington, D.C.).

To these I add:
(4) Provide a source of water if it is not naturally available, especially in areas subject to summer droughts.

B. Procedures to reduce squirrel populations:

(1) Prune mast-bearing trees to reduce crown volume. Remove mast trees and leave non-mast trees where possible.
(2) Plant small-seeded evergreen or deciduous species (e.g. birch, willow, elm) or exotics.
(3) Remove den trees and supplemental food sources such as bird feeders.

To these I add:
(4) Isolate the area from 'good' squirrel habitats.

Squirrel Control

Habitat management may help in reducing squirrel densities but whether it can reduce damage requires further research. Damage to agricultural or horticultural crops or buildings requires prompt action when it occurs.

Forest managers, however, must plan ahead and try and minimise damage before it occurs. The main grey squirrel damage period in Britain extends from May to July and decisions as to whether or how much control should be carried out must be worked out before this time. For each stand of timber, the forester may consider questions such as:

(1) Does the stand consist of a species usually vulnerable to damage?
(2) Are the trees in the stand at a vulnerable age for damage to occur?
(3) Has the stand been thinned recently or fertiliser applied?
(4) Were tree seeds abundant the previous autumn in the stand or neighbouring stands?
(5) Was it a mild winter?

If the answers to all these questions are yes then it is likely that squirrel populations will be high and damage extensive. Affirmative answers to questions (1) and (4) would also be enough to implement control measures providing the crop was of sufficient value (quality) to justify expenditure on control. Control is normally carried out before or during the main damage period. There are three ways to control grey squirrels in Britain. Firstly, they can be shot and this may often be done in conjunction with drey poking (there is no legal open or closed season in Britain), they can be trapped with live or humane kill traps (there are regulations with respect to this as laid down in the 1981 Wildlife and Countryside Act), or they can be poisoned according to the provisions laid down by the 1973 Squirrels (Warfarin) Order. Bounty schemes to encourage shooting do not seem to work and they certainly failed in Britain. (Where squirrels are managed as game animals in Europe, monetary compensation may be given by the government when damage occurs.) Cage trapping is one of the best methods for controlling squirrels but it is more labour intensive than poisoning. The anticoagulant poison, Warfarin, on a bait of whole wheat and at a concentration of 0.02%, is used in Britain. This is a chronic poison best known for its use in controlling rats. Animals have to eat several meals of the poison bait before they succumb. Poisoning is illegal in certain counties and, now that the red squirrel is a fully protected species in Britain (1981 Wildlife and Countryside Act), poisoning and trapping are illegal in any area where red squirrels are at risk. The poison is dispensed in hoppers of an approved design at densities of one to five per hectare. All poison should be removed from hoppers after poisoning operations have finished, and other precautions should be taken to protect non-target species. For example, hoppers should be secured firmly to the ground (to prevent deer or birds knocking them over and spilling the poison), or the hoppers should be fixed on platforms in areas where they may be disturbed by badgers. These guidelines must be strictly followed, and in fact when they have been followed, there have been very few reports of problems associated with Warfarin poisoning in the field. Laboratory trials suggest that mustelids are more at risk to secondary poisoning than tawny owls (Townsend et al, 1981; Townsend et al, 1984). Even though the use of Warfarin to control grey squirrels is an established practice, we should not be complacent and continual monitoring of the use and abuse of such poisons in wildlife control is essential (Rowe, 1983). In addition, research should be directed at possible ways of reducing squirrel populations which do not require the use of poisons.

In recent years, the potential use of the chemical control of reproduction in the grey squirrel has been examined by Elizabeth Johnson and her co-workers at Reading University (e.g. Johnson and Tait, 1983). Contraceptive chemicals, such as antiandrogens in males and oestrogins and progestins in females, would be dispensed on bait which would interfere with the normal reproductive physiology of the squirrels leading to sterility. Such a method would remove some of the objections to the use of poisons. Apart from stopping reproduction, studies on other animals such as rats indicate another possible advantage of chemosterilents in that the sterile animals would be left to deter the immigration of non-sterile animals from outside the population. The residents would gradually die through natural mortality. It is not clear whether this would occur in the case of squirrels, since the chemicals may affect their normal patterns of agonistic behaviour. Hopefully, future research will continue to examine this potential method of control.

Bibliography

Abbott, R.J., Bevercombe, G.P. and Rayner, D.M. (1977) 'Sooty bark disease of sycamore and the grey squirrel', *Trans. Br. mycol. Soc.* **69**, 507–8

Ackerman, R. and Weigl, P. (1970) 'Dominance relations of red and grey squirrels', *Ecology* **51**, 332–4

Aleksuik, M. (1971) 'Seasonal dynamics of brown adipose tissue function in the red squirrel (*Tamiasciurus hudsonicus*)', *Comp. Biochem. Physiol.* **38A**, 723–31

Alexander, L. and Olson, D.P. (1980) 'Grey squirrel influence on white pine establishment', *Trans. N.E. Wildl. Soc.* **37**, 23–31

Allen, D.L. (1943) 'Michigan fox squirrel management', *Michigan Dept. Conservation. Game Division Publ.* **100**, 1–404

Allen, D.S. and Aspey, W.P. (1986) 'Determinants of social dominance in eastern gray squirrels (*Sciurus carolinensis*): a quantitative assessment', *Anim. Behav.* **34**, 81–9

Armitage, K.B. and Harris, K.S. (1982) 'Spatial patterning in sympatric populations of Fox and Gray squirrels', *American Midl. Naturalist* **102**, 389–97

Ashbrook, F.G. (1951) *Raising small animals for pleasure and profit*, Van Nostrand, Princetown

Bahnak, B.R. and Kramm, K.R. (1977) 'The influence of environmental temperature and photoperiod on activity in the red squirrel (*Tamiasciurus hudsonicus*)', *Int. J. Biometeorol.* **21**, 164–180

—— (1979) 'The effects of temperature and photoperiod on activity in the red squirrel *Tamiasciurus hudsonicus*', *J. interdiscipl. Cycle Res.* **10**, 51–6

Bakken, A. (1959) 'Behaviour of gray squirrels', *Proc. Ann. Conf. S.E. Assoc. Game & Fish Comm.* **13**, 393–406

Baldwin, R.J., Howard, W.E. and Marsh, R.E. (1986) 'Debarking of conifers by western gray squirrel (*Sciurus griseus*)', in C. Richards (ed.) *Supplement to Tropical Pests Management*, Taylor and Francis, London

Bang, P. and Dahlstrom, P. (1974) *Animal tracks and signs*, Collins, London

Barash, D.P. (1982) *Sociobiology and behaviour* (2nd edn.), Hodder and Stoughton, London

Barkalow, F.S. (1967) 'A record gray squirrel litter', *J. Mamm.* **48**, 141

Barkalow, F.S., Hamilton, R.B. and Soots, R.F. (1970) 'The vital statistics of an unexploited gray squirrel population', *J. Wildl. Manage.* **34**, 489–500

Barnett, R.J. (1977) 'The effect of burial by squirrels on germination and survival of oak and hickory nuts', *American Midl. Naturalist* **98**, 319–30

Bateman, J.A. (1979) *Trapping: a practical guide*, David & Charles, Newton Abbot

Beale, D.M. (1962) 'Growth of the eye lens in relation to age in fox squirrels', *J. Wildl. Manage.* **26**, 208–11

185

Begon, M. and Mortimer, M. (1981) *Population ecology: a united study of animals and plants*, Blackwell Scientific Publications, Oxford

Benson, B.N. (1980) 'Dominance relationships, mating behaviour and scent marking in fox squirrels (*Sciurus niger*)', *Mammalia* **44**, 143–60

Berry, L.A., Michael, E.D. and Sanderson, H.R. (1978) 'Effect of population density on captive gray squirrels', *Trans. N.E. Wild. Soc.* **35**, 53–9

Black, C.C. (1972) 'Holarctic evolution and dispersal of squirrels (Rodentia: Sciuridae)', *Evolutionary Biology* **6**, 305–22

Blackmore, D.K. and Owen, D.G. (1968) 'Ectoparasites: The significance in British wild rodents', *Symp. zool. Soc. Lond.* **24**, 197–220

Bland, M.E. (1977) *Daily and seasonal activity patterns in the eastern gray squirrel*, Ph.D. thesis, University of Minnesota

Bobyr, G.Y. (1978) 'A contribution to the ecology of the Altaian squirrel (*Sciurus vulgaris altaicus*) acclimatized in the Teberdinskystate reservation', *Zoologicheskii Zhurnal* **57**, 253–59

Bolls, N. and Prefect, J.R. (1972) 'Summer metabolic rate of the gray squirrel', *Physiol. Zool.* **45**, 54–9

Bouffard, S.H. and Hein, D. (1978) 'Census methods for eastern gray squirrels', *J. Wildl. Manage.* **42**, 550–7

Brafield, A.E. and Llewellyn, M.J. (1982) *Animal energetics*, Blackie, Glasgow

Brenneman, W.S. (1954) 'Tree damage by squirrels: silviculturally significant?', *J. Forestry* **52**, 604

Britton, W.E. (1933) 'Injury to trees by squirrels', *Nat. Shade Tree Conf. Proc.* **9**, 85–91

Brooks, F.E. (1922) 'Note on a feeding habit of the grey squirrel', *J. Mamm.* **4**, 257–8

Brown, B.W. and Batzli, G.D. (1984) 'Habitat selection by fox and gray squirrels: a multivariate analysis', *J. Wildl. Manage.* **48**, 616–21

Brown, D.E. (1982) 'The use of "clippings" to index Tassel-eared squirrel population levels', *J. Wildl. Manage.* **46**, 520–5

—— (1984) *Arizona's tree squirrels*, Arizona Game & Fish Commission, Phoenix

Brown, J.G. and Twigg, G.I. (1965) 'Some observations on grey squirrel dreys in an area of mixed woodland in Surrey', *Proc. zool. Soc. Lond.* **144**, 131–4

Brown, L.C. and Yeager, L.E. (1945) 'Fox and gray squirrels in Illinois', *Illinois Nat. Hist. Survey* **23**, 419–536

Brown, L.N. and McGuire, R.J. (1975) 'Field ecology of the exotic Mexican red-bellied squirrel in Florida', *J. Mamm.* **56**, 415–19

Burger, G.V. (1969) 'Response of gray squirrels to nest boxes at Remington farms, Maryland', *J. Wildl. Manage.* **33**, 796–801

Busrick, S.W. and MacDonald, S.O. (1984) 'Seasonal food habits of marten in south-central Alaska', *Can. J. Zool.* **62**, 944–50

Capretta, P.J. and Farentinos, R.C. (1979) 'Determinants of selective herbivory in tassel-eared squirrels (*Sciurus aberti*)', in J.H.A. Kroeze (ed.), *Preference behaviour and chemoreception*, Information Retrieval Ltd, London, 205–15

Capretta, P.J., Farentinos, R.C., Littlefield, V.M. and Potter, R.M. (1980) 'Feeding preferences of captive tassel-eared squirrels (*Sciurus aberti*) for ponderosa pine twigs', *J. Mamm.* **61**, 734–7

Chaney, R.W. (1947) 'Tertiary centers and migration routes', *Ecological Monographs* **17**, 140–8

Clarkson, D.P. and Ferguson, J.H. (1972) 'Environmental temperature versus spontaneous running-wheel activity in the red squirrel *Tamiasciurus hudsonicus*', *Int. J. Biometeorol.* **16**, 269–76

Connolly, M.S. (1979) 'Time tables in home range usage by gray squirrels (*Sciurus carolinensis*)', *J. Mamm.* **60**, 814–17

Corbet, C.B. (1978) *The mammals of the palaearctic region*, British Museum (Natural History), Cornell University Press, London

Cox, C.B. and Moore, P.D. (1985) *Biogeography: an ecological and evolutionary approach*, Blackwell Scientific Publications, Oxford

Crawley, M.J. (1983) *Herbivory. The dynamics of animal—plant interactions*, Blackwell Scientific Publications, Oxford

Damuth, J. (1981) 'Home range overlap, and species energy use among herbivorous mammals', *Biol. J. Linn. Soc.* **15**, 185–93

Davis, D.W. and Sealander, J.A. (1971) 'Sex ratio and age structure in two red squirrel populations in northern Saskatchewan', *Can. Field Naturalist* **85**, 303–8

Degn, D.H. (1973) 'Systematic position, age criteria and reproduction of Danish red squirrels (*Sciurus vulgaris* L.)', *Danish Review of Game Biology* **8**, 1–24

Deutch, R.S. (1978) *Seasonal activity of the red squirrel* (Tamiasciurus hudsonicus) *in a southern Ohio deciduous forest*, MS thesis, University of Dayton, Ohio

Dice, L.R. (1921) 'Notes on the mammals of interior Alaska', *J. Mamm.* **2**, 20–8

Doebel, J.H. and McGinnes, B.S. (1974) 'Home range and activity of a gray squirrel population', *J. Wild. Manage.* **38**, 860–7

Don, B.A.C. (1981) *Spatial dynamics and individual quality in a population of the grey squirrel* (Sciurus carolinensis)', D. Phil. thesis, Oxford University

—— (1983) 'Home range characteristics and correlates in tree squirrels', *Mamm. Rev.* **13**, 123–32

—— (1984) 'Empirical evaluation of several population size estimates applied to grey squirrels', *Acta theriol.* **29**, 187–203

—— (1985) 'The use of drey counts to estimate grey squirrel populations', *J. Zool.* **206**, 282–6

Donohoe, R.W. and Beal, R.O. (1972) 'Squirrel behaviour determined by radio-telemetry', *Ohio Fish & Wildl. Report* **2**, 1–20

Dorf, E. (1960) 'Climate changes of the past and present', *American Scientist* **48**, 341–63

Drummund, H. (1984) 'The unequal struggle of the red squirrel', *The Field*, 1 December, 48–9

Dubock, A.C. (1979) 'Methods of age determination in grey squirrels (*Sciurus carolinensis*) in Britain, *J. Zool. Lond.* **187**, 27–40

Edlin, H.L. (1968) 'Woodland year: Cones in autumn', *Quarterly J. For.* **62**, 284–93

Eilb-Eibesfeldt, I. (1951) 'Besbachtungen zur Fortplanzungsbiologie und Jugendentwicklung des Eichhörnchens (*Sciurus vulgaris* L.)' *Z. Tierpsychol.* **8**, 370–400

Eisenberg, J.F. (1981) *The mammalian radiations*, Chicago University Press, Chicago

Elliot, P.F. (1974) 'Evolutionary responses of plants to seed eaters: Pine squirrel predation on lodgepole pine', *Evolution* **28**, 221–31

Ellis, L.S. and Maxson, L.R. (1980) 'Albumen evolution within new world squirrels (Sciuridae)', *American Midl. Naturalist* **104**, 57–61

Emmons, L.H. (1978) 'Sound communication among African rainforest squirrels', *Z. Tierpsychol.* **47**, 1–49

—— (1980) 'Ecology and resource partitioning among nine species of African rainforest squirrels', *Ecological Monographs* **50**, 31–5

Erlien, D.A. and Tester, J.R. (1984) 'Population ecology of sciurids in northwestern Minnesota', *Can. Field Naturalist* **98**, 1–6

Fancy, S.G. (1979) *Dispersal and daily movements of red squirrels* (Tamiasciurus hudsonicus)', MS thesis, Humboldt State University

Farentinos, R.C. (1972) 'Observations on the ecology of the tassel-eared squirrel', *J. Wildl. Manage.* **36**, 1234–9

—— (1974) 'Social communication of the tassel-eared squirrel (*Sciurus aberti*): a descriptive analysis', *Z. Tierpsychol.* **34**, 441–58

—— (1979) 'Seasonal changes in home range size of tassel-eared squirrels (*Sciurus aberti*)', *The Southwestern Naturalist* **24**, 49–62

—— (1980) 'Sexual solicitation of subordinate males by female tassel-eared squirrels (*Sciurus aberti*)', *J. Mamm.* **61**, 337–41

Ferner, J.W. (1974) 'Habitat relationship of *Tamiasciurus hudsonicus* and *Sciurus aberti* in the rocky mountains', *Southwestern Naturalist* **18**, 470–3

Ferron, J. (1975) 'Solitary play of the red squirrel (*Tamiasciurus hudsonicus*)', *Can. J. Zool.* **53**, 1495–9

—— (1979) 'Le comportement aqonistique de l'Ecureuil roux (*Tamiasciurus hudsonicus*)', *Biol. Behav.* **4**, 269–85

—— (1981) 'Comparative ontogeny of behaviour in four species of squirrels (Sciuridae)', *Z. Tierpsychol.* **55**, 193–216

—— (1983) 'Scent marking by cheek rubbing in the northern flying squirrel (*Glaucomys sabrinus*)', *Can. J. Zool.* **61**, 2377–80

—— (1984) 'Behavioural ontology analysis of sciurid rodents, with emphasis on the social behaviour of ground squirrels', in J.O. Murie and G.R. Michener (eds.), *The biology of ground-dwelling squirrels*, University Nebraska Press, Lincoln, 24–42

Ferron, J. and Lefebvre, J.L. (1982) 'Comparative organization of grooming sequences in adult and young sciurid rodents', *Behaviour* **81**, 110–27

Ffolliott, P.F. and Patton, D.R. (1975) 'Production rating functions for abert squirrels in southwestern ponderosa pine', *Wildl. Soc. Bull.* **3**, 162–5

Fisher, E.W. and Perry, A.E. (1970) 'Estimating ages of gray squirrels by lens-weights', *J. Wildl. Manage.* **21**, 341–7

Flyger, V. (1960) 'Movements and home range of the gray squirrel, *Sciurus carolinensis*, in two Maryland woodlots', *Ecology* **41**, 365–9

Flyger, V. and Gates, J.E. (1982a) 'Fox and gray squirrels, *Sciurus niger, S. carolinensis* and allies', in J.A. Chapman and G.A. Feldhammer (eds.), *Wild mammals of North America*, John Hopkins University Press, Baltimore, 209–29

—— (1982b) 'Pine squirrels. *Tamiasciurus hudsonicus, T. douglasii*', in J.A. Chapman and G.A. Feldhammer (eds.), *Wild mammals of North America*, John Hopkins University Press, Baltimore, 230–7

Formosov, A.N. (1933) 'The crop of cedar nuts, invasions into Europe of the siberean nutcracker (*Nucifraga caryocatactes macrorhynchus* Brehm) and fluctuations in numbers of squirrel (*Sciurus vulgaris* Lin.)', *J. Anim. Ecol.* **2**, 70–81

—— (1936) 'Migrations of squirrels (*Sciurus vulgaris* L.)', *Trans. USSR Academy Sci. Zool. Inst. J.*, vol. 3

Fox, F.J. (1982) 'Adaptation of gray squirrel behaviour to autumn germination by white oak acorns', *Evolution* **36**, 800–9

Fuente de la, F.R. (1972) *World of wildlife*, vol. 5, Orbis Publishing, London, 195–6

Golightly, R.T. and Ohmart, R.D. (1978) 'Heterothermy in free-ranging Abert's squirrels (*Sciurus aberti*)', *Ecology* **59**, 897–909

Goodrum, P.D., Reid, V.H. and Boyd, C.E. (1971) 'Acorn yields, characteristics and management criteria of oaks for wildlife', *J. Wildl. Manage.* **35**, 520–32

Grodzinski, W. (1971) 'Energy flow through populations of small mammals in an Alaskan taiga forest', *Acta theriol.* **16**, 231–75

—— (1985) 'Ecological energetics of bank voles and wood mice', *Symp. zoo. Soc. Lond.* **55**, 169–92

Grönwall, O. (1982) *Aspects of the food of the red squirrel* (Sciurus vulgaris L.), Ph.D. thesis, University Stockholm, Sweden

Grönwall, O. and Pehrson, A. (1984) 'Nutrient content in fungi as a primary food of the red squirrel *Sciurus vulgaris* L.', Oecologia **64**, 230–1

Gull, J. (1977) *Movement and dispersal patterns of immature gray squirrels (Sciurus carolinensis) in east-central Minnesota*, MS thesis, University of Minnesota

Gurnell, J. (1981) 'Woodland rodents and tree seed supplies', in J.A. Chapman and D. Pursley (eds.), *Worldwide Furbearer Conference Proc.* 1191–1214

—— (1983) 'Squirrel numbers and the abundance of tree seeds', *Mamm. Rev.* **13**, 133–48

—— (1984) 'Home range, territoriality, caching behaviour and food supply of the red squirrel (*Tamiasciurus hudsonicus fremonti*) in a subalpine pine forest', *Anim. Behav.* **32**, 1119–31

—— (1985) 'Woodland rodent communities', *Symp. zool. Soc. Lond.* **55**, 377–411

Guthrie, D.R., Osborne, J.C. and Mosby, H.S. (1965) 'Physiological changes associated with shock in confined gray squirrels', *J. Wildl. Manage.* **31**, 102–8

Hafner, D.J. (1984) 'Evolutionary relationships of the nearctic Sciuridae', in J.O. Murie and G.R. Michener (eds.), *The biology of ground dwelling squirrels*, University Nebraska Press, Lincoln, 3–23

Hall, E.R. (1981) *The animals of North America.* Vol. 1. Wiley, New York

Hall, J.G. (1981) 'A field study of the Kaibab squirrel in the Grand Canyon National Park', *Wildl. Monogr.* **75**, 1–54

Halvorson, C.H. (1972) 'Device and techniques for handling red squirrels', *Special Scientific Report Wildlife* **159**, 1–10

Halvorson, C.H. and Engeman, R.M. (1983) 'Survival analysis for a red squirrel population', *J. Mamm.* **64**, 332–6

Hampshire, R. (1985) *A study on the social and reproductive behaviour of captive grey squirrels* (Sciurus carolinensis)', Ph.D thesis, University of Reading

Hancock, D.H. and Nash, D.J. (1979) 'Dorsal hair length in agouti and nonagouti abert squirrels', *J. Colorado–Wyoming Acad.* **11**, 92

Hansen, L.P. and Nixon, C.M. (1985) 'Effects of adults on the demography of fox squirrels (*Sciurus niger*), *Can. J. Zool.* **63**, 861–7

Harper, J.L. (1977) *Population biology of plants*, Academic Press, London

Harestad, H.S. and Bunnell, F.L. (1979) 'Home range and body weight—a reevaluation', *Ecology* **60**, 389–402

Hatt, R.T. (1929) 'The Red squirrel: its life history and habits', *Roosevelt Wildlife Annals* **2**, 1–46

—— (1943) 'Pine squirrels in Colorado', *J. Mamm.* **24**, 311–45

Havera, S.P. (1977) 'Body composition and organ weights of fox squirrels', *Trans. Illinois State Acad. Sci.* **70**, 286–300

—— (1979a) 'Energy and nutrient cost of lactation in fox squirrels', *J. Wildl. Manage* **43**, 958–65

—— (1979b) 'Temperature variation in a fox squirrel nest box', *J. Wildl. Manage.* **43**, 251–3

Havera, S.P. and Duzan, R.E. (1977) 'Residues of organochlorine insecticides on fox squirrels', *Trans. Illinois State Acad. Sci.* **70**, 353–79

Havera, S.P. and Nixon, C.M. (1978) 'Interaction among adult female fox squirrels during the winter breeding season', *Trans. Illinois State Acad. Sci.* **71**, 24–38

—— (1980) 'Winter feeding of fox and gray squirrel populations', *J. Wildl. Manage.* **44**, 41–55

Havera, S.P. and Smith, K.E. (1979) 'A nutritional comparison of selected fox squirrel foods', *J. Wildl. Manage.* **43**, 691–704

Heaney, L.R. (1984) 'Climatic influences on the life-history tactics and behavior of the North American tree squirrels', in J.O. Murie and G.R. Michener (eds.), *The biology of ground-dwelling squirrels*, University Nebraska Press, Lincoln, 43–78

Hefner, J.M. (1971) *Age determination of the gray squirrel*, MS thesis, Ohio State University, Columbus

Hench, J.E., Kirkland, G. Jr., Setzer, H. and Douglas, L. (1984) 'Age classification for the grey squirrel based on eruption, replacement, and wear of molariform teeth', *J. Wildl. Manage.* **48**, 1409–14

Hight, M.E., Goodman, M. and Prychodko, W. (1974) 'Immunological studies of the sciuridae', *Syst. Zool.* **23**, 12–25

Hoglund, N.H. (1964) 'Uber die Ernahrung des Habichts (*Accipiter gentilis*, Lin.) in Schweden', *Viltrevy* **2**, 271–328

Holm, J. (1985) 'The real squirrel nutkin', *BBC Wildlife* **7**, 334–40

Horwich, R.H. (1972) 'The ontogeny of social behaviour in the gray squirrel, *Sciurus carolinensis*', *Advances in Ethology* **8**, Paul Parey, Hamburg

Hougart, B. and Flyger, V. (1981) 'Activity patterns of radio-tracked squirrels', *N.E. Wildlife Soc.* **38**, 11–16

Husband, T.P. (1976) 'Energy metabolism and body composition of the fox squirrel', *J. Wildl. Manage.* **40**, 255–63

Ingles, L.G. (1947) 'Ecology and life history of the California gray squirrel', *Calif.*

Fish and Game **33**, 139–58

Innes, S. and Lavigne, D.M. (1979) 'Comparative energetics of coat colour polymorphisms in the eastern grey squirrel, *Sciurus carolinensis*, *Can. J. Zool.* **57**, 585–92

Irving, F.D. and Beer, J.R. (1943) 'A six year study of sugar maple bark stripping by gray squirrels in Minnesota oak maple stand', *J. Forestry* **61**, 508–11

Jacobs, G.H. (1981) *Comparative color vision*, Academic Press, New York

Jacobson, H.A., Guynn, D.C. and Hackett, E. (1979) 'Impact of the botfly on squirrel hunting in Mississippi', *Wildl. Soc. Bull.* **71**, 46–8

Jennings, T.B. and Evans, S.M. (1980) 'Influence of position in the flock and flock size on vigilance in the starling, *Sturnus vulgaris*', *Anim. Behav.* **28**, 634–5

Johnson, E. and Taitt, A.J. (1983) 'Prospects for the control of reproduction in the grey squirrel', *Mamm. Rev.* **13**, 167–72

Jordan, J.S. (1971) Dispersal period in a population of eastern Fox squirrels, *USDA For. Res. Pap. NE-216*, US Dep. Agric.

Karpukhin, I.P. (1979) 'Habitat, distribution of the squirrel *Sciurus vulgaris* during spruce seed crop failure', *Byulleten Moscovskogo Obshchestva Isptatelei Prirody Otdel Biologicheskii*, **84**, 20–8

Kemp, G.A. and Keith, L.B. (1970) 'Dynamics and regulation of red squirrel (*Tamiasciurus hudsonicus*) populations', *Ecology* **51**, 763–79

Kenward, R.E. (1982) 'Techniques for monitoring the behaviour of grey squirrels by radio', *Symp. zool. Soc. Lond.* **49**, 175–96

—— (1983) 'The causes of damage by red and grey squirrels', *Mamm. Rev.* **13**, 159–66

—— (1985) 'Ranging behaviour and population dynamics of grey squirrels', in R.M. Sibly and R.H. Smith (eds.), *Behavioural ecology*, Blackwell Scientific Publications, Oxford, pp. 319–30

Kenward, R.E., Marcstrom, V. and Karlbom, M. (1981) 'Goshawk winter ecology in Swedish pheasant habitats', *J. Wildl. Manage.* **45**, 397–408

Kenward, R.E. and Parish, T. (1986) 'Bark stripping by grey squirrels', *J. Zool., Lond.* **210**, 473–81

Kenward, R.E. and Tonkin, J.M. (1986) 'Red and grey squirrels; some behavioural and biometric differences' *J. Zool., Lond.* **209**, 279–81

Keymer, I.F. (1983) 'Diseases of squirrels in Britain', *Mamm. Rev.* **13**, 155–8

Kilham, L. (1954) 'Territorial behaviour of red squirrels', *J. Mamm.* **35**, 252–3

Kirkpatrick, C.M. and Barnett, E.M. (1957) 'Age criteria in male grey squirrels', *J. Wildl. Manage.* **21**, 341–7

Klugh, A.B. (1927) 'Ecology of the red squirrel', *J. Mamm.* **8**, 1–32

Knee, C. (1983) 'Squirrel energetics', *Mamm. Rev.* **13**, 113–22

Koford, R.R. (1979) *Behavior and ecology of a Californian population of T. douglasii*, Unpublished Ph.D. dissertation, University of California, Berkeley

—— (1982) 'Mating system of a territorial tree squirrel (*Tamiasciurus douglasii*) in California', *J. Mamm.* **63**, 274–83

Korschgen, L. (1981) 'Foods of fox and gray squirrels in Missouri', *J. Wildl. Manage.* **45**, 260–6

Kotter, M.M. and Farentinos, R.C. (1984) 'Tassel-eared squirrels as spoor dispersal agents of hypogeous mycorrhizal fungi', *J. Mamm.* **65**, 684–7

Kramm, K.R. (1975) 'Entrainment of circadian activity rhythms in squirrels', *American Naturalist* **109**, 379–89

Kraus, B. (1983) 'A test of the optimal density-model for seed scatterhoarding', *Ecology* **64**, 608–10

Krebs, J.R. and Davies, N.B. (1982) *Behavioural ecology. An evolutionary approach*, Blackwell Scientific Publications, Oxford

Krebs, J.R. and McCleery, R.H. (1984) 'Optimization in behavioural ecology', in J.R. Krebs and N.B. Davies (eds.), *Behavioural Ecology* 2nd edition, Blackwell Scientific Publications, Oxford, 91–120

Laidler, K. (1980) *Squirrels in Britain*, David & Charles, Newton Abbot

Lair, H. (1984) *Adaptations de l'écureuil roux* (Tamiasciurus hudsonicus) *a la forêt mixte conifères-feuilles; impact sur l'écologie et le comportement des femelles reproductives*, Ph.D. thesis, University, Laval Sainte-Foy
—— (1985) 'Length of gestation in the red squirrel *Tamiasciurus hudsonicus*', *J. Mamm.* **66**, 809–10
Lampio, T. (1967) 'Sex ratios and the factors contributing to them in the squirrel, *Sciurus vulgaris*, in Finland', *Finnish Game Res.* **29**, 5–67
Larson, M.M. and Schubert, G.H. (1970) 'Cone crops of Ponderosa pine in central Arizona including the influence of Abert squirrels', *USDA. For. Service*, Fort Collins, Colorado
Layne, J.N. (1954) 'The biology of the red squirrel, *Tamiasciurus hudsonicus loquax* (Bangs), in central New York', *Ecological Monographs* **24**, 227–67
Lazarus, J. (1978) 'Vigilance, flock size and domain of danger size in the white-fronted goose', *Wildfowl* **29**, 135–45
Lemnell, P.A. (1970) 'Telemetry as a method for studying the home range: examples from a study on the red squirrel (*Sciurus vulgaris* L.)', *Zool. Revy* **32**, 51–6
—— (1973) 'Age determination in red squirrels (*Sciurus vulgaris* L.)', *Int. Congr. Game Biol.* **11**, 573–80
Lewis, A.R. (1980) 'Patch use by gray squirrels and optimal foraging', *Ecology* **61**, 1371–9
—— (1982) 'Selection of nuts by gray squirrels and optimal foraging theory', *American Midl. Naturalist* **107**, 251–7
Lindsay, S.L. (1981) 'Taxonomic and biogeographic relationships of the Baja Californian chickarees (*Tamiasciurus*)', *J. Mamm.* **62**, 673–82
—— (1982) 'Systematic relationship of parapatric tree squirrel species (*Tamiasciurus*) in the Pacific Northwest', *Can. J. Zool.* **60**, 2149–56
Lishak, R.S. (1982a) 'Grey squirrel mating calls: a spectrographic and ontogenic analysis', *J. Mamm.* **63**, 661–3
—— (1982b) 'Vocalizations of nestling gray squirrels', *J. Mamm.* **63**, 446–52
—— (1984) 'Alarm vocalizations of adult gray squirrels', *J. Mamm.* **65**, 681–4
Lloyd, H.G. (1968) 'Observations on nut selection by a hand reared squirrel (*Sciurus carolinensis*)', *J. Zool. Lond.* **155**, 240–4
—— (1983) 'Past and present distributions of red and grey squirrels', *Mamm. Rev.* **13**, 69–80
Longley, W.H. (1963) 'Minnesota gray and fox squirrels', *American Midl. Naturalist* **69**, 82–98
Lowe, V.P.M. and Gardiner, A.S. (1983) 'Is the British squirrel (*Sciurus vulgaris leucourus* Kerr) British?', *Mamm. Rev.* **13**, 57–67
Ludwick, R.L., Fontenot, J.P. and Mosby, H.S. (1969) 'Energy metabolism of the eastern gray squirrel', *J. Wildl. Manage.* **33**, 569–75
Lustig, L.W. and Flyger, V. (1975) 'Observations and suggested management practices for the endangered Delmarva fox squirrel', *Proc. Conf. SE. Assoc. Game and Fish* **29**, 433–40
Luttich, S., Rusch, D., Meslow, E. and Keith, L. (1970) 'Ecology of red-tailed hawk predation in Alberta', *Ecology* **51**, 190–203
Lyubetskaja, E.V. (1976) On a model of the eastern Sayan squirrel population. 1 Primary analysis of dynamics of squirrel population and cedar productivity. *Vestnick Moskouskogo Universiteta Biologiya* **31**, 3–10
MacClintock, D. (1970) *Squirrels of North America*, Van Norstrand Reinhold, New York
MacKinnon, K. (1978) 'Competition between red squirrels *Sciurus vulgaris* and grey squirrels *Sciurus carolinensis*', *Mamm. Rev.* **8**, 185–90
Marsh, R. and Howard, W.E. (1977) 'Vertebrate control manual. Tree squirrels', *Pest Control Manual* **45**, 36–48
Marshall, L., Webb, D., Sepkoski, J. and Raup, D. (1982) 'Mammalian evolution and the great American interchange', *Science* **215**, 1351–7

McComb, W.C. (1984) 'Managing urban forests to increase or decrease gray squirrel populations', *South. J. App. For.* **8**, 31–4

McNab, B.K. (1963) 'Bioenergetics and the determination of home range size', *American Naturalist* **97**, 133–40

—— (1971) 'On the ecological significance of Bergman's rule', *Ecology* **52**, 845–54

Meier, P.T. (1983) 'Relative brain size within the North American sciuridae', *J. Mamm.* **64**, 642–7

Merson, M.H., Cowles, C.J. and Kirkpatrick, R.L. (1978) 'Characteristics of captive gray squirrels exposed to cold and food deprivation', *J. Wildl. Manage* **42**, 202–5

Michelson, A. (1978) 'Sound reception in different environments', in M.A. Ali (ed.), *Sensory Ecology*, Plenum, 345–73

Middleton, A.D. (1931) *The grey squirrel*, Sidgwick & Jackson, London

Mikheeva, K.V. (1973) 'Squirrel population dynamics in the Sverdlovsk Province', *Ekologiya* **4**, 503–7

—— (1974) 'Dynamics of the abundance and ecological structure of the animal population in the northern Taigh Region of the Urals', *Sov. J. Ecol.* **5**, 171–3

Millar, J.C.B. (1980) *Aspects of the ecology of the American gray squirrel* Sciurus carolinensis *Gmelin in South Africa*, MS thesis, Stellenbosch

Millar, J.S. (1970a) 'Variations in the fecundity of the red squirrel, *Tamiasciurus hudsonicus* (Erxleben)', *Can. J. Zool.* **48**, 1055–8

—— (1970b) 'The breeding season and reproductive cycle of the western red squirrel', *Can. J. Zool.* **48**, 471–3

Mollar, H. (1983) 'Foods and foraging behaviour of red (*Sciurus vulgaris*) and grey (*Sciurus carolinensis*) squirrels', *Mamm. Rev.* **13**, 81–98

—— (1986) 'Red squirrels (*Sciurus vulgaris*) feeding in a Scots pine plantation in Scotland', *J. Zool. Lond.* **209**, 61–84

Moore, J.C. (1959) 'Relationships among the living squirrels of the sciurinae', *Bull. American Museum Natural History*, **118**, 157–206

—— (1961) 'Geographic variation in some reproductive characteristics of diurnal squirrels', *Bull. American Museum Natural History*, **122**, 1–32

—— (1968) 'Sympatric species of tree squirrels mix in mating chase', *J. Mamm.* **49**, 531–3

Mosby, H.S. (1969) 'The influence of hunting on the population of a woodlot gray squirrel population', *J. Wildl. Manage.* **33**, 59–73

Mosby, H.S., Kirkpatrick, R.L. and Newell, J.O. (1977) 'Seasonal vulnerability of gray squirrels to hunting', *J. Wildl. Manage.* **41**, 284–9

Mould, E.D. (1983) 'The role of tannic acid on palatability of forages of red squirrels', Abstracts 63 *American Soc. Mammalogists*

Mount, L.E. (1979) *Adaptation to thermal environment*, Edward Arnold, London

Muchlinski, A. and Shump, K. (1979) 'The sciurid tail: A possible thermoregulatory mechanism', *J. Mamm.* **60**, 652–4

Murie, J.O. (1927) 'The Alaskan red squirrel providing for winter' *J. Mamm.* **8**, 37–40

Murie, J.O. and Michener, G.R. (eds.) (1984) *The biology of ground-dwelling squirrels*, University Nebraska Press, Lincoln

Nash, D.J. and Seaman, R.N. (1977) '*Sciurus aberti*', *Mammalian Species* **80**, 1–5

Nixon, C.M. and Donohoe, R.W. (1979) 'Squirrel nest boxes—are they effective in young hardwood stands?', *Wildl. Soc. Bull.* **7**, 283–4

Nixon, C.M., Donohoe, R.W. and Nash, T. (1974) 'Overharvest of fox squirrels from two woodlots in western Ohio', *J. Wildl. Manage.* **38**, 67–80

Nixon, C.M., Havera, S.P. and Hansen, L.P. (1980) 'Initial response of squirrels to forest changes associated with selection cutting', *Wildl. Soc. Bull.* **8**, 298–306

—— (1984) 'Effects of nest boxes on fox squirrel demography, condition and shelter use', *American Midl. Naturalist* **112**, 157–71

Nixon, C.M. and McClain, M.W. (1969) 'Squirrel population decline following a late spring frost', *J. Wildl. Manage.* **33**, 353–7

—— (1975) 'Breeding seasons and fecundity of female gray squirrels in Ohio', *J.*

Wildl. Manage. **39**, 426–38

Nixon, C.M., McClain, M.W. and Donohoe, R.W. (1975) 'Effects of hunting and mast crops on a squirrel population', *J. Wildl. Manage.* **39**, 1–25

Ognev, S.I. (1940) *Animals of the USSR and adjacent countries. IV. Rodents,* Moscow, Leningrad. A USSR–Israel programme for Scientific Translations, 1966, Jerusalem

Ofcarcik, R.P., Burns, E.E. and Teer, J.G. (1973) 'Acceptance of selected acorns by captive fox squirrels', *Southwestern Naturalist* **17**, 349–55

Opdam, P., Thissen, J., Verschuren, P. and Muskens, G. (1977) 'Feeding ecology of a population of goshawk, *Accipiter gentilis*', *J. Ornith.* **118**, 35–51

Owings, D.H. and Hennessey, D.F. (1984) 'The importance of variation in sciurid visual and vocal communication', in J.O. Murie and G.R. Michener (eds.), *The biology of ground-dwelling squirrels,* University Nebraska Press, Lincoln, 169–200

Pack, J.C., Mosby, H.S. and Siegel, P.B. (1967) 'Influence of social hierarchy on gray squirrel behavior', *J. Wildl. Manage.* **31**, 720–8

Patton, D.R. (1974) *Characteristics of ponderosa pine stands selected by abert squirrels for cover,* Ph.D. thesis, University of Arizona

Patton, D.R., Wadleigh, R.L. and Hudak, H.G. (1985) 'The effects of timber harvesting on the kaibab squirrel', *J. Wildl. Manage.* **49**, 14–19

Pauls, R.W. (1978) 'Behavioural strategies relevant to the energy economy of the red squirrel (*Tamiasciurus hudsonicus*)', *Can. J. Zool.* **56**, 1519–25

—— (1979) 'Body temperature dynamics of the red squirrel (*Tamiasciurus hudsonicus*): adaptions for energy conservation', *Can. J. Zool.* **57**, 1349–54

—— (1981) 'Energetics of the red squirrel: a laboratory study of the effects of temperature, seasonal acclimatisation, use of rest and exercise', *J. Therm. Biol.* **6**, 79–86

Perry, R., Pardue, G., Barkalow, F. and Munroe, R. (1977) 'Factors affecting trap responses of the gray squirrel', *J. Wildl. Manage.* **41**, 135–43

Phillips, P.C. (1961) *The fur trade,* 2 vols., University of Oklahoma Press, Norman, Oklahoma

Pocock, R.I. (1923) 'The classification of the sciuridae', *Proc. zool. Soc. Lond.* I-II, 209–46

Poland, H. (1892) *Fur-bearing animals in nature and commerce,* Gurney & Jackson, London

Pruitt, W.O. and Lucier, C.V. (1958) 'Winter activity of red squirrels in interior Alaska', *J. Mammal.* **39**, 443–4

Pulliainen, E. (1973) 'Winter ecology of the red squirrel (*Sciurus vulgaris* L.) in northeastern Lapland', *Ann. Zool. Fennici* **10**, 437–94

—— (1982) 'Some characteristics of an exceptionally dense population of the red squirrel. *Sciurus vulgaris* L., on the southern coast of Finland', *Aquilo Ser. Zool.* **21**, 9–12

Pulliainen, E. and Lejunen, L.H.J. (1984) 'Chemical composition of *Pica abies* and *Pinus sylvestris* seeds under subarctic conditions', *Can. J. For. Res.* **13**, 214–17

Pulliainen, E. and Salonen, K. (1963) 'On ring-barking of pine by the squirrel (*Sciurus vulgaris*) in Finland', *Anales Acad. Sci. Fennicae* A IV 72, 1–29

—— (1965) 'On eating of pine-buds by the squirrel (*Sciurus vulgaris*)', *Silva Fennica* **117**, 5–22

Purroy, F.J. and Rey, J.M. (1974) 'Ecological and systematic study of the squirrel (*Sciurus vulgaris*) in Navarra: 1) Distribution, population density, food, diurnal and annal activity', *Boletin Estacion Central Ecologia* **3**, 71–82

Reynolds, J.C. (1981) *The interaction of red and grey squirrels,* Ph.D. thesis, University East Anglia

—— (1985a) 'Autumn/winter energetics of Holarctic tree squirrels: a review', *Mamm. Rev.* **15**, 137–50

—— (1985b) 'Details of the geographic replacement of the red squirrel (*Sciurus vulgaris*) by the grey squirrel (*Sciurus carolinensis*) in eastern England', *J.*

Anim. Ecol. **54**, 149–62

Rothwell, R.H. (1977) *The effects of forest type and mast crop on winter territories and population of red squirrels* (Tamiasciurus hudsonicus baileyii) *in the Laramie Range of Southeastern Wyoming*, Unpublished MS thesis, University of Wyoming, Laramie, Wyoming

—— (1979) 'Nest sites of squirrels (*Tamiasciurus hudsonicus*) in the Laramie range of southeastern Wyoming', *J. Mamm.* **60**, 404–5

Rowe, J. (1980) *Grey squirrel control*, Forestry Commission Leaflet no. 56, HMSO, London

—— (1983) 'Squirrel management' *Mamm. Rev.* **13**, 173–82

—— (1984) 'Grey squirrel (*Sciurus carolinensis*) bark-stripping damage to broadleaved trees in southern Britain up to 1983', *Quart. J. Forestry* **78**, 231–6

Rowe, J. and Gill, R.M.A. (1985) 'The susceptibility of tree species to bark-stripping damage by grey squirrels (*Sciurus carolinensis*) in England and Wales', *Quart. J. Forestry* **79**, 183–90

Rusch, D.A. and·Reeder, W.G. (1978) 'Population ecology of Alberta red squirrels', *Ecology* **59**, 400–20

Sanderson, H.R. (1975) 'Den-tree management for gray squirrels', *Wildl. Soc. Bull.* **3**, 125–31

Sanderson, H.R., Healey, W.M., Pack, J.C., Gill, J.D. and Ward Thomas, J. (1976) 'Gray squirrel habitat and nest tree preference', *Proc. Ann. Conf. SE. Assoc. Game & Fish Comm.* **30**, 609–16

Searing, G.F. (1975) *Aggressive behaviour and population regulation of red squirrels in interior Alaska*, MS thesis, University of Alaska

Seebeck, J.H. (1984) 'The eastern gray squirrel, *Sciurus carolinensis*, in Victoria', *Victorian Nat.* **101**, 60–6

Seton, E.I. (1920) 'Migrations of the gray squirrel (*Sciurus carolinensis*)', *J. Mamm.* **1**, 53–8

Sharp, W.M. (1959) 'A commentary on the behaviour of free-running gray squirrels', *Proc. Ann. Conf. SE. Assoc. Game & Fish Comm.* **13**, 382–6

Shenkan, Z. and Mingshu, L. (1979) 'On the age determination and age structure in the population of the squirrel *Sciurus vulgaris* at Wuying, Lesser King-an mountains', *Acta Zoologica Sinica* **25**, 268–76

Sherman, P. (1977) 'Nepotism and the evolution of alarm calls', *Science* **197**, 1246–53

Short, H.L. (1976) 'Composition and squirrel use of acorns of black and white oak groups', *J. Wildl. Manage.* **40**, 479–83

Short, H.L. and Duke, W.B. (1971) 'Seasonal food consumption and body weight of captive tree squirrels', *J. Wildl. Manage.* **35**, 436–9

Short, H.L. and Epps,. E.A. Jr. (1976) 'Nutrient quality and digestibility of seeds and fruits from southern forests', *J. Wildl. Manage.* **40**, 283–9

Shorten, M. (1951) 'Some aspects of the biology of the grey squirrel (*Sciurus carolinensis*) in Great Britain', *Proc. zool. Soc. Lond.* **121**, 427–51

—— (1954) *Squirrels*, Collins, London

—— (1962) 'Squirrels, their biology and control', *MAFF Bull.* **184**, 1–44

Shorten, M. and Courtier, F.A. (1955) 'A population of the grey squirrel (*Sciurus carolinensis*) in May 1954', *Ann. appl. Biol.* **43**, 494–510

Sibly, R.M. (1981) 'Strategies of digestion and defaecation', in C.R. Townsend and P. Callow (eds.) *Physiological Ecology: an evolutionary approach to resource use*, Blackwell Scientific Publications, Oxford, 109–39

Smith, C.C. (1968) 'The adaptive nature of social organization in the genus of tree squirrel *Tamiasciurus*', *Ecological Monographs* **38**, 30–63

—— (1970) 'The coevolution of pine squirrels (*Tamiasciurus*) and conifers', *Ecological Monographs* **40**, 349–71

—— (1978) 'Structure and functions of the vocalizations of tree squirrels (*Tamiasciurus*)', *J. Mamm.* **59**, 793–808

—— (1981) 'The indivisible niche of *Tamiasciurus*: an example of nonpartitioning of resources', *Ecological Monographs* **51**, 343–63

Smith, C.C. and Balda, R.P. (1979) 'Competition among insects, birds and animals for conifer seeds', *American Zool.* **19**, 1065–83

Smith, C.C. and Follmer, D. (1972) 'Food preferences of squirrels', *Ecology* **53**, 82–91

Smith, C.C. and Reichman, O.J. (1984) 'The evolution of food caching by birds and mammals', *Ann. Rev. Ecol. Syst.* **15**, 329–51

Smith, E.N. and Johnson, C. (1984) 'Fear bradycardia in the eastern fox squirrel, *Sciurus niger*, and the eastern gray squirrel, *Sciurus carolinenis*', *Comp. Biochem. Physiol.* **784**, 409–11

Smith, M.C. (1968) 'Red squirrels responses to spruce cone failure in interior Alaska', *J. Wildl. Manage.* **32**, 305–17

Smith, N.B. and Barkalow, F.S. (1967) 'Precocious breeding of the gray squirrel' *J. Mamm.* **48**, 326–30

Spurr, S.H. and Barnes, B.V. (1973) *Forest ecology*, 2nd Edn., The Ronald Press Co., New York

Stapanian, M.A. and Smith, C.C. (1978) 'A model for seed scatterhoarding: coevolution of fox squirrel and black walnuts', *Ecology* **59**, 884–96

Stephenson, R.L. and Brown, D.E. (1980) 'Snow cover as a factor influencing mortality of abert's squirrel', *J. Wildl. Manage.* **44**, 951–5

Streubel, D.P. (1968) *Food storing and related behaviour of red squirrels* (Tamiasciurus hudsonicus) *in interior Alaska*, MS thesis, University of Alaska

Sulkalva, S. (1964) 'Zur Nahrunqsbiologie des habichts *Accipiter gentilis* (L.)', *Aquilo Ser. Zoologica* **3**, 1–103

Sullivan, T.P. and Sullivan, D.S. (1982a) 'Population dynamics and regulation of the Douglas squirrel (*Tamiasciurus douglasii*) with supplemental food', *Oecologia (Berl)* **53**, 264–70

—— (1982b) 'Barking damage by snowshoe hares and red squirrels in lodgepole pine stands in central British Columbia', *Can. J. For. Res.* **12**, 443–8

—— (1982c) 'Influence of fertilization on feeding attacks to lodgepole pine by snowshoe hares and red squirrels', *Forestry Chronicle* **58**, 263–6

Tait, A.J. (1978) *Studies on the physiology of reproduction in the grey squirrel* (Sciurus carolinensis), Ph.D. thesis, University of Reading

Tamura, N. and Miyashita, K. (1984) 'Diurnal activity of the Formosan squirrel, *Callosciurus ertythraeus thaiwanensis*, and its seasonal change with feeding', *J. Mamm. Soc. Japan* **10**, 37–40

Taylor, J.C. (1966) 'Home range and agonistic behaviour in the grey squirrel', *Symp. zool. Soc. Lond.* **18**, 229–35

—— (1968) 'The use of marking points by grey squirrels', *J. Zool., Lond.* **155**, 246–7

—— (1969) *Social Structure and behaviour in a grey squirrel population*', Ph.D. thesis, University of London

—— (1977) 'The frequency of grey squirrel (*Sciurus carolinensis*) communication by use of scent marking points', *J. Zool., Lond.* **183**, 543–5

Thompson, D.C. (1977a) 'Diurnal and seasonal activity of the grey squirrel (*Sciurus carolinensis*)', *Can. J. Zool.* **55**, 1185–9

—— (1977b) 'Reproductive behaviour of the grey squirrel', *Can. J. Zool.* **55**, 1176–2284

—— (1978a) 'The social system of the grey squirrel', *Behaviour* **64**, 305–28

—— (1978b) 'Regulation of a northern grey squirrel (*Sciurus carolinensis*) population', *Ecology* **59**, 708–15

Tittensor, A.M. (1970) 'Red squirrel dreys', *J. Zool. Lond.* **162**, 528–33

—— (1975) 'The red squirrel', *Forest Record*, **101**, HMSO, London

—— (1977a) 'Red squirrel, *Sciurus vulgaris*', in G.B. Corbet and H.N. Southern (eds.), *Handbook of British Mammals*, Blackwell Scientific Publications, Oxford, 153–64

—— (1977b) 'Grey squirrel, *Sciurus carolinensis*', in G.B. Corbet and H.N. Southern (eds.), *Handbook of British Mammals*, Blackwell Scientific Publications, Oxford, 164–72

Tonkin, J.M. (1983) 'Activity patterns of the red squirrel (*Sciurus vulgaris*)', *Mamm. Rev.* **13**, 99–111

—— (1984) *Red squirrels in deciduous woodland*, Ph.D. thesis, University of Bradford

Townsend, M.G., Fletcher, M., Odam, E.M. and Stanley, P.I. (1981) 'An assessment of the secondary poisoning hazard of warfarin to tawny owls', *J. Wildl. Manage.* **45**, 242–7

Townsend, M.G., Bunyan, P.J., Odam, E.M., Stanley, P.I. and Wardall H.P. (1984) 'Assessment of the secondary poisoning hazard of warfarin to least weasels', *J. Wildl. Manage.* **48**, 628–32

Uhlig, H.G. (1955) *The gray squirrel. Its life history, ecology and population characteristics in West Virginia*, Pitman-Robertson Project 31-R. Commission of West Virginia

—— (1957) 'Gray squirrel populations in extensive forested areas of west Virginia', *J. Wild. Manage.* **21**, 335–41

Vahle, J.R. (1978) *Red squirrel use of southwestern mixed coniferous habitat*, MS thesis, Arizona State University

Vahle, J.R. and Patton, D.R. (1983) 'Red squirrel cover requirements in Arizona mixed conifer forests', *J. Forestry* **81**, 14–22

Van Horne, B. (1983) 'Density as a misleading indicator of habitat quality', *J. Wild. Manage.* **47**, 893–901

Viljoen, S. (1983) 'Communicatory behaviour of southern African tree squirrels, *Paraxerus palliatus ornatus, P.p. tongensis, P.c. cepapi* and *Funisciurus congicus*', *Mammalia* **47**, 441–61

—— (1985) 'Comparative thermoregulatory adaptations of Southern African tree squirrels from four different habitats', *S. African J. Zool.* **20**, 28–32

Viopio, P. (1970) 'Polymorphism and regional differentiation in the red squirrel (*Sciurus vulgaris*)', *Ann. Zool. Fennici* **7**, 210–15

Voipio, P. and Hissa, R. (1970) 'Correlation with fur density of colour polymorphism in *Sciurus vulgaris*', *J. Mamm.* **51**, 185–7

Walker, E.P. (1983) *Mammals of the world*, 4th edn, R.M. Nowak and J.L. Paradiso (eds.), John Hopkins University Press, Baltimore

Wauters, L.A. and Dhondt, A.A. (1985) 'Population dynamics and social behaviour of red squirrel populations in different habitats', *XVII Congress Int. Union Game Biologists*, Brussels, 311–18

Webley, G.E. and Johnson, E. (1982) 'The effect of ovariectomy on the course of gestation in the grey squirrel (*Sciurus carolinesis*)', *J. Endocrinology* **93**, 423–6

—— (1983) 'Reproductive physiology of the grey squirrel (*Sciurus carolinensis*)', *Mamm. Rev.* **13**, 149–54

Weeks, H. and Kirkpatrick, C.M. (1978) 'Salt preferences and sodium phenology in fox squirrels and woodchucks', *J. Mamm.* **59**, 531–42

Weiql, P.D. and Hanson, E.V. (1980) 'Observations on learning and the feeding behaviour of the red squirrel *Tamiasciurus hudsonicus*: The ontogeny of optimization', *Ecology* **61**, 213–18

Wells-Gosling, N. (1985) *Flying squirrels: glides in the dark*, Smithsonian Institute Press

Whittaker, R.H. (1975) *Communities and ecosystems*, MacMillan, New York

Widen, Per (1985) 'Goshawk predation during winter, spring and summer in a boreal forest area of central Sweden', in *Population ecology of the goshawk* (Accipiter gentilis *L.) in the boreal forest*, Ph.D. thesis, University of Uppsala, Sweden.

Wolff, J.O. (1975) 'Red squirrel response to clearcut and shelterwood systems in interior Alaska', *USDA For. Ser. Res. Note PNW-255*, Portland, Oregon

Woods, S.E. Jr. (1981) *The squirrels of Canada*, National Museums, Ottawa, Canada

Wunder, B.A. (1978) 'Implications of a conceptual model for the allocation of resources by small mammals', in D.A. Snyder (ed.), *Populations of small mammals under natural conditions*, University of Pittsburgh, Pennsylvania, 68–75

Wunder, B.A. and Morrison, P.R. (1974) 'Red squirrel metabolism during incline running', *Comp. Biochem. Physiol.* **48A**, 153–63

Zelley, R.A. (1971) 'The sounds of the fox squirrel, *Sciurus niger rufiventer*', *J. Mamm.* **52**, 597–604

Zirul, D.L. and Fuller, W.A. (1970) 'Winter fluctuations in size of home range of the red squirrel (*Tamiasciurus hudsonicus*)', *Trans. 35th N.A. Wildlife and Nat. Res. Conf.*, 115–27

Zwahlen, R. (1975) 'A contribution to the feeding ecology and the suppression of damage by the squirrel', *Jahrbuch Nat. Hist. Museum*, Bern (1972–4), 223–44

Index

INDEX